THE ART of POSITIVE THINKING

by
Acharya Shri Mahaprajna

Translated into English
by
R.K. Seth

Note from the Publishers

Any information given in this book is not intended to be taken as a replacement for medical advice. Any person with a condition requiring medical attention should consult a qualified practitioner or therapeutist.

THE ART OF POSITIVE THINKING

First Edition : 1993
Second Edition : 1994
Reprint Edition : 1998, 2002

All rights are reserved. No part of this book may be reproduced, stored in a retrieval system or transmitted, in any form or by any means, mechanical, photocopying, recording or otherwise, without any prior written permission of the author.

© Copyright with the Publisher

Price: Rs. 175.00

Published by Kuldeep Jain for

HEALTH 🌳 HARMONY

an imprint of

B. Jain Publishers (P) Ltd.

1921, Street No. 10, Chuna Mandi,
Paharganj, New Delhi 110 055 (INDIA)
Phones: 3670430; 3670572; 3683200, 3683300
Fax: 011-3610471 & 3683400
Email: bjain@vsnl.com
Website: www.bjainbooks.com

Printed in India by
J.J. Offset Printers
7, Printing Press Area, Ring Road, Wazirpur, Delhi - 110 035

ISBN : 81-7021-222-7
BOOK CODE : B-3934

CONTENTS

Translator's Preface i
Author's Preface iii

The Art of Thinking

    I.   How to Think (1) 1
    II.   How to Think (2) 9
    III. How to Think (3) 19
    IV. The End-product of Thought 27
    V.   "How I Look at Myself" (1) 37
    VI. "How I Look at Myself" (2) 47
    VII. "How I Look at Another" 57
    VIII. Freedom from Reaction (1) 65
    IX. Freedom from Reaction (2) 75

Change of Heart: The Basis and the Technique Thereof

    X.   Circumstances and Change of Heart 83
    XI. Environmental Influences and Change of Heart 91
    XII. Transmutation of the Mind (1) 101
    XIII. Transmutation of the Mind (2) 111
    XIV. Transmutation of the Mind (3) 121
    XV. Experiments in Heart-purification 129
    XVI. Negative Thinking 139
    XVII. Positive Thinking 147
    XVIII. Training in Methods of Mind Transformation 157
    XIX. Change of Heart—A Great Achievement 165

Freedom from Fear

    XX. Freedom from Fear 175
    XXI. Sources of Fear 185
    XXII. The Fear Complex 195
    XXIII. Reactions of Fear 203
    XXIV. Creative Fear 211
    XXV. Total Freedom from Fear 219

Glossary 229

TRANSLATOR'S PREFACE

It is fascinating to observe how Sri Yuvacharya Mahaprajna's most thought-provoking and breathtakingly lucid books come into being. At the appointed hour, a lean tall man with a calm, smiling face enters the hall the shivrarthis are gathered to practise dhyana. After initiating them into the precise mode and conduct of the day's meditation, he takes up a pad and jots down a few points—an outline of the discourse he would deliver an hour later. All through his writing, he is aware of the passage of time, glancing at the clock every now and then and giving further instructions to the sadhkas. At the conclusion of the meditation session, he smiles at his audience and asks, "How did it go?"

There is a short intermission for tea or lemon water and the great man returns and begins his discourse, without once looking at the pad on which he had earlier jotted down certain points. He speaks for nearly an hour in fluent and chaste Hindi. At the end of the discourse he answers questions. He does so everyday for the duration of the shivir. At the conclusion of the shivir, a new book is born, for it is his daily discourses duly recorded which are later edited and printed.

Sri Yuvacharyaji is a living embodiment of the truth enunciated by Acharya Sri Tulsi in his address to the sadhaks at Chavadia village near Marwar (Rajasthan). Speaking to the shivrarthis on that occasion, Acharya Tulsi proclaimed, "We do not ask whether you are a Jain; we only ask whether you are a man." For true religion, the great teacher maintained, has nothing to do with sects. Religion, in the right sense of the word, means the art of living sanely, intelligently so as never to create any problems at all.

It is this religion, transcending all sectarian considerations, and spreading the message of universal joy, which is the subject of Yuvacharya's discourses. Yuvacharyaji constitutes in himself an institution for helping men achieve self-realization and for bringing about a new world based on love and understanding through individual transformation. He is an inexhaustible fountain of supernal wisdom, born of profound experience in spiritual meditation. It is one's great good fortune to hear him speak. The next best is to read him in the original. But the wisdom embodied in his speech is so deep that even at second hand, in a translation, it leaves its impact upon the mind.

It has, therefore, been a joyful privilege for me to translate into English some of Yuvacharyaji's immortal works. (The present volume is a free translation of *Kaise Sochen*?) For earnest seekers who are keen on developing an integrated personality, his discourses have value beyond words.

I take this occasion to reiterate my heartfelt gratitude to my friend Dr. Prem Nath Jain who first introduced me to the great Jain saints of modern India. I am also most grateful to Jetha Bhaiji and Muni Shri Mahendra Kumarji, whose loving guidance and active co-operation have helped me rid this translation of many inadequacies. The title in English. "The Art of Positive Thinking' and certain modifications in the text in keeping with the spirit of the original were adopted in consultation with them.

Grateful thanks are due to Jain Vishva Bharati, the sponsors of the present series of translations, who have provided me with all amenities for the prosecution of my work. Indeed, Jain Vishva Bharati has become for me cherished home in the evening of my life. What I have gained here—supreme ecstasy—I regard to be the *summum bonum* of life. It would be my constant endeavour, through my work, to repay in some measure, however inadequate, the immeasurable benefits I have derived from living in close proximity with the *saints, sadhvis, samans* and *samanis*. For me, in the words of a poet,

> if there is a heaven on earth,
> it is here, here, here !

Finally, all great work in the Terapanthic order gets done with the benediction of its eternally dynamic Preceptor, Acharya Sri Tulsi. Both my wife and I are fortunate to have in ample measure his love and blessings. No words can repay our debt to him.

Jain Vishva Bharati   **R.K. SETH**
Ludnun-341 306.

AUTHOR'S PREFACE

The present book is devoted to a detailed discussion of the following three topics :

The Art of Thinking.
Principles Governing a Change of Heart; and
Freedom from Fear.

The Art of Thinking

Man is a living being endowed with a mind, and thinking is a function of the mind. Other animals possess a mind too, but their brain is not much developed; so their power of thinking is limited. However, thanks to his highly developed brain, man's capacity for thought is almost unlimited.

The body and the mind are intimately connected with each other. The body influences the mind and is in turn influenced by the mind. However, the mind affects the body much more. A study of the mutual interdependence of the body and the mind reveals that when a man's thinking is positive and constructive, his body too keeps in perfect condition. On the other hand, negative or destructive thinking results in the malfunctioning of the body. All thinking emanating from delusion and/or attachment is negative, whereas reasoning is ever positive and constructive.

Constructive thinking helps in bettering social and human relations and the path of development and progress is cleared thereby. Negative feelings create bitterness in social and human relations, thus obstructing the path of progress.

The practice of *preksha dhyana* serves to wipe out negative emotions and promote positive thinking.

Change of Heart

The evolution of our world is the evolution for change. Without change, there can be no development. While man has achieved tremendous success in changing the external environment, his success regarding the inner environment is limited.

A complete change of heart takes place only when there is inner transformation. The inner transformation is threefold—transformation of emotion, transformation of thought, and transformation of the body-chemistry. It is feeling which gives rise to thought and not vice-versa. Like feeling, like thought. With a change in feeling, there occurs a corresponding change in thought. When the mind undergoes a transformation and thought changes, the inner chemistry of the body also undergoes a change. That marks the beginning of a complete change of heart.

The technique of changing the feeling, the thoughts and the chemistry of the body is a composite one. It is technique of transmuting the endocrine output, of purifying the heart and the mind.

Five principles underlie this change:

    Concentration
    Equanimity
    Awareness
    Freedom from attachment
    Freedom from delusion
    Freedom from fear

There are four main sources of fear:

    Lack of vitality
    The fear-complex
    Constant thought of fear
    Secretion of the fear-producing hormones

There are five reactions of fear:

    Disease
    Old Age
    Death
    Forgetfulness
    Madness

The means of achieving freedom from fear (and how those means are employed in the technique of *preksha dhyana*) are all described here. I have thus discussed at length the art of thinking, the techniques of bringing about a transmutation in the mind, and some means of achieving total freedom from fear. In this process of thought-churning, I have been blessed with the inspiration of Acharya Sri and the editorial expertise of Muni Dhulheraj. The book, I hope, would provide the reader a refreshing dip into the purifying stream of thought.

Balotra (Rajasthan)   **Acharya Shri Mahaprajna**
1.9.1983

THE ART OF THINKING

I. HOW TO THINK (1)

Rene Descartes, the famous French philosopher said, "I think, therefore I am. That 'I Think' proves that 'I exist'—I exist because I think."

If I were to put it in dialectical terms, I would say, "I exist, and since I possess a developed brain, therefore I think."

Thinking does not characterise the brain ; it is only a function and hence cannot be a characteristic feature. Our existence and consciousness transcend thought. Thinking is merely a spark of light, not the entire flame. Freedom from thought is total illumination.

Through the practice of meditation *(dhyana)* we attain a higher level of consciousness which transcends thought and where direct experience begins. In the presence of direct experience, thought loses its *raison d'etre* and spontaneously comes to an end. Everything then becomes crystal clear because there is direct cognition. We see things as they are. There is no necessity for thought whatsoever. Where there is direct congnition, there is no thinking and where thought intrudes, there can be no perception.

There are three ways of experiencing—to know, to see and to think. Someone asked: "Has your servant performed the task entrusted to him?" The master said, "I don't know. I shall *find out* and let you know." Thinking is irrelevant when an event concerns another person.

To another query, "Have you got such and such article in your house?", the master said, "I don't know. I'll *see* if it is there." Here, too, there is no room for thought. The first question elicited the answer. "I'll find out", the second drew forth, "I'll see." To know (to find out) and to see require no thinking. The necessity for thinking arises only when 'knowing' and 'seeing' are not possible. Whatever is hidden, not evident, about which it is not possible to say anything with certainty, necessitates thought.

Thinking is a function of the cerebral consciousness. It is thus a mere ray of light, not total illumination. When, in the clarity of perception, one attains a direct vision, all thought stands transcended.

The objective of *dhyana-sadhna* (training in meditation) is to help the *sadhak* (spiritual practitioner) achieve direct experience. When there is direct experience, thinking comes to an end and knowledge in its wholeness is born. However, as long as the individual is bound to his body, as long as he is tied to cerebral consciousness which preoccupies him wholly, and until transcendental consciousness is awakened in him, thought has its utility, and it is not possible to do away with it altogether.

Two kinds of people are free from thinking. One who has attained direct perception, does not resort to thinking; nor does an idiot. The enlightened one does not have to think because he clearly perceives *what is*. The idiot or the foolish person does not know how to think; he is simply incapable of thought.

The master said to the servant, "Here are two tins of vegetable oil. Hide this oil somewhere in the garden." The servant took away the tins and returned after some time to say, "Master, I have hidden the oil in the garden; now where shall I keep the empty tins?" The master exclaimed, "What are you talking about? How and where did you hide the oil?" "Master!" said the servant, "I dug a pit near a tree and poured the oil into the pit and covered it with the earth. It is perfectly concealed; no stranger would be able to discover it. Now, what am I to do with the tins?"

The man who does not know how to think, one who is totally devoid of the faculty of thought, is a perfect idiot—he can pour the oil into a pit, but he can never utilize it. He can hide the oil but does not know where to hide the tins.

Thus two kinds of men enjoy freedom from thinking—the enlightened one and the ignoramus. What a juxtaposition! And yet such remarkable juxtapositions do occur. Only two kinds of persons remain unmoved by honour or disgrace; the entirely wise (who has freed himself from all passions) and the perfectly foolish. One wonders how the two can have anything in common. In a person freed from all passions, all disparities cease; his whole disposition undergoes a transformation. On the other hand, an idiot has no capacity to discriminate between honour and disgrace; he just cannot distinguish between the two. Therefore he, like the wise one but for a different reason, remains unaffected. What an irony! What a remarkable coincidence!

Thinking is an important factor in life. On the one hand we recognize the importance of thought; on the other we practise meditation for the attainment of a condition which is free from thought. Are we thus not caught in a paradox, an illogicality? However, we must not lose sight of the fact that though our ultimate objective is to achieve complete freedom from thought, such an achievement is not possible at the moment. It is a great illusion to think that a man can enter the transcendental state beyond thought the moment he starts practising meditation. If anything, during meditation the flow of thoughts becomes all the more powerful. Even thoughts which ordinarily never enter the mind, surface up during meditation. The moment a person assumes the posture of meditation or that of *kayotsarg* (relaxation with self-awareness), remote thoughts that never troubled him before flock to the mind. At that time the memory of things long forgotten comes to the fore and the spiritual practitioner finds himself assailed by all kinds of thoughts which bewilder him to such an extent that he even considers abandoning meditation altogether. However, the increased flow of thoughts is inevitable at that time, because the state of meditation furnishes an excellent opportunity for them to arise. When a man is in a state of tension, everyone is loath to approach him, thoughts being no exception. But when a man is in the state of *kayotsarg*, when he sits relaxed, when all tensions dissolve, thoughts say to themselves, "Now, here is a wonderful opportunity. There is no danger." So they unhesitatingly enter the mind. As long as the state of relaxation continues, they come without fear.

Meditation is a process which brings about a general loosening up of a person's attachments. There is an equal scope for ingress as well as egress. A spiritual practitioner welcomes all, the comers and the goers. Those not well-versed in meditation bind themselves to certain notions which they never can let go as long as they live. Such attachment results in much pain.

The moment a man starts practising meditation, he finds himself assailed by various thoughts. Let not the spiritual practitioner be disturbed by this thought-flow. Let him instead watch it and know it, i.e., let him observe the incoming thoughts without any interference. As his perception matures, the flow of thoughts would be weakened by itself. Similarly, with the awakening of consciousness, his capacity for direct experience would ripen and the thought-flow would grow more and more feeble. To expect thought to suddenly come to an end, to cease altogether on the very first day, would be unrealistic. It is, therefore, imperative that every spiritual practitioner should learn how to think rightly. He who, adopting the thorny path of spiritual practice, is yet desirous of leading his life without the least friction, without being embroiled with or in any way bruised by the prickly thorns, must learn how to think properly. He must at all costs master this art.

The vital question is, how does a man think?

Thinking is an art. Rarely does one come across a true thinker. But the man who knows how to think, finds his way greatly smoothened.

A mendicant, in the course of a discussion, said, "I've certainly learnt something from every kind of person." Someone asked, "What have you learnt from the thief?" The fakir said, "Once I sojourned into the house of a thief. At night, the thief would go out for stealing. On his return I would ask, could you get anything? He would say, nothing, I've come back empty-handed. But tomorrow might be fruitful. On the second day, and again on the third, I put the same question and he returned the same answer, 'I could get nothing today, have come back empty-handed, but I hope to get something tomorrow. Thus a whole month passed. For the entire month, the thief could procure nothing. I said to myself, 'The thief goes out for work every night. He spends 7 to 8 hours on it. He loses his sweet sleep, and yet gets nothing for his pains. For a whole month, he has not been able to procure anything. And yet, he has not lost hope. He always says, 'If not today, I'll get something tomorrow'. I said to myself, 'The thief has displayed exemplary patience. Even on returning home empty-handed, he never gave way to despair.' So from the thief, I learnt never to despair in the way of devotion. While engaged in a good work, one must never abandon hope."

But how strange and incomprehensible is man's disposition. A person engaged in good work is too soon disappointed, while the evil-doer never abandons hope. The thieves, the plunderers and the dacoits never despair.

This is a fact. After a great deal of thought I have arrived at the conclusion that the evil commands faith much more than the good. To have faith in goodness, one must have greater devotion. It is the absence of faith that spells despair. Faith and evil seem to be so bound together that a man takes to evil and his faith therein is strengthened by itself. Not much effort is required in that direction. But for the strengthening of faith in the path of goodness, a tremendous effort is called for.

What is right thinking and how are we to think rightly? It is essential to know this because a man with a negative approach would reject even the factual truth, while a man endowed with positive thinking accedes to truth and is thereby able to find a solution to his problems.

There are two ways of thinking—negative and positive. Much too often a man indulges in negative thinking; he does not think positively. The negative approach invariably results in despair, loss of enthusiasm, sentimentality, disdain of action, and deviation from duty. In short negative thinking means the beginning of failure in life.

The key to success lies in constructive, positive thinking. And only that man is capable of constructive thinking, who has understood the significance of meditation, who has learnt how to keep his heart pure, whose mind is capable of concentration, and who is free from attachment.

Both constructive and negative thinking have certain criteria by which we know them.

HOW TO THINK (1)

We must first of all determine whether one's vision is partial or whole, whether it is integrated or distorted, because a man endowed with a holistic, comprehensive vision can think constructively, but the thinking of a man afflicted with a partial vision is ever distorted.

In the absence of a total view of any given situation or incident, thinking based upon a partial view remains partial and therefore inadequate. A holistic vision is a must for right and balanced thinking. Confronted with a positive or comprehensive viewpoint, many a conflict is resolved, whereas a perplexed vision gives rise to prejudice and many unnecessary problems come to the fore.

Some travellers halted for rest under the cool shade of a mango tree. They fell to talking. One of them said, "As I came along, I saw a red lizard on a tree." Immediately, another countered, "You seem to be labouring under some illusion, because I too saw the lizard; its colour was green." The first wayfarer said, "You must have seen some other creature on another tree. For I saw it with my own eyes and I can vouch for it that it was a red lizard." The other protested, "I'm not telling a lie. It is you who are mistaken. It was a green creature that nestled on the tree." Accusation and counter-accusation went on till, gradually, they worked themselves up to a high pitch of excitement and came to blows. An intelligent companion intervened, "Why are you quarrelling for nothing? I too have followed the same route after you. Both of you are right. That creature on the tree was red as well as green. A total view involves no contradiction. It is only a partial, one-sided, perverted approach that spells mischief. That creature you saw was a chameleon. When the first traveller passed, it had assumed a red hue; when the second passed, it changed into green. You know a chameleon is continually changing its colour. Both of you reported right."

The world we live in is like a chameleon. Everything here changes from moment to moment and man is no exception. How many different faces does a man assume in the course of a single day? It appears that man is an image of God that manifests himself in a million ways. The person one saw in the morning as a model of tranquillity and dispassion shows himself by midday so exicted and agitated, as if he were a ruthless monster. In the course of a day a man assumes a thousand different forms. He presents himself in myriad different shapes. Only once during the day and again once during the night, does the sea display its tides. But the ocean of man's thought displays a thousand tides in the course of a single day. There is a continual rise and fall. No constancy or stability; only fickleness born of perversion. The situation calls for deep research, which means an enquiry into the meaning of the past and that of the present. Unless the two meanings coalesce, it will not be possible to know man fully.

To know and experience reality, it is necessary to investigate the essential significance of the past and the present. This in itself constitutes a holistic approach, a detached point of view in distinction with the perverted point of view based upon the perception of a part alone. There is little room for controversy in the holistic approach, but an impressionistic approach, based upon a one-sided view, vitiated by prejudice, inevitably gives rise to contention and conflict.

The healthy approach to thinking is the constructive, positive approach, the holistic point of view.

Emperor Shrenik's queen Chelna was sleeping. It was winter time, terribly cold. As she lay asleep, the following words escaped her lips, " I wonder what he will be doing now!" The emperor was awake. He heard these words which inflamed his whole being. He was proud of his queen's character. Now he thought, "The queen in whom I put my greatest trust, is muttering in sleep, 'I wonder what he will be doing now.' Who is she talking about? Has she a secret lover? O God!" His mind was in utter turmoil. He conceived a distrust of his own queen and instantly developed an extreme hatred for her.

The morning found the emperor desolate and angry. He called his prime minister Abhay Kumar who was also his son and said, "Burn this palace without delay! I'm going out to see Lord Mahavir."

Abhay Kumar was stunned at the emperor's command. He thought, "To burn the palace, to reduce Queen Chelna to ashes without any prior intimation—what sort of command is that!" On the one hand, there was his his father's command, on the other, the most heinous crime of burning his own mother alive! He knew very well what consequences his disregard of the king's order would lead to. He found himself in a dilemma.

Emperor Shrenik reached the meeting place of Mahavir, and paid his obeisance. In his discourse, Lord Mahavir discussed the topic of 'chaste and loyal women.' Incidentally Mahavir said, "Queen Chelna is the foremost among chaste and faithful women. She is very pious and dedicated to truth." The emperor could not believe his ears. He said to Mahavir, "Respected Sir, how is that? You say Queen Chelna is the most virtuous lady. But only last night these words escaped her lips in sleep, 'I wonder what he will be doing now!' Do these words symbolise her virtue or quite the contrary?"

Lord Mahavir said, "You know not the real meaning of these words. Queen Chelna came here yesterday to pay her obeisance. Afterwards on her way to the palace she came across a Jain ascetic who stood meditating under a tree. He was without any clothes. It was terribly cold. The queen did not stop there. Making her bow, she went on her way. While she slept at night, one of her hands lay outside the blanket. Because of extreme cold, her hand was benumbed, got so inert as if there were no life in it, The queen wanted to lift her hand, but could not. Whereupon the queen exclaimed, "O, the hand was exposed to the cold for a little while, and see what has become of it! It has become almost dead, completely paralysed. Homage to the ascetic who meditates in the open without any clothes! I wonder what he will be doing now!"

The Emperor was stupefied to hear it. He immediately took his leave. He thought, "If the palace has been burnt in accordance with my orders, a great injustice has been done." He walked briskly. On the way he met Abhay Kumar and anxiously enquired, "Did you carry out my order?" "Yes, Sir. How could I be negligent about any command of yours?"

The emperor said, "Abhay Kumar, a great injustice has been done."

Abhay Kumar said, "What do you mean?"

The Emperor related the whole story.

Abhay Kumar said, "Sir! don't you kindly worry. I've kindled the fire, as per your command, but it would take a whole day for the fire to reach the palace."

The emperor heaved a sigh of relief.

It would be apparent from this story how, because of perverted thinking, a terrible calamity could occur and how a man could commit a great injustice. God knows how many communal, national, tribal and social conflagrations arise from a perverted point of view. The wife says something. The husband does not pay full attention. And because of misunderstanding, a crisis develops in the family, sometimes leading to dreadful consequences. The husband protests he heard it with his own ears. But his ears are not fool-proof. He says he saw it with his own eyes. But his eyes are not the eyes of God. A great many of us have experienced for ourselves how a man is deceived by his eyes and ears. What stupidities does not a man indulge in on the basis of a partial view? Because of impatience and impulsiveness a great many injustices are perpetrated.

For correct and balanced thinking, for a constructive and positive vision, the first requirement is the development of a holistic point of view. No individual should allow himself to be swayed by a perverted vision, and he must never take a decision in any matter without first obtaining full information.

Once in China, compulsory enrolment of recruits was in progress. Someone came to Mao Tse-Tung, and said, "It is good that you have broken your leg. This saves you from conscription." Mao Tse-Tung replied, "You have said it, but I can't say so, because I don't have before me the whole picture without which it is not possible to determine whether it is good or bad."

Only when the whole picture is before one, one may determine whether a particular happening is good or bad. Such a conclusion cannot be reached on the basis of a partial view. When a man takes a decision on the basis of a partial view, half-baked alternatives and immature feelings, it invariably gives rise to conflict and war. A man must therefore develop a holistic point of view.

The positive and constructive point of view needs to be expounded at length. Its first principle, however, is the development of a holistic approach. When this principle gets activated in life, the constructive point of view starts maturing itself.

II. HOW TO THINK (2)

The sweltering summer! The scorching sun! In the hot season, one's brain too gets heated up. For right thinking, however, one must have a cool brain; a fervid brain hinders thinking. It also creates a number of unnecessary problems which invariably result in immoderate action. One chief sign of good health is that one's feet remain warm and the brain cool. But with most people the reverse is the case: the brain gets heated up and the feet grow cold. If the brain keeps tranquil, a man can live for a long time. Established in peace, he lives with zest. One objective of deep breathing is to keep the brain cool.

Today's scientists are busy developing a new technique which would enable man to live for 500 or even 1000 years. This is the technique of refrigeration, of deep freezing. A man is frozen cold. For 10 years he remains inert. Then he is exposed to heat and he gets up alive. The scientists experimented on ants and froze them alive. All the ants became dead and cold. After 10 minutes they were warmed up and they returned to life. They restarted their activity. We often see flies and ants falling into cold water and appearing as dead. But a little application of heat resurrects them to life.

If a man could be so frozen, he could live for a long time. Not to speak of the whole body, if only the brain can be kept cool, man's longevity would greatly increase. Untimely death occurs most often in youth, the chief reason being the frequent heating up of the brain. A young man flares up too soon and too often: the frequent heating-up destroys the brain cells.

Our brain cells constitute the basis of our life. As long as these cells are alive and active, a man does not die even if his heart stops beating. It has been observed that a man declared dead by the doctors, was found to be alive after some time. Occasionally, a 'dead' man carried on a bier to the funeral ground and laid down on earth for cremation, with firewood ranged all round ready to be ignited, comes to life and rises yawning on the pyre making the piled blocks go scattering. People mistake him for a ghost. But in fact he never died. He was alive all the time. Only the doctor had declared him dead. Actually his brain was active—it had not died, and as long as the brain does not die, a man cannot be said to be dead, despite heart- or pulse-failure.

The brain is the seat, the fundamental basis of life. The cooler the brain, the more wholesome one's life, and the more constructive one's thinking. Indeed, a cool brain is the essential pre-requisite for wholesome, constructive and balanced thinking. From this point of view, the second criterion for right thinking is whether thinking is being done in a state of frenzy or in a state of tranquillity. Agitation renders thinking defective. Thinking done in a state of turmoil can never be wholesome, right, balanced or constructive. It can be constructive only when the mind is not agitated. Thinking must be based upon facts for only factual thinking has any utility. Where the fact becomes secondary and emotion reigns supreme, thinking can never be practical or sane. The thinking of an individual who does not practise meditation and who has no control over his mind, whose mind is not tranquil and balanced, is ever abrupt and emotional—such a person is incapable of right thinking.

A politician's friend said to him, "I met such and such person today and he was abusing you." On hearing this, the politician flared up. He said, "Let me win this election and become a minister, and then I'll teach that man a lesson for abusing me."

This is what emotional thinking leads to. That politician should have first confirmed whether the person alleged to have abused him, actually did so. Otherwise one hears a canard and gets heated up for nothing. Who has not witnessed terrible fits of anger or pride? And we are also acquainted with the ill effects of these. The servant does not immediately carry out our order, our pride is hurt. In a highly wrought state we sometimes say and do abominable things. We indulge in abuse and give the servant a beating, and sometimes even dismiss him from service. All this is done in a frenzy of hurt pride. We never stop to consider for a moment as to why one man must always obey another. It is not always obligatory after all. To obey is good, but sometimes not to obey is better. The master is endowed with the faculty of thinking; so is the servant.

A master said to the servant, "Go and irrigate the garden." The servant said, "Master! it is raining like cats and dogs. Why irrigate now?" The master said, "You are a fool! If it is raining, why don't you take an umbrella with you?" Now, what is the servant to do ? The master who commands him does not even stop to consider that irrigating the plants in rain is utterly pointless. Why should the servant obey such a foolish command?

All those who give commands are not necessarily wise and many foolish orders are given. Sometimes these orders may result in great injustice. And yet the master becomes indignant if any of his commands is not immediately carried out. Later, of course, he has to face the music too. In a state of frenzy, all thinking becomes perverted. There is then little understanding between man and man. An overcharged brain is mainly responsible for deterioration in relationship between husband and wife, between brother and brother and between master and servant. With this wall of frenzy between them, one man can never fully understand another, nor can he see the other person as he is; his frenzy colours all that he sees. The man in front will appear to be the very image of his wrath. Frenzied thinking can never be right. Hence one of the criteria for balanced thinking is the practice of non-attachment. How is it possible? Is it possible to obviate wrath and pride? Most people never think in terms of obviating or mitigating pride. They think anger is natural; pride is man's second nature; these cannot be obviated. So man does not change, and pride and anger continue. Many people think that man cannot change, so the question of ending pride and anger which are part of human nature does not arise. The man who is engaged in the practice of meditation frees himself first of all from this false assumption, he who is not so freed cannot be a good spiritual practitioner. The first lesson that a spiritual practitioner has to learn is that man is capable of changing, that his nature can be changed. If man cannot be transformed, if his nature cannot change, it is better to abandon meditation altogether, for meditation then has no utility whatsoever. The significance of meditation lies in this that through it consciousness becomes so concentrated and pure as to wash away the long-accumulated dirt. When consciousness is unveiled, all habitual action disappears of itself. Habits have their breeding ground in impurity. Consciousness is so encrusted with layer after layer of impurities, that all kinds of habits take root there. One is often asked since the soul or consciousness is always pure, why should it be ever polluted?

Consciousness is ever pure. If we persevere in the practice of meditation, it will certainly become revealed, but the fact is that it is not so at present. Whatever is non-existent at the moment, must be seen as being non-existent. What is only a future probability must not be imposed upon the present, nor should a projection of the past be imposed on the future. Most of the time people project things which are not there at all. Imposition creates innumerable difficulties. The gold burnt in fire becomes purified; it is yellow and lustrous. But looking at the earth-incrusted ore dug out of the mine, one could never imagine gold to have such lustre. At that time it appears to be no more than a clod of earth. There is a great deal of difference between raw ore and the finished ingot. There is absolutely no comparison between lustrous gold that comes out of the fire and the metal mixed with clay in the ore. The sparkle of the finished ingot purified of all dirt and refuse is stupendous indeed. Similarly, the clarity and purity of a consciousness well-tempered in the oven of meditation is simply unimaginable in a consciousness vitiated by passion-dominated lust and desire. Wrath, pride, cunning, deception, hypocrisy, greed, hatred, fear, envy, approbation and condemnation, like and dislike— consciousness riddled with these emotions can never be accessible. What is it that is so riddled, so attracted by strong emotions? Not the inanimate, the unconscious. Wrath never descends upon the inanimate. Does the wall ever take offence? It the walls of our rooms were to be moved by anger, man's plight would be pitiable beyond thought. The coarse cloth upon which we sit is never hurt. We place our feet on it, and it says nothing. Just try to place your feet on another man's head! The bare touch would make the victim flare up. But the poor piece of cloth is never angry, never exhibits pride.

The inanimate displays no anger or pride, neither deceit nor hypocrisy. But man cheats man; the animate being deceives its fellows. That the inanimate should cheat the animate has never been seen or heard of. All the circumventions and deceits are conscious man's creation and man alone perpetuates them. It is the sentient, the animate which harbours all the vices; the inanimate, the insentient contains no evil. In the inanimate world, there is only *what is*— neither good nor bad. The 'good' and the 'bad' are the creations of a conscious mind. As long as the mind does not realize its true nature, evil is bound to continue.

Meditation is a process of realizing one's conscious self. It is a process of awakening awareness. As long as the true nature of consciousness is not seen, all the evils harbour in the mind, in it they find their base and support. In such a congenial atmosphere, they grow uninhibited. All the wickedness and the sins have their breeding ground in the mind; it is here that they find their nurture. Provided with a solid foundation, these grow even though the conscious being providing this support continues in pain. A queer situation! The landlord suffers hardship while the tenant prospers. It is not easy to evict the tenant. To free consciousness of all impurities is an arduous task. The general conception that one's nature is unchangeable is not altogether wrong. The conditioning of centuries cannot be easily done away with. However, meditation is a process which gradually washes away all accumulated grease and as the grease gets cleansed away, the elements sticking to it are also got rid of. The tenant enjoys certain rights by law. He cannot be evicted. But a house which is decayed gets demolished by heavy rain and storm and in that case all the tenants have to seek shelter elsewhere. The house stands evacuated by nature, meditation is such a potential downpour, such a terrific storm that razes the house of ignorance to the ground and then all the tenants—the evils and impurities—are obliged to fly. Everything stands changed. This is the transformation sought for.

In this world, there are some things which can be changed and others which cannot. All that is unchangeable and eternal must be left alone. However, every state of mind is changeable. There is no state which is permanent. The condition of wrath, for example, is transitory; likewise that of pride, of greed, of like and dislike and a thousand other passions which are forever fleeting. All these are changeable. All attachments and all actions are subject to change, and it is therefore possible to change them. Of course, the fundamental elements remain constant. There are two such elements— the sentient and the insentient, these abide. The sentient cannot become the insentient and *vice versa*. The states of mind change continually. When this truth is clearly understood, all irrelevant impressions by themselves fall off. This dissolution of irrelevant impressions is the beginning of transformation. The consciousness of a spiritual practitioner transcends all conditioning. His conduct then may appear to be somewhat strange though as a matter of fact all his interests undergo a sea-change, all his attachments die with the experiencing of Supreme Bliss; small pleasures become insignificant and lose their charm for him. Interest in material things lasts only as long as one has not experienced that state which transcends the previous one. Meditation marks the beginning of that suprasensuous state of complete non-identification. Matter is then seen as simply matter and consciousness reveals its purity. Attachment is the thread that binds the two, but meditation cuts off that bondage. Then matter is prized only for its utility. Breathing is vital to life, food and water are necessary for its sustenance, likewise clothing and shelter. Their procurement becomes purely a matter of utility, without any undue attachment. Thus comes into being an entirely new state of mind.

It is to meditation that thought owes the development of its creative power. Tranquillity is the means thereto—that is, the absence of emotional excitement.

Deceit gives rise to suspicion. Without deceit there can be no suspicion. The social atmosphere today has been so polluted that man has lost faith altogether. He does not trust anybody. The son does not trust his own father; nor the father his son. Napoleon once said, "There is no such word as 'impossible' in my dictionary." Similarly, the word "faith" has no place in a modern man's dictionary. Doubt and suspicion stalk the land. Nothing can be taken on trust. Distrust constitutes one of the flaws in thinking. A man is inclined to doubt. He feels threatened and therefore doubts. There is a saying that a burnt child dreads the fire. Once caught, twice shy. If society were free from deceit, a man would have no cause for suspicion.

A merchant was travelling with his consignment. On the way lay an octroi post. The merchant contrived to slip away without paying his dues. The incharge of the post came to know of it later and resolved to be more alert in future. Such an evasion had not occurred before. The merchants used to come to him and pay their dues by themselves. But when one of the merchants played foul and got away, the officer-in-charge began to suspect all the merchants that passed by his octroi post. He subjected them all to a rigorous search. No search was conducted earlier because no one had deceived before. One man deceived and now all were suspect. All thinking without faith is faulty and destructive. It can never be balanced or constructive.

Faith has a great significance in life. A life without faith has no foundation whatever. There can be no fulfilment in it. Faith rests on three pillars—capacity, accomplishment and a knowledge of the universal laws.

The first element is capacity. Each man must have faith, he must experience the truth that he is endowed with limitless capacity. The second element is accomplishment. Each man must have faith in his power to accomplish whatever he undertakes to do. The third element is a knowledge of the universal laws. Each man must know and abide by these.

To have faith does not imply dependence upon others. It only means that a man must depend upon himself. One cannot depend upon another; one can only depend upon oneself. A man may be said to have complete faith only when he believes in his own boundless capacity, in his power of accomplishing whatever he undertakes to do, and when he knows and abides by the universal laws.

We know that we have infinite capacity in ourselves. We also know that through right endeavour man can achieve what appears to be impossible. Self-exertion and effort are ever fruitful. However, there is a limit to what is possible. So one must understand the universal laws. If a man should say to himself, "I am going to exercise my will-power, and my power of concentration and the power of meditation and I'll never die," he is living in a fool's paradise. All his determination and will-power will be of little avail. In time, the man is bound to die. Only abysmal ignorance of the universal laws makes him assert otherwise. Death is inevitable; nothing endures. That is a universal law.

Change is the law of nature. One mode gives way to another. There may be an interval between birth and death—10 years, a thousand, or a hundred thousand, but ultimately there is dissolution and change; nothing endures. Let us take an atom. It may be black to-day but after some time it would change its colour. The transformation takes place of itself. There is no outside agency to bring it about. That is the universal law. It is so decreed. One colour gives place to another, one birth leads to another, everything changes, nothing endures. Nothing is everlasting. It cannot be

HOW TO THINK? (2)

otherwise. Birth and death are interchangeable. Whatever is born is bound to die.

Books on *hath yoga* repeatedly refer to a substance whose use would make one immortal. Such references are also found in books on *ayurved*. A particular substance is recommended whose use, they say, would keep one eternally young and immortal. It is possible that the man using it might keep young all his life, but that he should never die is altogether impossible. It is not necessary that every man should die of old age; one can die young or keep young for a long time. The talk of keeping young is intelligible but that of keeping alive for ever makes little sense. There is nothing which is eternal, which does not perish in course of time. The occurrence of such a reference in ancient texts along with details of experiments performed has created a misunderstanding that a man can live for ever. On that basis some people have gone to the extent of declaring publicly that they have conquered death through meditation. However, it remains an illusion. What the ancient writers wrote must be read in a specific context. "Eternally young and deathless" probably meant that a man would be healthy and not die prematurely. But the spirit was overlooked and the mere letter cherished, leading to a monstrous misunderstanding.

To doubt means to repudiate a probability. A sceptic rejects a probability outright; we must cultivate faith so as not to deny it blindly. Let us understand once for all the one great flaw in thinking: an original, an altogether new idea is presented, and the man immediately reacts by saying 'it's impossible!'

Today we see an aeroplane flying high in the sky. None can deny it. Nobody doubts. But in the days before the invention of the aeroplane, the principal of an American college is reported to have said to a parish priest, "It is not far when man would fly high in the sky." And the priest immediately retorted, "It's impossible! What rot you talk!" What an irony that after 35 years it was the two sons of the same priest who first flew in the air.

To deny a probability is the greatest flaw.

Some scientists today are reported to be busy developing genes. They have made some progress and it is quite possible that in course of time they are able to create synthetic genes. Yet many people today ridicule it as an impossibility. "How can genes be created ?" they ask.

It is sheer prejudice that stands in the way of our accepting something entirely new. Why should a probability be discounted after all? All development has been based upon recognizing a new possibility.

A Jain classic entitled *Yoniprabhrit* records in detail all possible combinations and permutations of the animate and the inanimate in various forms of existence. It is surprising that despite extraordinary advances in modern scientific research, the technique of developing an embryo in the test-tube has not been entirely successful. However, in *Yoniprabhrit* we come across the possibility of creating all kinds of living beings. There occurs a mention of this or that individual having created a thousand he-buffaloes, horses, etc. A particular instance is that of a king-disciple who knelt before his *guru*. "Master!" said the king, "The enemy has assaulted our town. I am not in a position to halt the adversary. You alone may do something to save us." The *guru's* heart was filled with pity at the plight of his devoted disciple. He made use of the knowledge gained from his study of *Yoniprabhrit*, and threw a bit of powder into the pond from where thousands of horsemen instantly emerged. It was an unending stream. The aggressors were quite baffled by the spectacle of a huge cavalry advancing to annihilate them and they took to their heels.

On another occasion the *acharya* was reading to his pupils from *Yoniprabhrit*. The subject was, "The Technique of Fish Production". A fisherman happened to be passing that way. His attention was arrested and he stopped to listen carefully to the whole account of the technique. The very next day he experimented with it. Soon his pond swarmed with fish.

The modern word for this technique would be genetic engineering; it is an ancient technique.

The point to be emphasized is that we should never shut the door on any probability. The cultivation of faith means openness to various possibilities. Wherever there is this openness, there is right thinking. There is then no prejudice. Prejudice exists only where there is no openmindedness.

Wrong thinking has its breeding ground in impulsiveness. A king was walking bare-footed. A thorn-prick caused him much pain. He called his minister and told him, "See, what pain a thorn-prick gives! Many of my subjects walk bare-footed. They are subject to this suffering. Why don't you cover the whole area of my kingdom with leather so that no one ever suffers a thorn-prick?" This order was the outcome of an impulse. In his irrational enthusiasm it did not occur to the king that if the whole earth was covered with leather where would the wheat grow and what would people and animals eat?

There is the tale of King Midas of Greece who prayed to God that whatever he touched might be turned into gold. His prayer was granted. Whatever he touched turned into gold. All food and drink, the moment he laid his hand on these, turned into gold, leaving him hungry and thirsty. His daughter came running to him and the king embraced her; instantly she too turned into gold. Thereupon the king realized how foolish he had been. He prayed to God again, desiring Him to take back His gift.

All passions lead to perverted thinking. No right decision is possible in a state of frenzy. If people come to see the truth thereof, many lawyers and judges would become superfluous. Men go to court when they are highly wrought. If their agitation could be somehow resolved, 75% of the cases in the law-courts would stand resolved too.

I am told that in West Germany an experiment is on. The man who goes to file a criminal case there, is made to sit quietly in a vacant room for 5-6 hours. Only then do consultations begin. It has been found that 70% of the would-be litigants return without filing a case, because what brought them to court was a highly wrought condition, and as soon as their agitation subsided they were at peace and disinclined to pursue the matter any further.

We have gone into some aspects of constructive and destructive thinking. There are other aspects too. To ensure constructive thinking, it is necessary to change one's circumstances and the only way to change one's condition of life is through an integrated and pure mind.

III.   HOW TO THINK   (3)

It is very pleasant today. Drizzling and light snowers. How delectable is a drizzle after sizzling heat! It is the nature of weather to change. Sometimes it is hot, at other times cold. Nothing in the world is eternal; everything undergoes a change. Man too is sometimes calm, at other times inflamed. Such is the inevitable law of change. Everything changes. Our thoughts too change. Some people say that thought is eternal. There is a contradiction here, for thought and eternity do not go together; no thought lasts for ever; it cannot stay for long; it gives way to another. It is variable and what is variable cannot be constant.

Change and fixity may coexist in matter, but whatever is in motion cannot be stationary and what is stationary cannot be in motion. What is eternal is not subject to change, and that which is subject to change cannot be eternal. Thought is inconstant, ever on the move. It is said that a particular man has changed his mind. There is nothing surprising about it. On the contrary, it would be surprising if the mind did not change. It is the nature of the mind to change. The reigning idea of yesterday gives way to some new thought. The present conception will not last till tomorrow. If a man clings to one idea all his life, he is said to be a fanatic. It is the nature of thought to move constantly, to be variable and transient. Some people accept a belief and stick to it for life. They even feel proud of it, saying to themselves, "I am a man of strong character. I don't change. I stick to my view at all costs." Such people think they are being very wise; however it is foolish to be so rigid. A stone is hard, not pliable, and one's bones too may grow rigid and hard like stone. In this is involved great danger. If the bones are flexible, a man keeps in good health; it is a sign of ill-health when the bones grow rigid. The more pliant one's bones, the healthier one is. The hardening of the spinal cord signifies loss of health. So clinging to one thing may be sheer obstinacy. In the absence of right thinking, one cannot differentiate between right and wrong. What is right appears to be wrong and *vice versa*. Some people never discover that they have been behaving foolishly all through.

A young wife said to her neighbour, "Many women these days find fault with their husbands. This is wrong. One should not criticise one's husband before others. My own husband is a lazy lubber, a thorough good-for-nothing. He is also very foolish, but I never talk of it!"

The field of thought is grossly perverted. A man goes on committing one folly after another, without once realizing that he is being silly. On the contrary he seeks to justify every action of his, even though it be riddled with all sorts of contradictions and incongruities, rank foolishness often appearing in the garb of wisdom. No such thing in the inanimate world.

There are three different states of thinking—(i) Irrational (ii) Rational and (iii) Supra-rational. The state of irrationality is that in which an individual is simply incapable of thought. Sub-human creatures know not how to think. Even among humans there are idiots—these do not know how to think; they are simply incapable of thought.

The second state is that of thinking in which a living being exercises his mind, entertains impressions and opinions. The third state is that of thought transcended. This is the state of meditation where all thinking comes to an end. No imagination, no memory, no reflection! This is the state of thought-transcendence. The experiencing of such a state in which thought is completely absent is a wordless realization which brings forth a super-consciousness which is beyond the senses, the mind and the intellect. This super-consciousness is an extrasensory state of mind. Here the soul is the only object of experience, all other memories vanish. It is an ultra-psychic condition which no words can describe. This state can only be experienced. All that falls within the sphere of the intellect can be expounded in words, but the world beyond the intellect is beyond language. All expression thereof is inadequate. At the same time, one cannot remain silent about it; it seems to demand expression. To talk about it or not is man's dilemma. However, the world we live in is a world of intellect and thought which is beset with many paradoxes; a person says one thing today, and something quite different tomorrow.

Churchill once said, " A perfect politician is he who says one thing in the morning, repudiates it in the evening, but with such tact as to convince his hearers that he spoke the truth on both occasions."

Contradiction is inevitable in the field of thought; each argument can be countered. Logic is ever exposing contradictions. That indeed is the office of logic. However, logic or thought is never productive of unanimity or harmony; instead, it creates paradoxes, for that is how thought moves. To expect stability in the dualistic world of thought is to be caught in illusion. It is to be far removed from fact, for conflict is inherent in thought, contradiction being its chief characteristic. We are here considering the nature of thought which is sometimes good, at other times evil; sometimes constructive, at other times destructive. We are interested in reducing to the minimum the element of destructiveness in thought; that is why we are posing the question, "What is right thinking?"

The question involves the purification of the mind, of thought itself. By emptying the mind of all thought, by maintaining our balance, we can make our thinking constructive and creative. We can thus reduce the element of destructiveness in it, whereas thought, which has in it the seed of contradiction and conflict, ever sullies the mind and destroys its purity. As the mind becomes silent with the emptying of thought, it progressively grows more subtle and refined; all its incongruities and contradictions gradually dissolve. There is no other way to achieve this purification.

There is the old legend of an extraordinary blanket which existed two thousand and five hundred years ago. It cost a fortune —more than a hundred thousand sovereigns. Why so costly? Because it was an air-conditioned blanket—it cooled in summer and warmed in winter. It was cleaned, not with water but with fire. The blanket was flung into the fire and all the dirt would go out of it. Unless it was so treated, it would not be clean. Similarly, the dirt of accumulated thought could not be got rid of through water, nor could one thought be purified by another; nor intellect or logic could make thought clean. For clearer thinking, for the purification of the mind, thought must be consigned to the fire of emptiness—a condition of total freedom from thought. Then all the refuse would clear of itself, and the mind will become fresh and creative. It would become constructive, imbued with faith, energy and light.

Thinking born of fear is ever negative and destructive. A fearful man is incapable of right thinking; fear dulls his mind and heart; his thinking becomes blunted. It would be idle to expect a fear-ridden brain to function normally. Such a brain cannot think constructively. The first condition for sane thinking is total freedom from fear. The mind must be absolutely fearless, and the brain, and indeed the whole environment, must be free from fear. Only in the right atmosphere will sane thinking become possible. A man oppressed by fear cannot think straight.

Why are you afraid? Why is man ridden by fear? In fact fear is the outcome of wrong thinking. A man's individuality is determined by his thought. He has accepted certain ideas and beliefs and the whole environment is vitiated by fear. A man who has understood even a little bit of spirituality, whose dry and anguished existence has been even slightly touched by the grace of religion, cannot but be fearless. He who is not fearless cannot be spiritual or religious; he cannot be sane. Fear is the root of all disease, of all conflict and of unspirituality. Can a fearful man experience truth? People talk of soul and of God endlessly, but they live in illusion. How can a man ridden by fear know anything of highly subtle and supra-sensual elements? The mind is never free of fear—fear of ill-health, fear of old age, fear of death and of separation; fear of loss of things and persons — the mind is ever dominated by fear and the power of consciousness quite overthrown thereby, and one talks of soul and of God! Will the soul manifest itself in a state of fear? Never. Fear can only give rise to a goblin; it cannot lead us to soul or God. Fear is the creator of evil spirits; with many people, it takes the form of a ghost or demon. It is a kind of mental projection; in the very moment of fear, a ghost begins to take shape before our eyes; it is the projection, the image, the reaction of a fear-afflicted mind. Is such a mind capable of any subtle penetration?

Lord Mahavir pronounced a subtle truth. He never said that non-violence alone constituted religion, despite the common belief. On the basis of my own understanding I can say that Lord Mahavir emphasized much more the importance of fearlessness than of non-violence. The spirit of non-violence is implicit in fearlessness; without fearlessness this spirit cannot manifest itself in life. A coward can never be truly non-violent. The man who is too much attached to life, who is afraid of dying, cannot be non-violent. A friend said the other day that the Jains in India almost outnumbered the Sikhs and yet the Sikhs managed to get their way while nobody paid any heed to the Jains. I said, "I don't want to enter into a lengthy discussion, but one thing is clear. The Sikhs are not afraid of dying; the Jains are. It has been reported that in the time of British rule, the English were opposed to the construction of a Gurudwara in Delhi. They were the absolute masters. And yet when the Sikhs began to offer sacrifices, the British Government was quite unnerved, and was compelled to grant permission. Nothing is impossible where there is no fear of death; for all incompetence owes its existence to this fear. One is greatly attached to life and is, therefore, afraid to die. But is one's removal from the scene, of much moment? Will one's death unpeople the world? Who cares! Of course, when a man is alive, his friends and relatives pretend to love him forever. But who remembers him after death? For a few days, there is a formal exhibition of grief; then all is forgotten. Once a year, on the occasion of the death anniversary, people do perfunctorily pay a tribute to the memory of the dead, "He was a good man", they say, "May his soul rest in peace!" That is all. As long as a man is infatuated with life, he cannot think straight. The first condition of constructive thinking is complete freedom from the fear of death.

Most of us are too fond of intellectual discussion. We give a great deal of importance to it. But a discussion without practical work by oneself is of little value. We churn the curd and butter comes out of it. But often there is no curd, and a man goes on turning the water. Sometimes there is not water even — only an empty vessel and the churning stuff. At times there is not even a vessel, nor the churning rod—all is imagination. And we hope to get butter out of it! For butter, we need the curd as well as the churning. Mere intellectual discussion is like churning the water. There is no curd, but the churning is going on. There is the empty vessel, or the vessel is filled with water. Discussion must be combined with practical work. No mere theory would do, practice must go with it.

There are two aspects of education (I say it on the basis of experience and ancient tradition)—theory and practice. Learn the theory and put it into practice! Then alone full understanding comes. Many people come to me in a hurry. They would say, "Sir, I have to go back immediately. I can hardly spare a few minutes. My mind is utterly restless; I am much perplexed, facing a great many problems. Kindly teach me the way to make the mind tranquil." I tell such a one, "You are an extraordinary creature. You have a tremendous problem on your hands—the problem of the mind, and you want a solution within two minutes! I don't possess a magic wand. I don't believe in sudden explosions of energy. Nor would mere blessing do the trick. I only believe in awakening a spiritual practitioner's own intelligence; I want to activate his own valour, so that he ardently seeks the truth on his own which alone is the liberating factor. One of the maxims of *preksha* meditation is : 'Find out the truth for yourself.' Let each individual find out the truth about himself. Let him not depend on anyone. Dependence upon another can prove very dangerous. Mutual dependence is a necessity of life. But there is a limit to it. Complete dependence upon another is often harmful. One must not depend even upon a *guru* beyond a certain point. Nor leave it to the *guru* to do everything, or one is in for disappointment. One must not depend even upon one's own father. What will you do when the father is no more? The father is not there for all time, is he? After all one will have to stand on one's own feet. What is required is an awakening of the pupil's own wisdom. Some masters make tempting offers to their disciples, give out sweet assurances that everything would turn out well even without their doing anything. All that turns out to be delusion. The disciple later complains "Sir, what you assured me would happen, has not come to pass."

The very belief in a *guru* is misleading. Why do you take the guru's word for granted, and later you start complaining? Whether it is religion, or God, or the *guru*, whether it is one's own self, or another, there is a limit to belief. Up to a certain point you have to trust another. But going beyond the limit would create complications. It is said in the context of *preksha* meditation, "Find out the truth about yourself. Discover your own path to salvation!" We are of course here to provide limited assistance. If the engine of a motorbus fails, the passengers get down and give the bus a push so as to restart the engine. So far so good. But you have to go far. Will you keep pushing the bus all the way for a hundred miles? It is just not possible. The engine must work by its own power. An occasional push may be in order, but pushing all the time would be utter madness.

Total freedom from fear is our ultimate goal. We must be brave, without fear of any kind. The thinking of a person afflicted with fear can never be right, it stands vitiated by his fear.

Equanimous thought is balanced thought. Any kind of superiority or inferiority complex results in perverted thinking. The one great criterion for wholesome thinking is to determine whether thought is born of equanimity or not. It seems to me that two kinds of feelings dominate a man's life—like and dislike; craving and aversion. All thought is actuated by like or dislike. Totally unconditioned thinking is rare. Someone dear to us says something and we appreciate it fully; but the same thing uttered by an adversary inspires in us a feeling of contempt or fear. Why? We are enquiring into the nature of wholesome thought. Thought conditioned by feelings of like or dislike is not wholesome at all.

Many things happen in the course of life. Two factors influence them all—like and dislike, approval and disapproval. All our action is conditioned by these. Passion or disgust, approbation or disapprobation, attachment or indifference, attraction or revulsion. There is no other motive for thought.

Man indulges in evil deeds or doubtful conduct; deceives others. Wherefrom do these tendencies originate? On the one hand operates attachment such as, "This is my family, my son, my wife—may they be happy! Let there be a bigger house, more money, no lack whatsoever." On the other hand, aversions prevail. Where there is 'like', 'dislike' is bound to be; the two go together. A man goes to the market and after a great deal of effort obtains pure *ghee*, because he does not want his son to partake of impure stuff. He does not want that his wife or other members of his family should consume adulterated foodstuffs. All because he is greatly attached to them. And yet the same person sells adulterated medicines to others, because he is indifferent to their fate; because he is not attached to them. Due to lack of affection, he indulges in corruption without any scruples. This feeling of attachment/unattachment powerfully affects one's approach and all perversions in thought and action originate therefrom. Without equanimity, all thought becomes shabby and the contradictions therein can never be resolved.

The chief function of meditation is to help a man go beyond like and dislike, beyond craving and aversion. It is to awaken in him a state of dispassion. Impartial and alert passivity in an individual is a great thing. Meditation which fails to develop equanimity is no meditation at all. Meditation is not mere entertainment; it is not merely relaxation or gratification; you sit idly, close your eyes, entertain no worry whatsoever. For 10 days you don't stir abroad; you squat immovably. rooted to the ground, in one fixed posture, and have complete rest. On being asked, one says it is wonderful! But what is the net result? What achievement, if any? To some meditation is nothing but mere relaxation and being confined to one place. When they go out of the meditation center, they continue as before, there is no change—the same world, and the same mischiefs. This kind of meditation is sorely limited by time and space. Even a naughty child grows quiet in sleep, barring some involuntary spasmodic movements. While sleeping, no man quarrels. In fact, in the state of sleep, every man appears to be virtuous. Of course, the evil-doer continues to harbour evil inside, but outwardly at least he does no harm while asleep. Evil dreams, imaginations and thoughts continue. With the conscious mind asleep, the unconscious becomes all the more active. But outwardly the evil-doer in sleep appears like any other person. As long as he lies asleep in bed, he cannot indulge in evil conduct, he tells no lies, nor tricks another; nor uses bad language—he does nothing whatever. In the unconscious state induced by sleep he keeps away from doing harm.

Meditation, however, is no true meditation, if it is does not bring about a complete transformation, if it does not purify one's thought or alter for the better one's whole approach. If, once outside the meditation center, there is no change in one's conduct, then such meditation is no more than sleep or unconsciousness.

Meditation on the other hand constitutes an awakening, a complete rousing of inner consciousness. The conscious mind becomes inert, but the inward consciousness becomes so active and expands so much that it transcends all conditioning. It remains steadfast and unchanging. If a meditator keeps tranquil enough in the meditation hall, but on returning home continues fighting and quarrelling, his family would rightly look upon such a person and his meditation with misgiving.

In the field of religion we witness a number of reactions. It is said that today's intelligent man does not care for religion. Such a reaction arises from the realization that the practice of religion hardly makes any difference. One practises religion for 50 years but there is no change in one's life. What is the utility of a religion like that. ? If there is no transformation whatever, religion loses all validity. A religion whose practice or non-practice makes little difference, can command no allegiance. If plunging your foot into the fire, or not plunging it comes to the same thing, who will dread fire? However, fire burns and so people avoid putting their feet into the fire. Because of its peculiar quality, fire demands attention and people tread it with care.

Religion too must become like fire to attract people's attention. If religion today holds no attraction for the modern man, it is because it has been divorced from meditation. Religion is no longer allied with inner consciousness. Mere outward conformity to meaningless rituals has rendered religion insignificant. Buried under ashes, the spark loses its power. Only when the ashes are shed off is the flame reignited. Meditation is a process of shedding off the ashes. Light manifests itself in a man who succeeds in removing the ashes and his thinking then is mature and responsible, like gold purified of all dross, imparting lustre to his whole life and conduct.

The approach is all important. And for inculcating the right approach, one must go into what thought is and what transcends thought.

IV. THE END-PRODUCT OF THOUGHT

Life is being and becoming. We exist, that is being. We desire, that is becoming. Each man wants to be something other than what he is; no man is fully contented with his lot—he wants to rise higher and still higher in life; he does not want to stagnate in one position for ever. This desire to be something gives rise to numerous possibilities. Becoming involves effort—a search for new ways of living, ending of laxity and the creation of a new environment. Man wants to attain the truth, he longs for success, health and growth —he wants all these.

It is man's nature to be preoccupied with results. It is this preoccupation with results that has given birth to a number of problems in the past as well as in the present—problems which apparently are insoluble. Man wants to achieve a certain result or he wants to do away with a certain situation or he wants to change it. And he wants to do all this on the basis of certain ideas he has arrived at. His whole attention is concentrated on achievement; natural aptitude or inclination are often quite ignored.

A newly appointed official was informed that the villagers have had an excellent potato crop. He went to inspect and saw field after field covered with green leaves. "What, just leaves! But where is the crop?" he exclaimed, "You have misinformed me. You said you have had an excellent crop, but here are mere leaves and no potatoes at all. What makes you tell lies to me ?" At this the villagers laughed and said, "Sir, potatoes grow underground; above the ground you find only leaves. Dig into the soil and you'll find potatoes everywhere."

The foliage above ground furnishes no idea of the crop below. Our mind is so disposed that we have only a superficial view of things; we do not try to go deeper. Without going deeper we shall not know the truth. The ultimate lies within. We must learn to distinguish between disposition and essential nature. The essential nature is fundamental. Only by laying hold of the essence, the fundamental nature of a person, can we understand his disposition and a comprehension of a man's disposition goes a long way towards an understanding of his final destiny. Mere preoccupation with an effect can be misleading and productive of illusion. We want to do away with anger, we want to remove all evil, ignorance, indiscipline, aggressive mentality, acquisitiveness and other ills. Not only we, but the whole society and the government want that. And yet all these evils continue to flourish. They seem to multiply despite our efforts to end them. Where do they get support from? Man is moving towards destruction. Evils are waxing strong every minute. Why this retrogression? What perpetuates evil and how is it that man cannot cope with it? What is it that he lacks? That is the big question confronting us. It seems to me that we have never seriously gone into this question. Had we done so, we might have discovered the truth about it and resolved the issue long ago. But we seem to be concerned only with removing evil, not with understanding it. Violence is an effect, an outward manifestation. So is anger, so is all evil. A man hoards money or indulges in adulteration. These are merely consequences. We want to do away with a particular result, without understanding the cause thereof. As long as the cause is there, the effect is bound to follow. If the root is not dissolved, the result flowing therefrom would remain. Anger does not come of itself; behind it lies a particular disposition, and behind that the fundamental nature of the person concerned. The inner overcomes the outer. We cannot remove outward evil without bringing about a fundamental inner transformation.

The psychologists have analysed man's essential nature. A particular nature gives rise to certain tendencies, with certain consequences. All scriptures too speak not of mere outward change, but deep inner transformation. I have also posed this question before would-be ascetics—those who want to renounce family and home to become ascetics. "Is it possible," I asked, "to achieve non-violence or continence or non-acquisitiveness through an effort of will?" They say it can be done. We exercise our will. We determine not to indulge in violence or sex, not to tell a lie, not to steal, or not to be acquisitive.

Well, I resolve to do or not to do something. I take a vow, for example, not to tell a lie. But is that any guarantee that I will no more tell lies, or give way to anger? If one could ensure non-violence through mere exertion of one's will it would be wonderful. Each man would take a vow not to remain poor, to annihilate poverty—and there would be no more poverty! One could resolve to remove a particular evil, but mere resolution does not end it. It would be wonderful if the mere utterance of a word could accomplish results. But the fact is that we have no magic wand that would instantly bring forth all that we desire. Mere determination would not do.

The religious thinkers went into the matter and have offered a way—the disciplining of the mind, of the body and the tongue. With discipline comes fulfilment. If the mind is still, non-violence comes into being. If the mind is pure and still, continence follows; also non-greed. But if the mind is restless, if it wanders like a monkey, if it is running after various objects, preoccupied with persons and things, how can there be non-violence or continence? Behaving like a monkey would not bring it forth. If it were so simple, I would urge the whole world to take to the monastic life; none should remain outside the fold. Just pronounce a word and the thing, whatever it is, is done! But in reality, it is not so. And a spiritual practitioner who tries to go forward without first maturing his meditation, is often obliged to retrace his steps.

There was a rat which lived in great fear of the cat. A sage conferred upon it a boon which transformed it into a cat. Having become a cat, it was no longer afraid of the cat but it was constantly haunted by the fear of the dog. The sage then turned it into a dog. After some time the sage said, "Now you must be utterly without fear." The rat said, "How can I be free from fear? The lion frightens me now." Thereupon the sage transformed it into a lion. But the fear was still not gone. The rat told the sage, "I'm no longer afraid of any other animal, but I'm still afraid of the hunter. Yes, I fear the hunter." Thereupon the sage asked, "What is it you want? Shall I transform you into a man?" The rat said, "Oh no! I have now seen for myself that every situation brings with it its own fear; there is no situation without fear, whether one is a cat, a dog, a lion or a hunter. Let me be my own self." The sage said, "Be it so!" And it became a rat again.

Fear would not go, whatever one might achieve. Without a change in his fundamental nature, man might become anything, it makes no difference. Only by getting rid of the root of fear, can a man be free of fear.

The importance of man's fundamental character, his essence, must be fully recognised. And it is only through discipline that man's nature undergoes a change. There are three kinds of discipline—the control of the mind, the control of speech and the control of the body. Violence is one consequence of our inner nature. As long as a man is caught in craving and aversion, it is not possible for him to be truly non-violent. Nor can he be truly continent; nor, as long as he is bound by like and dislike, can he be truly non-possessive. Our essential nature spells out our outer disposition. Our whole conduct is governed by our fundamental nature which gives rise to a particular mode of behaviour which in turn brings about certain results. It is a complete cycle, no one link whereof can be considered in isolation apart from the others.

The human problem is complicated by the fact that we want to bring about only superficial changes. Even the so-called religious people are out for material results, wiping off an undesirable effect and not the cause thereof. A man subject to fits of indignation straightaway wants to know how he can get rid of anger altogether. He says, "I really want to give it up for ever. I don't want to quarrel."

But anger is merely an effect; something else lies behind it. We must enquire into the root of anger; there may be some physical, psychological or material cause behind it. Anger is rooted in the past. There is a conditioning factor, a particular tendency, like or dislike, which gives rise to a particular mode of conduct. A man is attached to someone, or hates another, or he is afraid of one and loves another. All these tendencies arise in him and bring about particular results. When there is strife or controversy in the family, the members are advised not to quarrel or dispute among themselves. Such advice often falls flat upon them. People are boiling inside; they are out for a quarrel, all the causes of anger are active in them. Under the circumstances, how can they desist from fighting? You put fuel into the oven and light the fire, and then expect that there should be no heat or flame! How is it possible? Fire and heat are results flowing from the action of lighting the fuel. If you want to do away with the heat, you have to extinguish the fire. We do not want to quench the fire and yet seek to evade the heat! This is contradictory. Ways are often sought to get rid of a particular result immediately. Such efforts do not last long, and seldom prove effective. If we look at our problems and the ways in which we try to meet them, we shall find that all the time we are exclusively concerned with getting or doing away with particular results. So we go round and round, and the problem is never resolved. We never discover the root cause. We find ourselves caught in great illusion. The fundamental cause is there right in front of us, but we never perceive it. Our thinking is so vitiated that everything serves to distort our perception all the more.

A man took his wife to the election officer with the complaint that her name was not to be found on the electoral rolls. The officer examined the rolls and said that her name appeared in the list of persons since dead. The wife flared up, "Here I stand alive before you; how can you put my name among the dead?" The husband said, "You stupid! Do you think such a high official is telling a lie?" What an irony of fate! The root cause lies right before us, but we prefer to trust the official instead of paying heed to the living. All the jingoistic impulses are alive in us—the impulse to quarrel, to indulge in anger, pride, or possessiveness; all the impulses productive of evil are thriving within us. We trust the big official—he cannot tell a lie! We put our belief in a religious leader who tells us to seek refuge in him, so as to end all pain. We would rather seek the easier course in utter disregard of our inner compulsions. But if we really want to resolve our problems, we cannot afford to be exclusively preoccupied with effects. For the moment we are not concerned with effects or their removal. Rather we concentrate on the secret impulses; as to what particular impulse gives rise to what particular mode of conduct. We need not consider achieving a particular effect. That effect is bound to occur of itself. Why strive for that which is bound to happen of itself, irrespective of our efforts? How great is man's illusion! He strives for that which requires no striving; and the thing he must concentrate upon, which will effect a complete transformation in him, which will turn him into a good man, which will bring peace of mind, on which depends his success or failure, progress or deterioration, tranquility or disquiet, the attainment of truth or otherwise—that priceless jewel, the very origin and starting point of all creativity, he quite ignores. The technique of meditation is the technique of discovering that originating point; it is not the technique of achieving a particular result. The result-seekers, those who are after some immediate gain, wholly preoccupied with and constantly brooding on the problem of the moment, will never be able to master this technique; nor shall they ever perceive the deep significance of meditation. Unless one can look at a problem in the context of the whole, things are bound to go awry, and the problem is never resolved.

We have laid down five principles of right thinking. The first is holistic perception—a total view. If our vision is whole, we become receptive to truth and consequently attain it. But if our approach is partial or biased, all our efforts to arrive at the truth are doomed to failure. In that case, whatever we sieze upon as truth, ultimately turns out to be a partial view, not objective truth. And it all results in futile controversy. In fact no field, whether political, philosophical or social is free from controversy. And all controversy is born of narrow prejudice. Each system of philosophy, each individual is intent upon establishing the superiority of a particular tradition over others. The tradition itself may be good, and it is also right to have faith in a good tradition; however, a one-sided approach is not palatable to the discerning. It is also true that no words can contain the whole truth and any truth embodied in words becomes somewhat vitiated. It is a partial truth and though it may have its good points, yet it is not whole—the whole truth beggars description; it cannot be put into words. Truth is infinite whereas language is finite. No dictionary contains more than two to three lakhs of words. Language at all times is a limited medium. How can a limited medium (a few lakhs of words) adequately express the unlimited? Can the infinite be enclosed in finite terms? Impossible!

People talk about the soul, but they get confused. They talk about the Supreme Reality and stand perplexed. The man who seeks to perceive the soul through verbal definition is bound to be disappointed; likewise those who seek to describe the Supreme Soul in technical terminology. The word can never describe that which is beyond the word. It would be idle for a foreigner not rooted in the soil, to seek to represent the nation. He would command no recognition whatsoever. Similarly, a language is inherently incapable of representing the truth. It may be likened to a blind man's staff. Because he is incapable of vision, the blind man feels his way around with the help of his stick. Undoubtedly the stick has some utility. But while giving the stick its due importance, we must be on our guard against giving it more. It is true that without language social contact would be impossible; we shall not be able to establish right relationships; we shall not be able to accomplish any work. So language has to be accorded its rightful place. But we must not lose sight of the fact that its capacity is for ever limited. Something is expressed in words. But the nature of language is such that it might confuse instead of making things clear. Words have a way of causing confusion, and a man is caught unawares. How can one hope to arrive at the highest truth through such an unreliable medium? The very coining of words like the Truth, the Highest Truth, seems to be indicative of our mental confusion. What is after all the nature of the entity that talks about the soul? What is it that speaks? The soul itself is silent and does not manifest itself. It abides deep within, the subtlest of the subtle. Then what is it that gives expression to it? There is a big question mark about it.

So we must not put immoderate trust in language; nor in the mind. A man comes up and says, "I want to talk about the soul." I ask, "Why?" He answers, "I want to know it." Others too express a desire for soul-realization. I invariably say, "Do you really want to realise your soul? Or do you merely want to talk about it." All of them maintain they are interested in self-realization, not in merely talking about it. But if you really want to experience your soul, practise meditation. Let your mind be tranquil, quiet, let your body be motionless, still. Get to the door which leads to the soul, i.e., come to know the body first. It is strange how some seekers of the supreme truth want to have nothing to do with the door. They want to experience the soul direct. Well, the direct approach is all right; one needs no intermediary to take one to Truth, but then one has to traverse the way, every inch of it, by himself. You cannot jump into the truth without traversing the whole path. Most of us have taken it for granted that he who talks about the soul or God is the true seeker; and he who talks about the body, goes astray. "The body is dirty, not worth talking about," we say.

I find that those who practise control of the mind, of speech and the body, ultimately realise the soul and the Supreme Reality; others go on talking about these for years together and never come to know either soul or Truth. On the contrary, a vast confusion overtakes such idle talkers and they never can find a way out.

THE END-PRODUCT OF THOUGHT

Ordinarily a man gets preoccupied with the things of the moment, renders himself incapable of holistic perception, without which there can be no real progress.

Four friends were taking a journey together. The three of them were scientists, and the fourth one a layman. To be a scientist is one thing, to be wise quite another. The scientists were not wise, but the fourth man who was not a scientist was nevertheless very wise. While walking in the forest, they found the skeleton of a lion, the sight whereof inspired their scientific curiosity, and they immediately wanted to do some experimentation to see if they could enkindle life in the dead skeleton. They sat together in consultation with one another. One of them said, "I'll provide this skeleton with skin and flesh." The second scientist said, "I'll make the blood flow in it." The third said, "Well, I shall breathe life into it." The fourth man said, "Very good. But let me first climb up a tree!" So the fourth man climbed up a tree and witnessed the doings of his three friends. Each one of the three performed his experiment, made good his word, with the result that they found themselves confronting a roaring lion. The lion was hungry and appeased its hunger by devouring the three scientists standing before him. The fourth friend, the non-scientist, wisely kept his perch and escaped death.

We must inculcate a total view. A partial view would not do. If our perception is one-sided and not whole, our impulses and actions and the consequent results cannot be good. Holistic perception implies thinking not solely dictated by one's instinct, nor wholly based upon one's inherited disposition, nor with a view to achieving a particular result alone. Rather a total view would embrace all the three aspects together.

Behavioural psychology commands great prestige today. Man's inner states and instincts are being studied on the basis of his conduct. It appears that man is at last moving in the direction of total perception. A child does not obey his parents, is very insolent, quarrels with everybody, beats his younger playmates, calls them names. All these tendencies are found in him. His parents naturally want their child to be free of these tendencies. So the mother, as soon as she comes to know that her child has quarrelled with someone, slaps him. But does the evil tendency stand removed thereby? If it could be so removed all the children would stand reformed in no time. But, generally speaking, the more they are punished, the more recalcitrant and rebellious they become, instead of being reformed. The children grow worse. Why this deterioration? Because we are solely concerned with achieving a particular result instead of understanding the child's essential nature. The mother is interested only in curbing a particular tendency in her child. She does not want her child to quarrel or to be disobedient or indisciplined. She wants to change his outward conduct. But will the child's disposition change? Until the child's essential character is transformed, the tendency would remain. So all our effort should be concentrated on bringing about a fundamental transformation in the nature of the child. In the context of *preksha* meditation, we stress the fact that in order to change a child's disposition, we must carefully study his fundamental nature. Until the pituitary and thyroid glands are activated, no amount of effort will bring about a transformation in the child. There is only one way to do it. In order to change a child's habits, make him concentrate on the *Darshan Kendra* (the Centre of Intuition) and his disposition will automatically change. The change in disposition can be wrought only by changing the fundamental nature which would release a different kind of action with different results. People are generally very rigid. Instead of going in for total comprehension, they mostly rely on a half-truth and take a decision on the basis of a partial view. They revel in their ignorance and do not listen. On mere hearsay, they would take a stand. "He said so?" they would mumble angrily. When he said it, in what context, in what tone, under what circumstances, they do not want to inquire. If only they would take the trouble to inquire, the whole thing would perhaps appear in a different light, leaving no room for anger or pride. But nobody seems to be interested in knowing the whole truth. A mere supposition would make a man flare up. "So he said this; I'll teach him a lesson! I shall make him eat his words." The conflict has begun, and sometimes a whole life is wasted in such trivial controversies, adversely affecting society as a whole.

The parents wanting to bring about a transformation in their children, or the teachers in their pupils, or the political leader in the masses, generally concentrate on changing the outer circumstances. They are mostly preoccupied with achieving a particular result. They would emphatically declare that there should be no smuggling, no black-marketing. This or that must not be allowed to happen or particular actions would not be allowed to vitiate the atmosphere. However, to think of changing certain actions with evil consequences without first bringing about a complete transformation in man's inherent inclination, is to live in illusion. If actions and effects could be so altered, our earth would have become a heaven before long. But it does not so happen. We must once for all realize the fact that there is no possibility whatever of changing the existing behaviour without first bringing about a transformation in man's inherent inclination, and that without changing the existing behaviour, the actual state of affairs would continue to be what it is. That is the whole truth. So let us inculcate this total view, which has three aspects—result, action, and inherited inclination or primal

THE END-PRODUCT OF THOUGHT

tendency. That is the order from above; if we start from below, the primal tendency as the fundamental cause, particular behaviour arising therefrom and particular results, the outcome of that behaviour, would form the chain of cause-effect in that order. We must experience these three truths together; we must concentrate our attention on these. In the field of religion, we are guilty of having committed a grave error in abandoning meditation altogether. We have adhered to things other than meditation. We do not seem to have any desire to transform our primal tendencies. We are after immediate gain. We say that a religious man must change. People often ask: "How is it that despite a great deal of religious revival, society has not changed"? But people may talk about religion for ages together, society is not going to change through mere talk. A society, a religious community which does not harbour any desire for fundamenal transformation, will continue to writhe in pain; it cannot be awakened. Meditation was primarily discovered to enable man to change the inherent inclination which gives birth to a particular disposition. Without a complete transformation of our primal tendencies, all our efforts to change the existing state of affairs are bound to fail.

In the field of education, efforts are on to effect vital changes in the brain; but no effort is made to change and refine man's primal tendencies.

We feel that a change of attitude and character is possible through the practice of meditation. Two kinds of delusions confront us in life — the delusion that perverts our attitude and that which sullies our conduct and behaviour — until we remove these, we shall not be able to bring about any refinement in our outlook or character. Those who have come here to practise *Preksha Meditation* and experience the truth for themselves, must clearly understand that their primary objective is not to annihilate anger or pride, or any other visible evil; rather they are here to investigate their true nature which alone is responsible for all that happens to them. What happens to a man happens to him because he is the kind of man he is. The man himself must undergo a transformation for the present state of affairs to change.

One man said to another, "I saw your wife talking to her lover." The second man immediately flared up. He picked up his gun and said, "Where are they?" The first man said "In the garden." The other man immediately started for the garden in great rage. He would shoot them both dead, he said. Then, as he reached the garden, he recollected with a shock, "Oh, what a fool am I! I've no wife! I'm not yet married !"

There is the general belief that a wife cuckolding her husband deserves to be shot dead. The mind is heavily conditioned by it, and the very idea of an unfaithful wife is maddening and inflames a man so that he quite loses his reason and does not even stop to inquire into the truth of the matter. One thought absorbs him to the exclusion of everything else: he must avenge the insult to his manhood!

Such is the atmosphere that prevails today. Inflamed by passion and subscribing to current conventions, a man takes decisions in a state of sleep walking without really knowing what he is doing.

Let meditation bring about an awakening in us so that we are capable of a total view and of dispassionate observation, and take the right decision and seek a resolution of our problems through full exploration and understanding of the root thereof.

V. HOW I LOOK AT MYSELF (1)

A man is limited by his physical organism, which in itself constitutes a natural limit. No one is free of his body, or from the limitation thereof. The limitation marks a separation. However close one person may be to another, however intimately related, the natural separation caused by the body cannot be done away with. Imagine two men sitting together. They are close to each other, and yet might experience different sensations, one drowned in anxiety, the other exalted by joy. They may be blood-brothers, father and son, bosom friends, deeply intimate and very well-known to each other, and yet their feelings are different, one happy, the other unhappy. Why so? It has been said that one's knowledge or experince is one's own. The *guru's* experience is of little avail to the pupil; or that of the father or the elder brother to the son or the younger brother. If experience were trasferable like money from one person to another, then it would suffice for one member of the family to study; all others need not go to school or college at all. If one member of the family can earn enough money, the life of the family goes on undisturbed even if nobody else makes any money. Not so with knowledge or experience.

One's experience is exclusively one's own. Similarly, the sensation experienced by one person cannot be transmitted to another. Each person's sensation is personal and incommunicable. The same event happening to five different persons would call forth different sensations and different responses from each. One man is so much affected by a particular event that he cannot even eat or drink and life becomes for him a great ordeal, while the same event leaves the other indifferent. "Life is like that!" he says and there is an end to it.

A man came to me and said, "Everything affects me terribly. Any little happening haunts me for days together; I cannot get free of it. What am I to do?" I said, "Why don't you adopt this maxim? Whenever anything happens, say to yourself, 'Life is like that!' Such a happening is just in the nature of things. There is nothing novel about it. Rather it would be surprising if such a thing did not happen!"

You are deceived by a friend and wonder at it. Actually you have not observed the truth of life; you have not really understood the true nature of your friend. That a man should deceive his friend, is an everyday occurrence; there is nothing very astounding about it. When one comes to accept the ways of the world, there is no more perplexity.

Each man's sensations are different. So also are his experiences and physical processes. Birth, childhood, youth, old age, death—all these relate to the body and are distinctive in case of each individual. Each particular organism has its own childhood, youth, old age, birth and death which are unique to that organism. All these are conditioned by that particular organism.

Our life has two aspects—individual and social. That which is personal is individual. But we live in a world where everything is related to everything else, where contagion spreads from one organism to another. Thoughts are also transmissible. A particular thought arises in an individual. Sometimes the same thought arises in the minds of thousands of people simultaneously. Thought, like some diseases, is contagious. And since we are organisms open to contagion, no individual can live alone, in perfect isolation. Our individuality thus comes to have two aspects — personal, that is, particular to an individual, and social that relates to society as a whole. If both these aspects are taken into consideration, then our thinking is wholesome and our approach to ourselves and the decisions flowing therefrom are right. If our thinking is entirely personal, isolated, it cannot be said to be right. Nor can it be right if it is wholly social, completely ignoring the personal factor.

There are thus two patterns of living—the social and the individualistic. The social pattern discounts the individual. The individual is like a mere cog in a machine and has no intrinsic worth of his own. Those subscribing to this communistic way of thinking give all the importance to society, even to the point of total extinction of individuality. What matters is the state; the individual is not at all important; he is expendable, can be hanged or shot dead at will. He is merely a part of the machine. As long as a part has utility, it is maintained. The moment it ceases to have utility, it is dispensed with and replaced by another. It was customary at one time in Japan to convey the old, superannuated parents to a forest to die. A superannuated doting fool had no utility whatsoever. Only that which had utility had the right to exist. For many ages this tradition was prevalent in Japan. Old worthless parents were conveyed by their own children to the forest to rot and die. Man is capable of strange things, caught in a stream of utter selfishness. Even a social approach to a problem then becomes woefully partial and inadequate.

The other extreme is the totally individualistic approach, in which a person thinks only of himself. The individual alone is of value to the exclusion of everything else.

The totally individualistic approach or a totally communistic approach are both pervasive in society today. Both of them are, however, partial, giving rise to endless problems.

We are discussing the possiblity of a different approach altogether in which the individualistic and the communistic points-of-view are harmoniously synthesized, giving rise to a holistic view which takes everything into consideration and excludes nothing whatever.

Three things are vital for man: freedom, self-reliance and self-effort or exertion. Indeed, these are the three great principles of any man's life. Freedom is a great boon; without it man is nothing more than a machine. There can be no greater prostitution than that a man should sell his freedom for bread, comfort or gain. A tradition of slavery has subsisted in our society. There is a difference between a servant and a slave. A servant works for salary, he may leave at will; or the master may dismiss him. However, the terrible thing about slavery was that a slave was sold for good, just like cattle, a cow or a buffalo. All his life, he remained a slave, without any will of his own. The master might ill-treat him, beat him unto death, do what he will, the slave could never leave,. The slavish mentality is permanently ingrained in a slave. To sell oneself for bread or comfort betokens a slavish mentality. That is why a real man would not willingly sell himself or become a slave. He wants to maintain his independent existence. The dearest and the most cherished thing in the world is freedom.

Manu the great law giver very aptly says, "Independence is joy; dependence is sorrow." In the very moment of becoming dependent upon another you purchase sorrow. To be a slave and to be unhappy are not two different things; rather to be a slave is to be unhappy. Likewise, freedom and happiness go together.

Freedom is our greatest joy. No food can be as delicious as independence. Eating is a joy, but only in freedom; eating in slavery can be no joy.

The king once asked the members of his court, "What is the sweetest thing on earth?" One courtier said, "Milk-pudding". "Chocolate", said another. "Curd", "honey", "raisin", "sugar", each person named his favourite delicacy. Still another said, "It is different with different people and depends upon individual taste." Each man gave his opinion, but Birbal kept silent. The king accosted him, "Birbal, what do you say? Which according to you is the sweetest thing on earth?" Birbal said, "The human tongue." The king said, "What rot you talk! How can the tongue be sweet or sour? And how do you make it the sweetest delicacy? Prove it!" Birbal said, "I'll, but on some suitable occasion." And there the matter ended for the time being.

After a few days, Birbal, with the king's permission, invited the queen to dinner at his residence. On that occasion innumerable delicacies were prepared. The queen was enthralled at the variety and the exquisiteness of the dishes and showered encomiums on Birbal for a most delectable feast to which she had been treated.

Presented with an exquisite dish, a civilized human being is prone to eat less but praise the cook most extravagantly. He does it while eating and also later. Four things are discussed too often - food, sex, nationalism and politics. A great deal of one's life is spent in pointless discussion. If we analyse the lives of people who are continually complaining of lack of time for work, we shall discover that a great deal of their lives is frittered away in discussions about food, sex, nationalism and politics, leaving them no time at all for serious work. A man is advised to do some meditation and he immediately objects, "But where is the time? I'm too busy. There is so much to do!" They have no time for anything worthwhile. A very large number of people are continually talking politics. "Our minister, or our Prime Minister," they say, "is no good. Our policies are all wrong. Look at what is happening to the country!" They seem to be so anxious about the fate of the country, as if the entire responsibility for national security devolves upon them. We fritter away our time in useless pursuits and then complain of lack of time.

To return to our story, the queen highly commended the glorious dinner hosted in her honour by Birbal. She was all praise for the exquisite preparations. "What a wonderful treat!" the queen kept saying. She was immensely gratified by the reception accorded to her. After some time, she rose to go. Just then Birbal whispered to a servant, "Sweep and wash the whole courtyard thoroughly. A Turkish slut has sat here and partaken of her meal; the spot is profaned by her touch. Wash it clean of all profanity!" The queen overheard the direction and was beside herself with rage and humiliation. The exquisite provisions she had earlier praised so highly as being most sweet, all turned into vinegar. When on her return to the palace, the king asked her, "How did it go?" she impatiently burst out, "Why in God's name did you send me there?"

"Why, what happened?"

"Oh, everything turned into poison!"

"What, were the dishes not properly cooked?"

"O, no, that's not what I meant."

"What do you mean then?"

"Your Majesty! After a most excellent repast, Birbal said something terribly nasty. I still keep wondering how he had the temerity to say it! The meanest rascal would not say it of his enemy." And then she recounted what she had overheard.

The king was also nettled beyond measure, his brows clouded. He immediately summoned his court and when Birbal arrived, he did not once glance in his direction and showed no awareness of his presence. Birbal immediately understood what had transpired. Those clouded eyebrows plainly told their tale. But he quietly took his place. After some time the king's curiosity overtook his temper and he addressed himself to Birbal thus:

"You're guilty of a great crime!"

"I'm not guilty of any crime, Your Majesty!" said Birbal.

"What did you say when the queen was leaving?"

"Nothing, whatever."

"But did you not say to the servant, "Wash this spot clean of all profanity — it's unhallowed by the touch of a Turkish slut!"

"That, I did say. I remember now."

"But why did you? And how dare you!"

"Well, I had to provide you with a proof."

"What proof? What are you talking about?"

"Your Majesty has quite forgotten. Don't you remember saying, 'How can the tongue be sweet or sour?' and you wanted me to prove it. Now see how my tongue set at naught all my great preparations and hospitality. What prodigious amount of effort and money I put in to provide that 'excellent' dinner to the queen — an equivalent of my whole year's salary! I've gone bankrupt, and yet all my effort was of little avail. You only remember what my tongue uttered; everything else is quite ignored. Well, you know now how delectably sweet or how terribly bitter the human tongue can be!" The king sat motionless and still.

The tongue is sweet; it can also be bitter. This truth applies to the whole of our life. Freedom is most sweet. A dry crust of bread tastes sweet in freedom; whereas in a state of slavery, the most exquisitely prepared viands taste flat, even poisonous.

But most of us have no direct experience of sweetness. Only yesterday I said to a young camper, "Do not take your chapatis with cooked vegetables, if you want to know the real flavour of wheat-bread." Those who eat their bread with spiced preparations, can never know the real taste of wheat. All that they know or can know is the taste of salt or sugar; they do not and cannot know the true taste of wheat-bread or the vegetables. What do we really know of the taste of ribbed gourd or of cucumber, for instance? Their sovereign taste is quite supplanted by that of salt and chillies in profusion.

Freedom has its own unique flavour, but the freedom that we know is overlaid in profusion with spices of slavery, so much so that we never experience true freedom. Only the man who has tasted wheat-bread in itself, unmixed with the spiced victuals, knows how sweet it is. Similarly only the man who has experienced freedom, in all its purity, knows its true flavour.

Maharana Pratap wandered in deserts and mountains and repeatedly withstood all kinds of temptations. He suffered intolerable hardships. Sometimes no bread was available for the prince, his son; the poor child was denied bare means of subsistence. But Rana Pratap knew the taste of freedom, before which all other tastes paled into insignificance—neither rulership, nor magnificence, nor kingdom, nor power, nor any other temptation meant anything to him as compared to freedom.

Individual freedom is a priceless treasure. To deny the individuality of a person is to deny freedom itself. Look at our system of government and our modern city organisation, where the individuality and the freedom of a citizen are gradually being laid waste. The individual is fast becoming a mere cog in a gigantic machine. What slavery, what dependence! You want to instal a window in your room, but you are not free to do so. You have to obtain sanction from the municipal corporation. That you must not cause any inconvenience to your neighbour is intelligible but even when there is absolutely no harm in it, and even if your neighbour has no objection to it, you are not free to execute your plan! One is hedged in by so many laws as to leave no room for freedom anywhere.

The second great blessing of individual life is self-reliance. But where is self-reliance to be found today? There is so much relying on others that men are gradually becoming more and more dependent. You must have heard of *amar bel*, the evergreen creeper. It has a beautiful name, but is a very dangerous creeper. The plant it settles upon is as good as finished. The creeper cannot stand on its own; must find something or the other to lean upon. And it begins to eat into the plant that supports it. Sometimes this creeper spreads up to an area of one kilometre. Whatever it leans upon, it devours. *Amar bel* aptly exemplifies the pernicious effects of dependence. Man too is no less dependent on others, and is consequently no less dangerous than *amar bel*. He too resorts to ruthless exploitation and destruction of others in order to maintain his own prosperity and luxurious living.

A monied man keeps servants upon whom depends all his glory and grandeur. Without his attendants, he would be no different from any other man. The so-called 'greatness' of the master is manifest as long as there are 10-20 hands to work for him. He then thinks he is really somebody. If the 'great' man is obliged to work with his own hands like any labourer, all his 'glory' and 'greatness' would instantly disappear. There would be no occasion then for false pride to subsist. Why does a man want to be a millionaire? In order to secure for himself all kinds of comfort. In the process he becomes so terribly dependent, that without his servants he can do nothing. And yet, though he recognizes the utility of the servant, he turns a deaf ear to his basic needs. When the servant falls ill, he blames it on his fate. When the servant is in health the master takes out of him as much work as he can, but if an exigency befalls the servant, the master is of little avail to him. Is this dependence on the servant less dangerous than that of *amar bel?*

On entering his room an officer found a telegram on his table. He glanced at it hurriedly. It read, "Mother dead. Come at once." His mother was very old. He felt extremely sad and started making preparations to go. Just then a worker entered the office and said, "Sir, my mother has died. You must kindly grant me leave to go. Earlier, I left the telegram on your table." It was then that the officer glanced at the address which he had overlooked in the first instance. So the telegram did not relate to him. He felt immensely relieved. But then he became conscious of the expectant worker who stood before him, awaiting the acceptance of his leave application. The officer pulled a long face and said, "Old people are always dying. Today your mother is dead, tomorrow someone else may die. You cannot just abandon work like that!"

How is that? Here is a man who works for you, and who is instrumental in making available all kinds of facilities for you. But when he is in trouble, you simply ignore him. You become quite insensitive and blind to his most importunate need. It is this subjective, highly self-centred mentality that has given birth to the idea of a socialistic society. The advent of socialism has not occurred without cause. There is a definite inspiration behind it. There is a cause to every effect. The subjective individualistic approach had crossed all bounds, the self was so predominant as to preclude any awareness of another's difficulty or need. This situation inevitably led to a reaction, it ignited a spark and produced a conflagration.

Dependence and subjective individualism are intimately related. Today man has become so dependent that he is not at all interested in self-reliance. It seems that as long as someone is there to work, some people would not be inclined even for a little exertion. Left to themselves, they would not even put a morsel in their own mouth. Perhaps they secretly wish for the invention of a machine which not only would cook food but also convey it to their mouth. Later they would want a machine to digest it for them. This comfort-seeking mentality obliges a man to look up to others for every little thing. It has had a calamitous effect in that man has almost forgotten to exert himself.

The human body is naturally meant for exertion. Indeed the capacity for exertion is the third great blessing of life. The man who has no faith in his own valour achieves little in spite of all kinds of facilities available to him. However, many people ignore this truth. The so-called 'big' man thinks it beneath his dignity to make any effort. To do work with one's own hands is looked down upon as something despicable. We must come to realize the truth that exertion is absolutely necessary for the upkeep of the body.

I used to lament how a labourer was obliged to work so hard! Also what extraordinary toil the ascetics had to endure! They had to go begging for alms, to fetch water, to carry heavy loads in scorching heat. How great an effort it all involved! But gradually I came to realise the truth that exertion is necessary for physical health and that any part of the body, deprived of healthful exercise is liable to turn morbid and sick and utterly useless. The great secret of health is work. Each part of the body requires exercise. For perfect health, the hands, the feet, and every other part must be fully exercised. There can be no proper blood circulation in a part which is not so exercised. Without proper blood-circulation, any part is likely to grow morbid. It requires no germs, or contagion to make it sick. The root cause of multiplying diseases today is lack of exercise. People come to attend meditation camps where they do *yoga-asanas*. Why? Doing *asanas* involves no great spiritual endeavour. Though the effort may partake of spirituality, yet doing *asanas* is not purely a spiritual exercise. The first objective here is body-perfection: to train the body, to keep it in good form. For without a healthy body there can be no meditation, nor any spiritual development, no breath- or body-perception, nor any perception of the psychic centers, nor any perception of colours. All these perceptions become impossible for a sick organism. The body must be in perfect health. Doing *yoga-asanas* is conducive to physical well-being.

It is useful to distinguish clearly between self-reliance and self-exertion. The latter is a physical process. To exercise different parts of the body and employ them in work, to utilize the power latent in them is self-effort or valour. Self-reliance is trust in one's own strength, in one's capacity to exert. Self-reliance comes first; it leads to valour. Without self-reliance, the question of effort or valour does not arise. He who cannot stand on his feet, has to take the help of a stick, or walk on crutches. To have faith in one's own power is the first requisite — that is self-reliance. And to utilize this power, to employ it in work, constitutes valour.

The first attraction of a meditation camp is the prospect of spiritual development; the second the maintenance of physical health. As it is, the desire for physical health comes to be the prime attraction, though it should be the other way round. Spirituality should be the first consideration which in itself ensures physical well being. But with most people the intangible is not easily reached, whereas the tangible is readily grasped.

It is often said that a particular person attended a meditation camp, practised meditation and was cured of his disease. Another says the same thing and still another. And the news spreads far and wide. One suffering from a disease is naturally attracted. I just happened to talk to a camper and I said, "You come from far-away Maharashtra. What for?" He said, "I have not been keeping good health. I got myself thoroughly examined. Doctors are unable to diagnose what is wrong. So I've come here. Since I came here, I have felt better."

To want to be in good health is most natural. One cannot expect much from a sick organism. If the knife is not sharp, how will the housewife pare the vegetables? One needs an instrument, some sort of appliance for doing work. Our body is our instrument. It is the edge of the knife which shaves everything clean. How is it that one generally keeps good health during the camp period? The campers stop taking pills. For an hour daily they are required to practice *asanas* and *pranayam*. Any obstruction in blood-circulation in any part of the body gets automatically removed; the blood begins to flow freely in the veins. You must have seen the policeman directing traffic on the cross-roads. A minute's delay in free passage sometimes causes hundreds of vehicles come to an abrupt halt, causing a traffic jam. For years together our body has put up with a great many obstructions, innumerable blood-particles awaiting free passage.

The body cannot keep in good health unless it is properly exercised everyday. Unless the blood-vessels are thoroughly unblocked, good health is not possible. Physical activity is a must. In the absence of other toil, one might as well take recourse to *yoga-asanas*. Through the practice of *yoga-asanas*, the body gets its needful exercise. Physical activity is thus an essential health requirement.

Freedom, self-reliance and exertion are the three blessings of life which make up a man's unique individuality.

A man's life has two aspects — individual and social. We have briefly considered the individual aspect. But each individual is an inalienable part of society, and we must also consider his relationship with society.

VI. "HOW I LOOK AT MYSELF!" (2)

Without utility, without need, an individual would stand isolated. Each man is bound by need to another, thus giving birth to society. Without union with another, without relationship, an individual would stand alone. But one individual unites with another; he is capable of relating himself to another and this capacity for relationship creates society. Utility and capacity for union become factors of mutual cooperation. The third factor is influence. If one individual were not influenced by another, there would be no society. Society has thus come into being on the basis of utility, mutual dependence and cooperation. The individual is no more isolated; he lives in society, in relationship with others. Utilities are various since needs are many. One requires food, drink, shelter, clothing and what not. There are many needs. Alone, in isolation, an individual would never be able to provide for these. But utility and need are linked together.

The other day we were talking about self-reliance, which is characteristic of an individual. However, if probed in some depth, self-reliance also turns out to be a relative term. Man's need makes him self-reliant. But in the context of the totality of needs, no man can be completely self-reliant. What holds greater validity here is the principle of interdependence which means that men are mutually dependent upon one another; they rely on each other. It is mutual dependence that forms the basis of society. One man ploughs the fields, the other is engaged in business, a third moulds implements, a fourth provides other farm equipment. Through cooperation of them all, wheat flows into the market. The farmer farms the land, but he cannot do it without implements — he uses tractors to plough the fields; without tractors he would be idle. The farmer also needs other equipment. Where does he procure them from? The craftsman makes ploughs. But if there is no iron or wood available, how will he create them? For iron you need the ore, and labourers who would extract the ore from the mine. Everything is connected with everything else. All are interdependent. A particular individual strolls alone by himself. It seems as if he lives alone. But he is not alone. There are others who are walking along with him. Shades of a thousand individuals are accompanying him. His belly is full, and so he walks. If his wife had not served him food, he would find it difficult to walk. His feet would grow cold, his knees would sink; deprived of food, he would not have the requisite energy to stand and walk. When he walks, his stomach along with the food in it moves with him. And also moves with him the provision merchant from whom he procured the wheat flour; and the farmer who produced the wheat, and the craftsman who moulded implements for the farmer. Numberless shadows move with him. Alone he would not be able to take a step forward, would become immobile. Every movement of ours implies the collaboration of a thousand men. The belief that one can live alone, in total isolation, disregards the fact of interdependence; it is a purely subjective illusion. But the moment we perceive that without mutual cooperation, no man can achieve much, the whole picture of our society presents itself before us, clearly showing the inevitable link between the efforts of different individuals. A man by himself can achieve nothing. All work gets done through mutual cooperation.

This cooperative relationship is so subtle that a gross mind is likely to miss it, but to a subtle mind it is apparent at every step. A man is going to a friend's house. He is moving in a particular direction because of his relationship with his friend. He is attached to him and that is why he is going there. It is the need of being related that takes him there.

Relationship, utility and influence — the three together impel mutual cooperation. Without mutual cooperation, no man can live in this world; he cannot even maintain his existence without it. All things are interdependent. The second storey rests on the first, and the first storey on the foundation; the foundation itself rests on the earth. There can be no foundation without the earth. Everything has a base. That which has no material base, belongs to the subtle world. It is not to be found in the material world. In the world of matter, everything rests upon something else. That is why we seek a basis for everything.

A logician was carrying a basin brimful of *ghee*. A question arose in his mind: Does the basin hold the ghee or is it the *ghee* that holds the basin? Naturally, nothing can rest without a foundation. It was apparent that the basin held the *ghee*. And yet could it not be otherwise? May it not be the *ghee* that holds the basin? He would make an experiment, he thought. He turned the basin upside down. All the *ghee* was spilt. The basin was empty. Now all his doubts were cleared. It was conclusively proved that it was the basin that held the *ghee* and not otherwise.

The very basis of society is in question. Society runs on a basis —that of mutual cooperation. Where this is ignored, many difficulties arise. If we analyse today's problems, we shall find that poverty is not so terrific a problem as that posed by lack of mutual cooperation. Man lives in society, yet he is disregarding the principle of interdependence.

"HOW I LOOK AT MYSELF!" (2)

Delhi is a magnificent city. The place where the meditation camp is being conducted is situated between two hotels. Yesterday a friend said, "I don't feel like living between two hotels. The mind is invariably diverted from the purpose in hand. That is why I did not attend this camp." Those magnificent hotels, so very commodious! And the rich people residing therein!. These wealthy people living in splendid apartments present a fascinating picture. Yet, when the creators of those great buildings are quite forgotten, the whole thing becomes problematical. The principle of mutual cooperation implies mutual support, give-and-take, interdependence. If we could keep it in view, no problem would ever arise. The problem arises because of lack of mutual consideration and reciprocity. Society is based upon mutual support. When the very nature of society is denied, when the principle of mutual interdependence and mutual consideration is violated, problems are bound to arise. It is surprising that the people who raised those buildings, whose contribution was the greatest, stand totally ignored.

Two things are necessary for any creation — intelligence or craft and labour. Whether intelligence or craft commanded greater recognition cannot be said with certainty, but the value of labour has never been adequately appreciated. This imbalance between intelligence and labour has posed a great problem which can never be resolved as long as the imbalance continues. A man of intelligence can earn one lakh in a day, even a crore of rupees or more, without putting in any effort. And yet the labourer who executes what intelligence dictates, is denied the bare necessities of life. This great imbalance has vitiated the nature of society that we have created. When the essential nature stands corrupted, problems are bound to arise.

A man was passing through the forest. He felt thirsty. He could not find any water in the vicinity. His thirst meanwhile was becoming more and more intense. Imagine the heat of mid-day in June! But presently he espied a well. On reaching there he saw there was water in the well. There was also lying a bucket, with a piece of rope attached to it. But there was no one who could draw water from the well. At first he thought he should draw the water himself and slake his thirst. But instantly he dismissed the thought as unworthy of him, he being an *amirzada* (the son of a wealthy man). What will people say if they saw him drawing water from the well? It would be perfectly disgraceful! For a man in his position to be found engaged in a mean task like that! He must wait till some servant or other lowly man should come to draw water from the well.

In a little while, another traveller arrived. He too seemed to be in a pitiable condition because of extreme thirst. He saw the bucket with the rope attached to it and a man sitting beside the well. So he said, "Brother, I am very thirsty. Will you please draw some water and give it to me?" But the man replied, "I can't do it! I am an *amirzada*. But why don't you do it, and let me too have some water." The traveller said, "I can't do it, because I am a *nawabzada* (the son of a *nawab*)." The two of them sat idle, waiting for someone to come and draw water for them.

After a short while, still another man came. He called for water from afar, but his precursors bade no reply. He came nearer and said, "I'm dying of thirst. Why don't you give me some water?" Then one of them explained the situation. "I am an *amirzada*," he said, "I can't draw water. It would be beneath my dignity to do so. My companion here is a *nawabzada*; his position too forbids his engagement in a lowly task. We are as thirsty as you. Why don't *you* draw water and let us all have a drink." The new-comer replied, "I'm sorry I can't do it — I'm a *shahzada*, the son of a king."

After some time a fourth traveller arrived. He too was thirsty. He immediately took up the bucket with the rope attached to it, and lowered it into the well. At this, the three of them burst out, "Brother, we too are thirsty; get water for us as well." The new-comer said, "Here are the means ready to hand — the bucket and the rope. Why don't you draw water for yourself?" The first man said, "I am an *amirzada*; it will be beneath my dignity to draw water from the well." The second man said, "I'm a *nawabzada*". The third said, "I'm a *shahzada*, the son of a king. I was born for greater things than merely drawing water from a well." The fourth man said, "Well, sirs, please yourselves!" And he immediately proceeded to slake his own thirst. The other three looked up to him and said, "We too are thirsty. Give us some water!" But the man ignored them quite and while departing said, "I'm a *haramzada*, a bastard. It's not my way to offer water to anyone."

"How is that?" they all cried.

The bastard made a parting thrust "These bloody *amirzadas*, *nawabzadas* and *shahzadas* can produce nothing but *haramzadas!*"

A telling satire! It justly depicts the state of our society where there would be no bastards if there were not a sizable class of *amirzadas*, *nawabzadas* and *shahzadas*, living in idleness and luxury, inevitably giving rise to a bastard race. Here is mirrored before us the face of our perverted society, where the principle of mutual cooperation is thrown overboard; and the natural feeling that one is dependent upon and should be grateful to others is non-existent. When this happens in a society, it is already sick. All social life is vitiated at the core, with increasing violence and cruelty and a host of other maladies.

The first and foremost principle of social life is mutual cooperation, people helping one another. Other things come later

— discipline, for instance which evolves out of mutual cooperation; without the active feeling of interdependence, there can be no growth of discipline.

The master wants his servant to be disciplined, but if the servant finds the master lacking in proper appreciation of his services, if he feels degraded as a human being, he will never be inspired by true discipline; on the contrary, a feeling of reaction to injustice would grow. With the active feeling of interdependence, however, discipline comes of itself.

It is very difficult to take work from another, unless there subsists an active feeling of interdependence between men. However, with mutual cooperation, it is the easiest thing in the world to receive or offer assistance. In our religious order there was a learned and highly-celebrated ascetic, Muni Magan Lal, lovingly nicknamed as "Mantri muni". He was greatly revered, almost second to the *Acharya*. He had grown old and there were many young monks to look after his needs. At times, the monk assigned to the *Mantri muni* would forget to fetch drinking water for him—an hour would elapse and the Mantri muni would suffer thirst in silence, without saying a word. Nor would the Mantri muni reproach the young monk on the latter's return. Sometimes, out of his own sense of guilt at neglecting his duty, the monk would ask forgiveness of the Mantri muni and then Mantri muni would say, "Don't mention it please! You've much to do. You keep so busy, and yet you find time to look after an utterly useless old man like me, who cannot even get up by himself, who cannot even walk. I say this is great!" No amount of reprimand or reproach would have awakened in the young monk the feeling which the artless words of the old man did. The young monk was filled with an ardent desire to do his utmost in the service of his revered Mantri muni.

How does it come about?—that reverent feeling. Out of mutual consideration, of course. A mere upbraiding of the attendant-monk would have created reaction and unkind thoughts in his mind. But the right appreciation of his services, notwithstanding his omissions, served to fill the young monk with reverence.

Mutual cooperation is the one great attribute of social life. The more fully is this truth appreciated, the greater the evolution of discipline in a particular society. Discipline cannot be imposed from without; it is inborn. It is not like the stagnant pond-water, the result of rain from the outer atmosphere. Rather it is like the water of an eternal fountain springing from the earth. There is the water which rains from the sky, and there is the water emanating from the earth. The water in the well is part of a running stream and wherever water comes out of the earth, it flows from running springs and reservoirs. Water flows in mighty currents from the mountains.

Likewise, discipline is a mighty stream. It is not standing rain-water which is essentially limited. You can draw from the pond only that water which is collected there; much of it evaporates and is lost. But a running spring sprouting from the earth runs for ever; it never dries up. You draw water from a well today, and the next day and the next. Just one well provides for the whole village, because it is an ever-running source. It is not the accumulation of rain-water. Similarly discipline flows in our life like an immortal current, a never-ending stream.

The master told the servant, "Listen! You're not to do anything without my permission." The servant said, "All right, master!" Something happened the very next day. The servant came running to the master and said, "Master! The cat is drinking the milk. What am I to do?" The master was exasperated. "Fool!" he said, "Why have you come to me? You should have driven away the animal." The servant said, "Well, Sir, didn't you tell me yesterday not to do anything without permission?"

Here is a case of limited water in the pond! Doing just what you are told! But discipline is a much larger matter. It is vitally connected with intelligence; it cannot be imposed from without; it prospers with the feeling of togetherness, the feeling of mutual cooperation and understanding.

The other day we were talking about freedom which is related to individual life just as dependence or slavery is related to social living. Both these words — freedom and dependence are used by us pretty often, we cherish them both. There is nothing wrong in being free; nor need 'being dependent' have any adverse connotation. We give great importance to freedom — it is considered to be something entirely good, whereas dependence has a pejorative ring since we often use the term as an opposite of freedom. But the meaning of each word is relative. Truth is relative; to be absolute is to falsify. For example, the white colour can be good as well as bad, depending on circumstances. Likewise, the blue colour. And who would say that the black is unconditionally bad? It is the right colour for winter. With the advent of winter, we find everyone clad in black, for it is well-known that the black has great capacity for absorption of heat and is therefore a good protector of skin in winter.

In courts of justice, the judges are clad in black. The black is opaque to influence of any kind. In fact, colours are symbols of feeling, conduct and character. The choice of the right colour is a serious matter, requiring discrimination. The black dress worn by the judges and the lawyers signifies impartiality. A judge must not take sides, nor be influenced by any person or thing; the atmosphere of the court room must be free from prejudice. If a judge were clad in red, he would not be disposed to listen to the lawyers; inflamed by his own importance, he would talk much more than listen to the lawyers. So the red is not the right colour for the courts. Neither red, nor yellow. There is a saying in Hindi, "he turned red and yellow", which means he was beside himself with anger. Both 'red' and 'yellow' are provocative. Yes, colours are of two kinds: hot and cold. The blue is cool, whereas the red and the yellow are hot. So no red or yellow for the judge, since they are provocative and in a state of provocation, a judge cannot deliver justice. He must keep cool; hence the choice of black for the judge is a very significant choice.

To say freedom is always good and dependence altogether bad is a one-sided view. In order to arrive at the truth we require a holistic approach, a many-sided view, according to which freedom can be good as well as bad; similarly dependence can be bad as well as good, depending upon circumstances.

When India achieved independence, people interpreted it in strange ways. On being asked to deposit income tax, the businessman tells the income tax officer, "Now that the country is free, why should I pay income tax at all?" The farmer likewise refuses to pay land revenue, "I'm a free man now. Why should I pay anything?" Here is a satirical anecdote: A man sat in the middle of the road. A truck came along. The driver stopped the truck and said to the man, "Why are you sitting in the middle of the road causing needless obstruction?" The man said, "I'm a free man, the citizen of a free country. I'll do as I please." The driver said, "All right, I, too, am then free to drive this truck without stopping."

Freedom is not always good; the word has many connotations. Likewise dependence is not always bad. If a child were not dependent upon his parents, if it continually disobeyed them, it would get spoiled. Again, a man of inferior intellect has little capacity for independent thought or decision; if left free to act by himself, he is liable to go wrong. It is better for him to heed a wiseman's counsel. All discipline is based on that. It is not right always to have one's own way. Up to a limit, one is free to act on one's own; beyond that one must obey a superior intelligence. There are occasions when one must function independently; there are also occasions when one must depend upon another.

A student recognizes his teacher's superior knowledge. Likewise the pupil his guru's. If the pupil were to occupy his *guru's* seat, he would not thereby become the *guru*. To be a *guru*, one must possess the *guru's* intelligence. One has to acquire learning and wisdom before one can impart it. True freedom flows from right guidance; he alone can command who has served well.

Here is a leaf out of my own book. When we were studying under Acharya Tulsi, he used to say, "Be disciplined! Do what the *guru* tells you; no doing as you please. No talking to one another! No wastage of time! If you adhere to strict obedience for five to seven years, you will feel free to do anything for the rest of your lives. Nobody will object to anything you do; nobody will stand in your way. But if you refuse complete surrender to the *guru* now, you will have no freedom and will always be dependent upon another. Only a good disciple will make a good *guru*; he who has not lived fully the life of a disciple, will never know the fulness of a *guru's* life.

So dependence is no unmitigated evil. Discipline is one aspect of social life; the other is dependence, that is obedience to another. Dependence need not always mean slavery; it is merely an acceptance of another's authority on the part of one whose faculties are yet undeveloped, with a view to fuller development of one's own capacity.

This is what happens everywhere. Thousands of students go to America or Germany for specialized studies. Students from those countries come here. The exchange of students goes on because some arts are more developed in a particular country, and students from all over the world repair there, which means they depend on another country for acquiring mastery in a particular field. Not all disciplines are fully developed in each country, nor all faculties in each man. To acquire what you don't possess, you have to go to another.

In olden times, a tradition was prevalent among various religious orders. A student-monk belonging to one order would go to the head of his order and say, "Master! I'm interested in studying this subject, but there is none in our organisation who can teach it. With you kind permission, I should like to migrate to another religious order where a teacher of this particular discipline is available. On completing my studies, I shall come back to you." The *guru* would give permission and the monk, after relinquishing his own order, would go to enrol himself as a disciple of the other order, accepting their authority and discipline. After completing his studies, the monk would return to his former *guru*.

The third plank of social life is synthesis or harmony. One man living alone cannot come into clash with another. But wherever there live more than one, a conflict of interests is inevitable; there are bound to be differences of opinion and thought. With these differences, there can be no harmonious living. The husband insists that they must shift to another house; the wife wants to continue where she is; the conflict begins. Struggle, conflict and dissensions prevalent in society disrupt life altogether. It is in this context that a synthesis of different points-of-view becomes important. Indeed it becomes the one great principle of humanistic, many-sided approach. Find a coordinating factor between two opposites to ensure harmony. Consider the pros and cons of each move to arrive at a balanced view. And this coordination is possible on the basis of mutual toleration. Without toleration, there can never be any coming together. We have to consider others. Sometimes the father has to accommodate the son; at other times the son has to accommodate the father.

The son said to his father, "Daddy! All this time I have been taking my meals with you, but I'll dine with you no more." The father was a sensible man. He said, "O, sonny, it's all right. All these years *you* have been taking your meals with me, but from today, it is *I* who will take my meals with you." Nothing was changed; things continued as before. The father's humorous approach to the problem side-tracked the conflict and brought about harmony.

Acharya Shri Tulsi often says, "Look, a teacher must know when to speak and when to keep silent. It is not necessary that a teacher should always speak. At times it is good to speak, at other times it is good to keep still, to suffer in silence."

When you consider others, others consider you. But often one does not tolerate anyone. The father knows no toleration nor the mother! But they want the son and the daughter-in-law to show them utmost consideration! It's impossible! To be endured, you have to endure.

Toleration is the fourth principle of social living.

The fifth is co-existence — to live together. Co-existence is possible only with the development of coordination, toleration, mutual cooperation and interdependence.

We are discussing the art of thinking. How to look? How to think? What is the right approach to oneself? Our life has two aspects — individual and social. Both these aspects must be kept in view. A partial, one-sided view, whether wholly individual or wholly social, can prove misleading. Consider both aspects together, without any equivocation.

The modern man is a great equivocator. Actuated by self-interest, he would adopt an individual or socialistic stance to suit the occasion. A man said to another, "O brother! beware of wrong doing! Never be dishonest! Your conduct must be unexceptionable!"

His colleague replied; "Well, It's not me alone; the whole society is corrupt. I can't live in isolation!" Here is an example of an egoist adopting a social stance to serve his own ends.

On another occasion, a man said to his friend, "You've wealth in abundance. People are suffering grievously on account of floods. Why don't you do something?"

The friend said, "Well, each man must endure his fate! What can I, a mere individual, do except take care of myself?"

Here is an example of self-centered individualistic thinking. While committing a heinous crime, a man justifies his conduct on social principles; and where there is some good to be done, he avoids doing it on an individualistic score, saying, " It behoves each man to take care of himself. For as you sow, so shall you reap. I did good in my past life, and am therefore prosperous; the other man did evil, and he must suffer for it now. I can't be made responsible for him!"

Thinking is thus often vitiated by a wrong approach.

For one practising meditation, right thinking is essential. Right thinking means adopting the right approach, that is an individualistic, subjective response where such a response is called for and a socialistic and collective response where society as a whole is concerned. One must have the wisdom to adopt the right course at the right time.

VII. "HOW I LOOK AT ANOTHER!"

A man approached his *guru* and asked him, "Master! How can I be free of sorrow?" It was a big question. To live in a world of sorrow and yet be free of it.

The *guru* said, "Well, we shall talk about it. But first bring me the cloak of a man who is entirely happy."

The man entered a house and asked, "Brother, you are all happy here?"

Everything is all right as long as the question is not posed. The sea is calm as long as there is no storm. But let the winds blow and the storm arise, and it is all commotion. The stillness vanishes as if it were never there. Likewise, it is all right as long as the question is not posed; when it is posed, nothing seems to go right.

The householder said, "Happy? My neighbour is such a scoundrel, creating new problems for me everyday. How can I be happy? In fact, I'm terribly unhappy!"

The man entered another house, and asked, "Brother, I hope you are all happy here and have no problems?" The second householder said, "What a question! Sir, I've a termagant for a wife, who has made my life impossible. I cannot even imagine what being happy is!"

The man went to another house, and still another. He met housewives complaining of their husbands' rages; and husbands complaining of their wives' ruthlessness. He met fathers harassed by insolent sons. He went into thousands of houses and found no happiness anywhere.

He was fed up with his unprofitable rounds, and went back to the *guru* and said, "I am exhausted, Sir. You asked me to procure the cloak of a person who was entirely happy. What to speak of complete happiness, I found no one who was even tolerably satisfied!"

The *guru* said, "Why are they unhappy? What is their grief?"

He said, "Some are in conflict with their neighbour, others complain of a son's misdemeanour; everyone has a grievance against something or some person. Each one of them is unhappy on account of another."

The *guru* said, "The secret of being happy is not to look up to another, but to look at yourself. That's the way to abiding joy."

The man said, "Is that all? You could have told me this before. Why did you make me go round and round to other people's houses for nothing?"

The *guru* said, "Truth is not easily digestible. If I had told you before, you would have rejected it outright. But now that you have gone round and seen for yourself, you will understand that most people are unhappy because they look up to others for happiness."

That's the truth. He who looks up to another, will never be happy. Every man is unhappy, and he is unhappy on account of another. In each case, the other is the cause of one's sorrow. Illness, cruelty, hatred — all occur because of another.

The "swa" meaning 'the self', and the "par" meaning ' the other', 'the alien', 'the opposite', are intimately connected with our individuality and constitute its frontiers. Either we think of "ourselves" or we think of "another". The "par" has two meanings — 'independence' and 'difference'; it has an independent existence, and it marks a separation from and an opposition to the 'self'.

We accept the independence and the difference. Thinking can be from various angles. It is always relative. In itself it makes no sense; its origin and development demand a base, something other than itself — the object may be some individual or thing, matter, space, time, a situation. But without some object which serves as its basis, thought cannot be. Without the fuel there can be no fire. Fuel is also required to ignite the fire of thought. That fuel is "par", 'the other'. No thinking is possible without 'the other'.

We think about ourselves. We have already discussed "How I look at myself!", one's approach to oneself. We must also discover "How I look at another!", one's approach to others. It is an important theme. When we live in society, we have to consider *swa*, "the self", as well as *par*, "the other". Without the other, there would be no society. If there were only *swa*, the self, it would constitute pure spirituality, without any need for social conduct. The whole of our social behaviour is based upon "the other", differentiated from "the self". How do we approach this other-consciousness?

There are two kinds of thinking — constructive and negative. Whether we think about ourselves or about another, our approach can be positive and constructive, or negative and destructive. It has been observed, however, that our approach to another is seldom constructive; for the most part it is destructive. Man is so constituted that he gives greater importance to the self and ignores the other. The most intelligent man, when questioned about the other, tends to depreciate the latter, espies many faults in him. Rarely do we meet a person who would see in another all the virtues and praise him for that. It is but seldom that he would shower such praise. The not-so-intelligent is incapable of recognising merit in another. Such a man looks upon himself as the wisest soul in the world and seeks gratification in displaying to advantage his own virtues. About others, he maintains very strange notions.

A man in power perceives many shortcomings in the general public. He would criticize everything and every person except himself. Of course, he does not directly claim that he alone is virtuous, but then he does not seem to see anything wrong with himself. This negative approach to another makes us find fault with another. Consequently, we are not able to appraise another rightly and give him his due importance.

Values are of great importance in social life; for society cannot do without them. However, to determine what is of real value is very difficult. We find ourselves incapable of right evaluation, because our approach is largely negative. Without first establishing non-violence, no right appraisal is possible in any social set-up.

Indeed, the first condition of right appraisal is non-violence. The mind is steeped in violence. By violence is not meant merely the obvious 'killing and being killed' that goes on in society; rather it is intimately connected with the whole of our consciousness and colours our vision. The greater the identification of our consciousness with persons and things on the principle of pleasure and pain, the more vitiated our vision. But so deeply ingrained in the individual is this consciousness of like and dislike that apart from love and hatred, no third dimension seems possible. Like and dislike ever colour our vision. Our perception of people and things just as they are seems well-nigh impossible. It does not seem possible to see a man as he is. Someone may say, "I see that man as he is." Actually, there is no real perception. A thousand hurdles block our vision. There are so many impediments, such walls of prejudice, that the object is quite lost from sight. The feeling of enmity, friendship, love, pity, etc., stands like a wall between the perceiver and the perceived. It is rare that a man perceives another man just as he is. No man seems capable of pure perception.

Someone asked, "Who is your friend? Who is your foe?"

We are caught between the opposites. Either a man is our friend or our enemy. Either there is love or there is hatred. Either we like or we dislike. There is no other alternative. "Who is your friend? And who is your foe?" seems unanswerable. One must first know another before one can determine whether he is a friend or a foe. If one does not know another at all, there is no basis for determination. And most people do not know. But there must be some who know. For those who know and are capable of seeing things as they are, there is no friend, nor enemy. He who knows transcends like and dislike; he who is caught in like and dislike does not know.

The *guru* made a very significant observation: "Nobody knows." One might say, "I know the members of my family, I know my neighbour, I know people in Delhi," but as a matter of fact, nobody knows anything. Each man is enclosed within the walls of prejudice and illusion which he cannot penetrate. We do not know the man in front of us; we only have an image about him. It is always the images of our own creation that we deal with; reality is far off. We only perceive the shadow, the substance is ever out of our reach. There is no real contact between man and man; it is all a relationship between images which ever breeds conflict. Reality eludes us and we are caught in mere images, shadows without substance!

While crossing a road we saw the solid front wall of a house with a huge lock on its door. Quite impenetrable it seemed, nobody could enter that house. But as we went a little further, we saw the house was a ruin, with its back and side walls all gone. Only the front wall stood with that huge lock on the door which seemed impenetrable. No side walls, no back wall, nothing whatsoever. No basis for living. Only a huge (but utterly useless) lock on the front. Man's condition is not very different — only a shadow of a house without any substance!

To find substance in a world of shadows is not easy. All friendship or enmity is imaginary. We really know neither our friends nor foes. The man we call our friend turns out to be a secret foe, and he whom we look upon as our bitterest foe reveals himself as a friend. We command no pure vision; our perception of friends and foes is faulty. In trust lies the greatest danger, and the greatest security is to be found where danger is. All this reversal of values is the outcome of *par*, 'the other'. Our approach towards another is such that the very word, "the other" has become synonymous with danger. On the contrary, the word *swa*, the self, seems to offer us the greatest satisfaction. How did we come to have such a view? Obviously because of prejudice; because of lack of understanding. It is the attitude of like and dislike which colours all our relationships.

The thinking of a meditator undergoes a transformation, becomes refined; his approach changes; he comes to realize the unique individuality of the other, which is a great breakthrough. Generally a man, preoccupied with himself, is incapable of recognising the independent existence of another.

The father says he loves his son. But he does not recognize the son's right to an independent existence. Any free move on the part of the son causes the father great perturbation. The husband would not admit his wife's free and separate existence. The master, likewise, would give the servant no freedom; he would curb each and every want of his. We have evolved all kinds of controls because we are not inclined to accept dispassionately another's independent existence. Of course we accept it in theory. But in practice it is not acceptable to us. The question of freedom always gives rise to a number of problems.

Without deep meditation, without analysing the manifold layers of our consciousness, without experiencing for ourselves the content thereof, the fact of another person's unique individuality, though acceptable in theory, cannot be directly apprehended by us.

Infinite and wonderfully subtle is the world of our consciousness, but rarely do we inhabit this subtle world. Our perception is wholly conditioned by matter, and so is our thinking.

The father is mightily pleased with a son who earns for him ten to twenty lakhs of rupees per year, irrespective of the means, fair or foul, employed by him. The other son may be more true and honest, even though he does not earn much money. He just makes both ends meet, and is able to save a little. The father says to him, "How much did you make last year? How much did you save?" To which he answers, "Just enough to make both ends meet; not much to save." And the father is displeased, "You are a good-for-nothing", he says, "You just don't know how to get along. How will you marry your children? Or shoulder other family responsibilities? Or maintain your prestige? Who will pay any heed to you?"

The son is roundly blamed and branded incompetent. The one who makes lots of money is declared as good and honourable; the other good-for-nothing. Our whole approach is materialistic, not spiritual. Honesty in itself is not much prized; truth and goodness command no premium. Compassion is discounted. Money, on the other hand, however earned, commands great prestige.

To aspire to a happy and conflict-free life, while our approach and thinking remain materialistic, is to be lost in futility. The secret of joyful living, the evolution of a constructive viewpoint and the development of our creative powers — all stand forestalled by materialism.

It is a very complex problem. We never do justice to another. We cannot do justice even to ourselves! So how can we be just to another? One who is not just to himself cannot be just to anyone. One whose thinking is limited by worldly things, can never come to know the reality about himself, and so cannot do justice to his own innate capabilities. Only that man is capable of justice whose mind is firmly established in truth, non-violence and non-acquisitiveness. A thousand echoes go rumbling about us, proclaiming that people are not considerate to one another, that good conduct, kindness, is valued no more; that evil is thriving and goodness on the wane, that morality is declining and immorality waxing strong. The situation is causing great anguish and concern to the serious-minded.

However, such anguish and its expression are ineffective in meeting the challenge.

As long as thinking is materialistic, non-violence cannot flower. Nor can truth or non-acquisitiveness be established. And without non-violence, without truth and without the spirit of non-possessiveness, our thinking about the other cannot be constructive.

For the growth of constructive thinking, it is essential that non-violence and non-possessiveness are fully established in life and society. For this it is necessary for us to recognize the individuality of the other, his independent existence. What advantage accrues to us through the other? How is one man benefited by another? In this context, a new science, fast developing these days, has significant insights to offer. The modern theory of environmental influences can play a big role in developing a positive approach, by bringing home to man the most remarkable fact that even a slight displacement of a particle can cause a great upheaval in nature.

A campaign for the extermination of rats is on these days. However, a total extermination could give rise to a great many problems; the extinction of a living species is fraught with grave consequences.

The flies, the mosquitoes are not utterly without worth; they too contribute towards human welfare. The mosquitos bite and yet they have their utility. This applies to all the insects that are apparently harmful. The rats, for example, devour huge quantities of grain; they cause a lot of damage, but they also have their utility. The extinction of rats would result in the extinction of cats, and of many other species responsible for the destruction of a number of pests. Everything in nature is interconnected; one particle with another; a million threads combine to make a counterpane; or a sack to carry a load. One thread by itself has little utility, but many threads unite to produce useful articles.

The whole of our world is a unity, a synthesis, not a breaking-up or disintegration. Living is possible only through cooperation. All the species, and the sub-species in nature, all that exists is the result of synthesis, of integration. Disintegration means decay. The whole order of the universe stands disturbed by division and discord.

The science of environment underlines the importance of union for survival, of the desirability of not interfering with the natural processes, of not disturbing nature's equilibrium, so as not to create disorder and confusion.

As a result of present-day atomic and nuclear experiments, the very atmosphere of the earth stands adversely affected. It is causing great concern all round. The solid atmosphere surrounding the earth affords us protection from the intense heat of the sun. The disintegration of this protective cover could mean the end of the human race, the end of the world, for man will not be able to endure direct contact with the sun.

It is therefore essential that we develop a constructive approach. For the evolution of constructive thinking, it is necessary to purify our consciousness. As it is, our consciousness is riddled with impurities; it is very much identified with things and ideas. It must rid itself of all identification, so as to be capable of fitting in with the 'other' and with society. The feeling of violence, of untruth, of possession, of dominating the other, characterising our consciousness, has to be got rid of. Our consiousness must be freed from these impurities, otherwise our approach will continue to be negative and destructive.

For the evolution of a constructive approach towards nature, it is essential for us to be fully considerate to all conscious beings, instead of being guided by materialistic considerations. Without full awareness, it would be difficult to transform our materialistic outlook.

It is possible for an individual to radiate sobriety, simplicity and tolerance, but only if he is firmly established in self-observation and awareness.

The whole problem of negative thinking is caused by our materialistic approach—too much attachment to material things. The moment we attain to the boundless depths of meditation and see things for what they are, we shall be able to adjudge the true value of material objects, and shall never aspire to dominate over another. We shall then come to realize the essential humanity of 'the other' and our approach towards him will be constructive. Life in this ever changing world is full of problems and these problems go on multiplying without any possibility of a solution. Even the so-called religious people are riddled with problems and the net of problems has become so wide as to embrace everything. The one and only cause thereof is the rigidity of our ways of thinking and feeling. Our whole outlook is stereotyped, and so is our conduct. We live in a kind of limbo, totally unmindful of what we do and how we live. There are two kinds of insensitivity—a befuddled vision and thoughtless conduct.

A meditator must clearly understand that the first priority is for chastening one's approach, to dissolve the state of oblivion, of unawareness, in which a man usually lives. This would require experimentation and experience. Here in the meditation camp, people are experimenting—they are directly experiencing the truth of things. Not merely accumulating knowledge, not merely theorising (for it is not a matter of knowledge or theory). Theory without practice is of little use. But practice combined with theory yields fruit which is most valuable.

This present moment is very sacred for us, for it is in this moment that we have gained an insight into the combination of theory and practice. May we benefit from this discovery! Whatever hard work we have put in, whatever experience we have acquired, let us mature it further in the light of this knowledge. May our hearts be filled with an intense longing for liberation and may we advance undeterred on the path of freedom!

VIII. FREEDOM FROM REACTION (1)

It is my birthday today. I mention it only because you know it already. I begin the new year with a fresh resolve: "Development and still greater development of non-violence in my life!"

People want to know about my progress in life. They say, "How is it that you have been able to write so many books? How did you achieve such mastery over yourself?" I should like to tell them of a great maxim which has effortlessly permeated and transformed my life. That great maxim is : "Freedom from reaction".

There are two forms of violence — reaction and revenge. Killing, too, is violence, but no man is engrossed by a desire to kill all the time. Nor does he actually commit a murder everyday. If he kills some one every day, he would himself go mad in course of time. Only rarlely does the spirit to kill overpower a man? It is only a hardened criminal who commits a murder. The other two forms of violence are more common, i.e., reaction and revenge. Even among these two, reaction is more frequent.

During the course of a single day, we react a hundred times; and a hundred times we indulge in violence. Many times it so happens that one's very breath, the ingoing as well as the outgoing, is thoroughly steeped in violence. Occasions for reaction are never wanting in life. Since childhood I have made it a rule not to react, so as to be able to do something in life. One who is caught in reaction, loses his creative powers; such a one can only indulge in destructive activity. He can accomplish no great work, for one can use one's energy this way or that, for construction or destruction. How you utilize your energy is for you to determine. You can use it for constructive purposes or lay it waste in acts of destruction. Each man must determine for himself if he is going to utilize his energy constructively or destructively.

I made a strong determination and I am happy to report that most of the time I have been free from reaction. I don't remember entertaining any malice towards others. The moment I found that some one intended to cause me harm, I told myself he was wasting his energy, that his powers declined. I see a man vomiting. It is not necessary for me to vomit also. In actual everyday living, it does happen that one man's vomit causes nausea to another and makes him vomit too. But if one's morale is high, one does not succumb to the morbid inclination.

The problem of violence is a formidable one. There are many occasions for committing violence in life. But not to indulge in violence or reaction, despite provocation, to maintain still one's equilibrium and lead a life of vigorous action in perfect non-violence, is a great achievement.

To lead an active life is to utilize to the full one's independent nature; it is to experience for oneself the joy of free uninhibited action. Whatever one does then, one does it with full awareness and responsiblity, and not because of any compulsion. The reactionary is ever the victim of another's will.

Here is a tale, primarily meant for children, but truly significant. A father and his son went riding a horse. People saw them and said, "Look at that heartless pair riding a poor sickly horse!" The father immediately reacted to this observation by getting down and walking beside his son on the horse. A little later, someone remarked, "Look at that hefty shameless young fellow riding the horse and his poor old father footing it along!" At this sarcastic remark, the boy got down and made his father ride the horse. A little way farther, an onlooker remarked, "It's really strange, the old man himself riding in comfort and making the poor boy plod on foot." On hearing this, the father also climbed down, and both walked beside the animal. A little later, another group, met them and one of the party said, "See those fools going on foot beside the horse while they could easily ride the animal!"

The man caught in reaction finds himself in a quandary. He knows not what to do; all the ways are closed to him. His mind is restless and he cannot determine on any single thing.

There was a youngman newly turned monk. He lay resting beside a village pool, with a brick under his head for a pillow. The women of the village came to the pool to fetch water. As they were passing by, one of them said, "Look at him! He has become a monk, yet he must have a pillow, even though it be of brick!" The young monk heard it and said to himself, "I haven't done well in using the brick as a pillow." And he pushed the brick away from under his head and lay without any head-support. The party of village maidens, on their way back home, noticed him again and the same girl who had spoken before, now remarked in passing, "What a feeble-minded creature is this monk! We said he should not have a pillow, and he has pushed aside his brick!" The monk heard it and put the brick under his head once again. On her next trip to the village pool, the same maiden saw the monk lying with the brick under his head and remarked, "What kind of a monk are you! We criticized pillow-keeping, and you shove aside your brick; we criticized the latter act, and you put the brick back under your head. If you so readily submit to our criticism, you will not be able to do anything. Have you not taken to the monastic way of life? Why then, let the world say what it will, you must keep your own counsel, or you'll never be a true monk!"

To live in this world, blindly reacting to what others say is an impossible undertaking. The great blessing of non-violence is to live in accordance with what is right, irrespective of worldly criticism: As long as the mind is caught in reaction, a man cannot be said to be truly non-violent. Most men's understanding of non-violence is rather gross. The accidental crushing down of an ant under the feet is pronounced to be an act of violence; not so the most reactionary deed!

What is the cause behind the prevailing indiscipline? Blind reaction. We do not even listen to another, not to speak of accepting what he says. Indeed each man is inclined to have his own way without any consideration for another. To learn from another is no longer considered to be good form. Amongst the new generation, intolerance, the tendency never to accept what another says and to flout discipline—all of which constitute voilence—are increasing day by day. There are two reasons for this—those privileged to speak know not what to say or how to say it; and those obliged to hear do not know how to listen.

Discipline is essential for right living. Social life without discipline is a mere skeleton from which the spirit has evaporated. Each man's body, each living organism, is a skeleton but it moves. What makes it move? The breath of life! It is the power of breath that makes the body move, without this power, it remains a useless apparatus without any movement or life of its own.

Discipline is the life-breath of our being, but without non-violence, there can be no discipline. In fact the greater the violence, the greater is the indiscipline, and conversely, the more mature the spirit of non-violence, the more perfect the discipline. Non-violence manifests itself in action-oriented life, in total freedom from reactionary mentality and consequently from all reaction.

There is the fable of the monkey and the sparrow (weaver-bird) from *Panchtantra*. The sparrow sat in its nest in a tree and the monkey sat on a branch nearby. The rainy season was in full swing and it was raining hard. The monkey was shivering. The sparrow saw him shiver and said, "O monkey, you resemble man very closely. You have hands and feet like him. You can do anything. Why don't you build a shelter for yourself?" At this the monkey was filled with great anger. He leapt furiously and tore up the sparrow's nest into shreds and throwing down the bits, exclaimed, "What cheek in you to tell me what I should or should not do! How dare you preach to me! I have hands and feet all right, but I shan't stand your sermonising. If I can't build a house for myself, I can at least bring another's down."

The tale illustrates a life of reaction. The sparrow meant well and spoke out of charity, but the monkey's pride (and man's too) knows no bounds; he resents any kind of interference, however well-meaning He looks upon himself as the wisest and the best — a superior being. Who could advise him then, when all advice is looked upon as an affront? Most cruel and vicious is the serpent of the ego that is firmly established in a man's heart; withal, it is very poisonous and perverse, ready to deal a mortal blow to anything or person that dare confront it.

With pride in our heart, the development of non-violence is just not possible. Will reaction ever lead us to freedom? This discussion is pertinent not only to a mendicant's life, but also to society. Even for living in society, it is desirable to curb one's pride. For the monk, of course, it is absolutely necessary. But the worldly man must also exercise restraint.

Queen Victoria knocked at the door of Prince Albert's apartment. "Who is there?" demanded the Prince from inside. "Empress Victoria", said the Queen, but the door continued shut. She knocked again, and once again the same query greeted her ears : "Who's there?" "Your dear wife, Victoria" said the Queen this time and the door was instantly flung open. For the Empress there was no admission, but for the sweetheart there could be no bar. Hauteur is productive of tension and engenders still greater arrogance in another, whereas humility begets humility. The one great reason for reaction is pride, and when both the parties are filled with self-importance, the situation becomes impossible.

Pointing out another's error also invites a reactionary response. To tell another that he is in the wrong is a dangerous thing. Ninety-nine persons out of one hundred would passionately resent such a charge. To indicate another's lapse is to turn him into a foe. This applies not only to worldly people, but also to the spiritual practitioners. Why should I then try to reform another and buy his enmity in the bargain? Because the man whose mistake is brought to the fore, seldom accepts it with grace. Instead of responding to it positively and saying "Thank you very much for pointing out my error! You have done me good. I'll be more careful in future," the man very often starts quarrelling with his reformer, saying "What the hell do you think of yourself? A slip of a boy and finding fault with me? What do you know of life? I've lived longer and know better. What cheek to discover any faults in me! I'll teach you a lesson!" A terrible reaction is born which soon changes into a desire for revenge, and is ever destructive.

One man casually tells his friend, "You're in the wrong" and immediately there develops a knot in the friend's mind, and moved by an impulse to refute, he hurls the same charge at his accuser fifty

FREEDOM FROM REACTION (1)

times a day, iterating, "It's *you* who are in the wrong". The poor remonstrator knows not what to do. He says to himself, "What a spectre have I raised! I only pointed out his mistake in all goodwill and affection, with a view to saving him from unpleasant consequences, but this man has taken it amiss. Reacting to a supposed insult, he is now dominated by a feeling of revenge and is for ever finding fault with me." Without non-violence, there can be no freedom from reaction.

I look upon Acharya Bhikshu's life as a model of non-violence. In the past two centuries, there have been only two apostles of non-violence—Acharya Bhikshu and Mahatma Gandhi. There is a good deal common to them both.

A devotee came to Acharya Bhikshu and said, "That man over there is picking faults in you. He says you have this defect and that — indeed a thousand imperfections!" Acharya Bhikshu blandly replied, "What's wrong with that? I became a monk simply to get rid of my imperfections. I'm practising austerity to be free of my defects. That man is my great benefactor, since he is cooperating with me in the task of removing my faults. I am grateful to him."

Here is a life of pure action. Acharya Bhikshu had not a trace of reaction in him. An average person, when told of someone picking faults in him, would react with a vengeance.

A politician standing for election was told that a particular person was calling him names. He immediately reacted by saying, "All right! Let me win this election. As soon as I become a minister, I'll set him right, teach him a lesson for calling me names."

Most people think it manly to pay back in the same coin. Tit for tat! Someone hurls abuse at you. If you endure it in silence, you are no man! You must hit back. Very few people are able to maintain their equilibrium in the face of an insult. Very few return good for evil.

Here's another leaf out of Acharya Bhikshu's life. He was preparing to sojourn in Pali for the rainy season. He obtained permission from the owner to stay in an old shop. Later some people came to know of it. There are all kinds of people in the world. At that time there were a great many opponents of Acharya Bhikshu. These adversaries went to the owner of the shop and instigated him against the Acharya. The shop-owner was thus misled into turning the Acharya out. "You can't stay here," said the shop-owner. Acharya Bhikshu smiled and said, "All right!" and walked out of the shop. He found shelter elsewhere. The rains set in. Very heavy rains! It so chanced that under the impact of the heavy downpours and the cyclones accompanying it, the shop where he had earlier stayed collapsed. When he came to know of it, the Acharya said, "Look! Those people who turned me out did me a good turn. If I had stayed in the shop, I would not be alive today. They are my saviours! God bless them!"

A man caught in reaction would think otherwise. He would feel insulted at having been turned out and he would want to avenge his insult. Or at least he would speak ill of his tormentors. Reaction is productive of violence, tension, disequilibrium, obstruction in the smooth flow of blood, and sometimes this blockage is so extreme as to cause haemorrhage. Brain haemorrhage is the result of extreme tension and behind every tension lies the spirit of violence, reaction and revenge.

The doctrine of non-violence is not merely a religious doctrine. It is the principle of good, harmonious living. Most people are a great deal preoccupied with diseases. Newer and newer medicines are being evolved but the diseases go on multiplying. One must thoroughly explore this phenomenon of disease-multiplication. Diseases multiply not only due to germs, but also because of psychological violence.

It has been found that people participating in meditation camps get rid of their addiction to medicines. Even chronic diseases get cured. What makes these diseases disappear? Most diseases are psycho-somatic in character. They originate from the mind, from the violence latent there. Meditation helps dissolve all psychological tension and brings about freedom from reaction. In that climate, diseases cannot survive. The very basis of their existence is destroyed. One of the principles of logic lays down, "Every effect has a cause; without the cause there is no effect." But we do not search for the underlying cause. We get preoccupied with extraneous matters, and the fundamental cause is lost sight of. If we realize for ourselves the truth as to how diseases multiply because of psychological pressure, we shall not then resort to drugs, nor become valetudinarians. In fact, many people come to attend meditation camps because they are fed up with doctors and drugs. The prescription is usually for the eradication of germs; the medical practitioner can do no more than prescribe antibiotics. That's the limit of his cure. But how will antibiotics help? The germs of the disease will of course be killed. But at the same time these drugs damage the vital force of the organism. Antibiotics are meant to destroy. These do not possess the intelligence to kill only the disease-germs, and not the life-saving elements in the body. The function of antibiotics is to destroy—they would destroy the germs all right, but they also destroy the life-saving elements.

It cannot be that a man who takes to antibiotics is free from worry. He has also to take vitamin pills in order to make up for the loss caused by the antibiotics. The physician would always prescribe Becosules along with the antibiotics. Now, how long is one going to take B. Complex? The doctor prescribes a drug to destroy the disease-germs and the patient takes it regularly, whereas the cause of the disease may lie elsewhere. How could a cure be effected in such a case? The disease may not be due to the germs alone. A great many diseases are caused by psychological pressure. With the removal of that pressure, the disease is automatically cured.

Meditation has been found to cure a number of diseases— diabetes, ulcer, high blood-pressure, etc. How does it happen? No medicine administered and yet the disease is cured! Practise meditation and the eczema disappears. Why? Simply because many of these diseases are primarily psychological; they are rooted in mental tension. We have never seriously inquired into the matter. Subtle implications of violence evade us — we are totally preoccupied with its gross manifestations. It is said that the Jains recognise non-violence to be the first principle of religion. It does not appear so to me. If they really regarded it as the most important thing in their life, they would not be afflicted with so many diseases. The fact is that the Jains are no less sick than other people. It shows that they have accepted non-violence only in theory and they do not practise it. *Preksha Meditation* constitutes in itself the practical aspect of religion. We are so involved in futile discussions, that this practical aspect itself stands sadly neglected.

Let us evolve a new approach. Let us not be too much concerned with mere theory; instead let us fully establish ourselves in the doctrine of non-violence through practice. What is required is constant evaluation of our efforts. It is only through practice that non-violence flowers in our life.

An hour's practice of non-violence through *Preksha Meditation* is far more valuable than a thousand theoretical discussions thereof. One who meditates for an hour, has a direct experience of non-violence. Only then does he become capable of fine discrimination. Freed from the tyranny of like and dislike, the mind becomes innocent and pure. This dissolution of like and dislike, no argument, however prolonged, could effect; on the contrary, argument only serves to strengthen the habit of love-hate relationship.

I remember an incident during Acharya Sri's visit to Haryana. A resident of Bhiwani approached Acharya Sri and said, "Sir, I wish to hold a religious debate with you." "What for?" asked Acharya Sri. He answered, "I just want to have it!" "But why? What is your objective?" insisted Acharya Sri. At last he blurted out, "I wish to vanquish you in argument." Acharya Sri laughed and said, "Aren't you making a mountain of a mole hill? What good will it do? If you are so keen to outwit me, I hereby accept defeat. Go and broadcast it all over the town. Tell them you have overthrown Acharya Tulsi; I shan't contradict it!"

The man stood still, without a word. On Acharya Sri's next visit to Bhiwani, he was among the foremost of his devotees. He was also at the head of the Reception Committee to welcome him and later it was he who conducted the public meeting.

When we ourselves are free from reaction, when there is no violence within us, it becomes difficult for others to indulge in violence. Even if they were previously so inclined, something holds them from proceeding as per plan.

On the other hand, if my mind is full of violence, even though I might discuss the doctrine of non-violence a hundred times so as to understand it fully, it would come to nothing. The whole attempt is doomed to failure from the very beginning.

There is only one way of establishing oneself firmly in the doctrine of non-violence—*Preksha Meditation*. This is practical living. If religion becomes impractical and conventional, if it is divorced from direct experience, it would be a lifeless thing. We do not believe in a dead, stereotyped religion. What we are after is a living religion—a religion which would resolve our present-day problems. We have nothing to do with that religion which is solely preoccupied with life after death.

"Practise religion—you will not go to hell." "Practise religion—you will go to heaven, find salvation." When? In the hereafter? Your present life stands untransformed and you are talking of paradise and salvation! The individual who cannot find salvation in the present, will never find it after death. If there is salvation for man, it is here and now. One who does not properly value the present, would lose himself in the illusion of heaven and salvation, both heaven and salvation ever existing beyond his reach. He would never be able to establish any contact with them, like the parallel straight lines which go along side by side but never meet.

Religion aims at reforming the present, bringing about a transformation in everyday living. A very strange thing has come to pass. In the so-called religious families, men and women practise religion, visit religious places, pray and worship, but also they quarrel among themselves. Whatever evils are found in the irreligious, are also very much present in the so-called 'religious'; they are in no way different. They seem to practise meditation, work for salvation, but at the same time, they are very much involved in petty jealousies and wrangles. If heaven and salvation were so easy to attain, no one need transform himself!

It is a vast subject. We might devote a whole camp-period to the consideration of non-violence which is a great power. Non-violence is a peerless light, at present beclouded; a radiant flame almost deadened with ashes; its brilliance quite vanished.

FREEDOM FROM REACTION (1)

The man who has had a direct experience of non-violence, is filled with unlimited energy. In him is awakened the capacity to die, which constitutes in itself the greatest power a man can know. The ultimate power wielded by the rulers of the world is the power to kill; they can do no more. And the man who has awakened in himself the capacity to die can face all the world powers with equanimity; he becomes insuperable. Nothing can frighten or suppress him; he becomes invincible.

The development of such power is possible only through non-violence. India once witnessed this power, appreciated it fully. But during the Middle Ages, a change occurred.

The historians perhaps indulged in gross misrepresentation and a feeling grew up that non-violence had weakened the nation. That such a feeling should grow is most surprising, for where there is non-violence, there can be no fear. And *vice-versa*. Fear and non-violence cannot exist together. Such a powerful weapon is non-violence that gives a thousand men ready to die, a hundred-thousand – strong army cannot destroy them. The army indulges in killing when the enemy confronting it is actuated by the same motive. If the persons in front display an altogether different mien, if their countenances show no violence within, no aggressive design whatsoever, the biggest army is rendered inactive; its posture of violence, too, undergoes a transformation. But we have made non-violence appear to be utterly worthless. The frightful prospect facing us today is that of psychological violence.

In the context of *Preksha Meditation*, I should like to dwell at length on psychological violence alone, because the observance of non-violence forms the practical aspect of *Preksha Meditation*, which aims at doing away with violent impulses and ruthlessness, and to awaken compassion. Our hard-heartedness has created innumerable problems. All the corruption, evils and lack of authenticity originate from insensitivity. If a man were really humane, there would be no ground for evils to flourish.

Shrimad Rai Chandra was like a teacher to Gandhiji. He was a great spiritual practitioner. He dealt in jewellery. After a merchant had entered into some bargain with him, the prices shot up and the merchant stood to lose around Rs. 50,000/-. In those days, about 70 years ago, it was a tremendous sum. The merchant was quite flustered. Shrimad Rai Chandra came to know of it and called at him. He found the merchant greatly upset. Shrimad said, "What's the matter?" The merchant said, "Sir, have no fear on my account. I'll pay what I owe you even to the penny." Shrimad said, "Don't you worry about paying. Let me know your actual position. How are you getting along?" But the merchant was preoccupied with his debt to Rai Chandra. He said, "Sir, I'm fully sensible of my obligations. I'll pay as early as I can. You don't kindly insist on an immediate payment." Shrimad replied, "I have not said a word about payment. It is *you* who are reiterating it tiresomely. Are you reading from a prepared statement?" But the merchant was grossly preoccupied with the matter and he said again, "I've got the promissory note ready with me. Here it is. I'll pay as early as I can." Shrimad took the promissory note and said, "What do you take me for? A harpy, a blood-sucker?" and while saying so, he tore up the promissory note. The merchant stood still with wonder.

Compassion from the heart, from the deepest layers of the mind—that is the first characteristic of a truly religious man. If there is no compassion, if hard-heartedness continues, a person cannot be said to be religious—indeed, to call a ruthless person religious would be a mockery of truth.

The practice of *Preksha Meditation* is an effort to awaken compassion. It is an endeavour to make the heart pure and innocent. The aim is to transform our consciousness so that we can establish an intimate relationship with one and all.

IX. FREEDOM FROM REACTION (2)

'Action and reaction' are natural phenomena. A thornprick and the hand immediately reaches the affected spot to pull it out! The pricking of the thorn is action; extracting it immediately, reaction. A thorn pricks, the message is instantly transmitted to the central nervous system through messenger-nerves. A direction is given, the muscles get activated, and the hand reaches out to extract the thorn. That is the theory of action and reaction. To every action there is a reaction. It is inevitable. Nevertheless, we must avoid those reactions which do not further our well-being, which are positively harmful, and which stand in the way of our fulfilment, perverting our habits. Merely saying that reaction is natural, would not do. Many people think that it is natural for a man to be angry if somebody abuses him. If he does not get angry, he is dubbed as 'timid' and 'weak'. One is not supposed to pocket an insult quietly; a man who does so is not considered manly. However, every response cannot be said to be natural; we must exercise discrimination. All those responses which are natural for the continuation of life require no thought on our part; we don't have to make any effort to change them. But there are reactions which are not natural, which proceed from some belief, some conclusion, almost unconsciously. These we must avoid. But how? That is a complex problem. Because one has formed certain habits, because the constitution of one's brain is such that given a particular situation, a particular reaction automatically comes off, despite one's will to the contrary.

A good deal of work is necessary for ushering in light; darkness requires no exertion! Light comes and goes but darkness is eternal! One strives to cultivate forgiveness, but in the moment of action, forgiveness is lost sight of, and anger arises automatically. How to be free from these reactions? We need some support — a sound maxim. For we want no excuses ; we want the work done.

A story from the history of *Terapanth*. Acharya Rishirai directed Jaicharya to proceed from Bidasar to Bikaner. It was formidable weather, terrifying heat, the sizzling sands of the desert — those frightful dunes ; there were no roads! A 70-mile journey in the hottest month of the year and no water anywhere! To traverse those scalding dunes, all the way to Bikaner! Such was the command of Rishiraj from Mewar to Jaicharya: "Proceed from Bidasar to Bikaner!" It presented serious difficulties to the monks. Also to the camp-followers. Anything could happen. It posed the greatest danger to life itself. And a very critical situation arose soon after the foot march began. We have on record Jaicharya's word for it. On the very first day a fierce dust-storm threatened to bury them alive! The alarmed travellers gathered round Jaicharya and respectfully said, "Sir, it's a question of discipline. The Acharya's word must not be slighted, but perhaps a way could be found so that we are not guilty of disobedience, but at the same time we avoid this seemingly fatal journey." Jaicharya said, "Let rustics and slaves find excuses for evasion! I am going to carry out the Acharya's command!"

All evasion is vain. The intelligent man boldly confronts the issue. He ever keeps his aim in view and steadfastly works for its fulfilment. But we do need a sound doctrine with which it is possible to avoid reaction and to turn the tide thereof.

A sound basis for action evolves through practice. There can be two kinds of support — theoretical and practical. Both have their utility.

The ancient Preceptors have laid down specific maxims for the ascetic's daily conduct. They say, "In such and such situation, seek refuge in such and such maxim."

A particular situation arises. For instance take food. The right kind of food is not available. How to appease one's hunger? The relevant dictum reads: "It is my *dharma* (moral duty) to endure hunger in a particular situation. It is my *dharma* not to eat anything uneatable. If the right kind of food is not available, it is my *dharma* to go fasting."

Somebody utters hard words, indulges in downright abuse. Anger is the common reaction in such a case. One gets agitated. But a sound maxim might save one from falling. In this context a very important doctrine was laid down: "Whatever another says, in whatever way, however uncomplimentary and hard, go into it; find out the truth or falsehood thereof. 'Am I really guilty of this? Is there any truth in what is being said?' If there is, anger is out of question. Rather one should say to oneself, 'This man is speaking the truth. I have been negligent. I have unwittingly committed a mistake. I must simply accept this fact. I'll tell my accuser that he is right and I'm guilty.' If what is said is not true but the result of illusion, sheer imagination, one should say to oneself, 'What is being said does not apply to me! Why should I be agitated for nothing?" This is sound doctrine. "If it is a fact, I must simply accept it. There is no room for anger. If untrue, it does not apply to me. Either way I need not be agitated." If carried into practice, this doctrine would help one avoid many a pitfall; one would not get easily excited or enraged. On the other hand, it would help a man maintain his equilibrium under all circumstances.

In a different context, a man condemns somebody. The person condemned is displeased. If there is praise, the man is pleased. Both pleasure and displeasure are reactions. And the mind is so conditioned as to react to pleasure and pain automatically. A little praise sets the face aglow; the slightest censure makes it crestfallen. Is it possible to avoid such extremes? Here is a beautiful maxim that can prove helpful:

> No one becomes a thief if called so by another; no one becomes a saint if called so by another. One's conscience tells one whether one is a thief or a saint.

This is a good maxim and if only one can assimilate it thoroughly, one can be free from reaction.

Given self-confidence, confidence in one's own capacity and valour, another's opinion can do one no harm. People generally do not want a man to rise. Particularly the older people, one's own parents, stand in the way of the younger generation. They go on harping on the goodness of their own times, everlastingly decrying the succeeding generation, calling it feeble and worthless.

The conflict between the young and the old has been there from time immemorial. The older generation and ancient accomplishments command easy recognition; the younger persons and contemporary achievements have to struggle for recognition. Man is not generous enough to grant recognition to another easily. The new generation is impatient to win recognition and the older one is full of pride, has its own standards, and is reluctant to accord recognition to the younger generation on the basis of newer values. This conflict is to be found in all fields — literature, *ayurved* or religion. "Just because a thing is old, does not make it good" — the renowned poet Kalidas sounds here the characteristic note born of two generations of conflict. The old scholars had treated his poetry and plays with slight respect, and the poet was obliged to observe that mere antiquity was no guarantee of excellence in literature; that contemporary poetry could not be said to be inferior just because it was new. A thoughtful critic would declare a poem to be good or bad only after a thorough examination, whereas a foolish one would thoughtlessly continue to sing praises of antiquity, discarding the new.

Acharya Vagbhatt wrote a book entitled *Ashtanghriday*, which the leading *ayurvedic* practitioners did not recognize. Even Vagbhatt was slighted by the older generation whose attitude made him pen the following lines: "For the mitigation of wind take oil, for gall use *ghee*, and for cough honey is most wholesome. It does not matter who says this; the speaker is not at all important. The important thing is the nature of the materials. What is required is a balanced approach without malice."

The approach of the poet Kalidas and of Vagbhatt towards this controversy between the old and the new is very significant. But Acharya Siddhasen's contribution thereto is even more spectacular, and almost rare in ancient Indian literature. According to him, nothing can be termed as 'new' or 'old'. The division between the two is unnatural, for what we look upon as antiquity was once novel and whatever we consider to be novel today will become antiquity in course of time. Those who are living right now, after their death, will rank among the old for the new generation. The concept of antiquity is not a static one. So, the word of antiquity should not be given credence to without examination.

In every tradition, whether that of *ayurved* or classical literature, or philosophy or religion, the older generation has looked down upon the newer one as weak. If we act on the basis of what other people say, we shall be afflicted with an inferiority complex, and our power of doing things adversely affected. We shall have to make our own decisions and act independently. We shall have to determine for ourselves what we ought or ought not to do. "Don't follow another!" is sound doctrine. If somebody calls you 'great', beware of being hoodwinked into a complacent sense of self-exaltation. On the other hand, if somebody condemns you, you need not feel small or inferior. Some people would extol a non-descript person so that he loses himself in an illusion from which he never comes out. There can be no poison greater than flattery. Conversely a sense of inferiority born of adverse criticism can make even a genuinely great man falter; his power declines under severe condemnation. All because of a man's tendency to be influenced by another. The truth about oneself can only be discovered by oneself. Only you can know what under your particular circumstances is feasible or not. You can only depend upon yourself and nobody else.

At times a situation arises when one is greatly provoked. Confronted with an angry man, one is liable to lose one's balance. At such times, one should say to oneself, "This man is ignorant. And it is because of ignorance that he is angry. He is getting worked up over something which can be resolved in a peaceful way. Now, I need not follow him. If he is ignorant, must I follow suit? If he flares up, must I too lose my balance? He is simply being silly, must I too behave foolishly? I am not going to act silly or in a childish manner or ignorantly!" That is a good resolve.

A sound doctrine awakens wisdom. Wisdom tells us that a problem cannot be resolved through excitement; that it can only be resolved through a balanced approach. It is not a matter of mere intellect. Intellect is essentially limited. If we are guided by intellect alone, we shall be inevitably caught in a vicious cycle of 'tit for tat', meet anger with anger, abuse with abuse, resulting in endless mutual recrimination. The intellect will tell us it is but right to pay back in the same coin; that if you do not return violence with still greater violence, life would become impossible for you; your very survival will be jeopardized. One man cheats, another abstains from cheating; one man indulges in abuse, the other keeps tranquil; one man, impelled by the fury of anger, becomes all dominant, the other is pushed to the wall. This is no good. "The other must counter another with greater violence. Tit for tat!" This is what intelligence dictates. But wisdom functions on a different level where intelligence can never reach. Wisdom is insight, inner perception; its yardstick is different. Its standards too. The criteria resorted to by the intellect are no longer valid. We must build on a different foundation, different values.

Wisdom is introspective. It looks within, not outside. It is the awakening of our *darshan kendra* (the centre of intuition). As this centre is gradually awakened, as it becomes activated, wisdom is kindled inside; ideas, conclusions and beliefs undergo a sea-change. The whole world stands transformed.

Two brothers got to the point of separating. All the hereditary possessions were equally divided between them. Two rings remained to be distributed — one of diamond and the other of silver. Who would get the diamond ring? Both contended for it. At last, the elder brother said to himself, "This quarrel is unseemly. Let my younger brother have it if he wants it so badly!" So the younger brother got the diamond ring. But the silver ring proved to be much more valuable; it was the ring of wisdom. It had these words engraved upon it: "This too would pass!"

The younger brother who kept the diamond ring gave himself up to a life of idle luxury. He spent money lavishly in vain exhibition, till nothing was left and he was steeped in poverty and degradation from which he could never come out.

It so happened that the elder brother too lost all he had. In this time of hardship he happened to look at the silver ring he had on his finger. "This, too, would pass!" Today's problem in the very nature of things, could not, would not last for ever! The wise saying gave him fortitude. His morale and self-confidence remained unimpaired. The days of adversity passed away in due course, and once again he regained wealth and power. All problems stood resolved.

Both the brothers faced adversity. One survived it because his morale was high; the other went down because he had no inner resources, no means to keep up his spirits.

A man rises, falls and rises again. Rise and fall is a natural process. The sun rises and sets everyday. Day is followed by night, night by day, and the cycle of life goes on. The important thing is never to let one's morale go down in adversity, for the man who loses his spirits when things go wrong, can never rise. But the man who maintains his equanimity under all circumstances never has any problem. And wisdom is the key to equanimity; courage and moral supported by wisdom can never weaken a person. The man who has on his finger the ring of wisdom, survives the worst calamity whereas one with only a diamond ring is lost. Morale is thus much more valuable than diamond. With mental poise one can acquire much wealth, but no mere wealth can give us equanimity. The rich man is not necessarily equanimous.

An army commander sat in a pensive mood. His face was lined with anxiety. His wife said, "What's the matter? Why are you so sad?" He said, "I have received very bad news. My army is losing." The wife said, "I too have received bad news—far worse than yours!" The commander was puzzled. What could be worse than his army's defeat? The wife said, "Yes! my husband has lost his courage; he has turned a coward. It is a thousand times worse than any defeat."

Immediately the commander got up. One word stung him into action. Setting aside his despair, he ran to the battlefield and fought with such exemplary valour as to lead his army to victory.

The greatest misfortune is the weakening of the morale; the destruction of self-confidence. With the loss of self-confidence, all kinds of evils crop up. But with self-confidence, with fortitude, evil days pass away quickly.

Wisdom helps one maintain one's morale. The practice of meditation is not merely a matter of sitting crosslegged with one's eyes closed; it is not aimed at merely seeking comfort; rather its purpose is to develop one's faculties to the full. It is a technique of expanding one's capability. If the practice of meditation does not lead to increased self-confidence, something is wrong with such meditation. It is not meditation at all, rather some illusion or self-deception. The food which does not enhance one's power of resistance, is no proper nourishment. The tonic which fails to impart a sense of well-being to its user cannot be said to be genuine; rather something spurious under that label. The greatest benefit that flows from meditation is the increase of power. Indeed three things happen simultaneously—the heightening of consciousness, the upsurge of joy and enhanced strength. Without these, meditation is no meditation, but something else—perhaps illusion and unconsciousness masking as meditation.

FREEDOM FROM REACTION (2)

We have been exploring the nature of non-violence; also of freedom from reaction. Shall a weak man be able to achieve this freedom? The feebler a person, the more readily does he react. Such a person cannot achieve freedom from reaction.

The habit of reaction has been continuing for generations together, since the beginning of time. It has entered our bloodstream, become second nature. It is not easy to change it; rather an uphill task. You are not actually responsible for the way you react; it is a bequest from your parents—a hereditary influence.

The mother of a very smart child complained that her son was very naughty and that he flared up easily. I asked her if she herself was given to anger. She said she did have her angry fits. I said, "Then, how do you expect your child to be free from anger? In fact he has got it from you. It is a hereditary influence. The child gets it either from his mother or father." Even the physician inquires if a particular disease is hereditary. Genealogy is important. Before granting initiation, we here too are interested in knowing what kind of family tradition our novices bring with them—what virtues and what defects! The match-makers also want to know the family background of the prospective bride and bridegroom. The reactionary mentality is not a sovereign trait of your own; it is a bequest from your parents. To change this hereditary influence, this inveterate habit, is not easy. One needs a very powerful inspiration to accomplish it. No tall building can be erected without a strong foundation. To be free from reaction also requires a strong base.

We have discussed certain inspirations in this context—theoretical helps in the form of doctrines, verbal aids such as maxims. Experimental aids we need not dwell upon at length, since you are already practising these. An occasion for anger arises, and you immediately take to deep breathing. You need not strain your mind too much. Just start observing your breath, and the situation is bound to change. The other person is boiling with rage but you concentrate all your attention on the nostrils and start observing the incoming and outgoing breath—while you are so engaged, the other man's anger is entirely wasted on you. It would have been fruitful if it had succeeded in exciting an answering anger in you. One man flares up, but if his opponent does not react, the man feels somewhat depleted. Many people want to make a person mad, but if that person does not oblige and keeps tranquil, their ire boomerangs and fills them with irritation. The practice of deep breathing and meditation on the psychic centres are powerful aids. In the face of anger, concentrate your attention on *Darshan Kendra* (the Centre of Intuition) or on *Vishudhi Kendra* (the Centre of Purity), and no reaction would develop. As soon as anger arises, control your breath. Hold it for a minute or so, and all anger would evaporate. By means of these theoretical and experimental aids, we can avoid blind reaction and maintain our equilibrium.

We have presented a non-violent view of right thinking in the context of meditation. This analysis of psychological non-violence is bound to prove immensely useful to us. Generally our conception of violence and non-violence is extremely limited; to kill a living being is violence, not to kill is non-violence. In the face of such simplistic treatment, no further discussion is possible.

But if we consider the matter from various aspects, we shall discover that without non-violence, no two persons can live together. If each man is after running the other down, there can be no society, no family. Non-violence ensures that one man will not be devoured by another, that people will cooperate with one another. From the time when society came into being till the present day, non-violence has mattered much more than violence, that is why non-violence has developed so much. All this is intelligible on the psychological level. A person practising meditation must go into it deeply, otherwise he would not be able to achieve a correct appreciation thereof. Meditation develops our sense of affection and friendship for all; it helps us achieve total freedom from reaction.

The moment you decide to practise *Preksha Meditation*, you also accept five directive principles of conduct: (i) living in the present; (ii) freedom from reaction; (iii) amity towards all; (iv) austerity in eating; and (v) observing silence or moderation in speech.

The practice of these principles is in effect the practice of non-violence. Without practising non-violence, no man can be temperate in speech or abstemious in food, or exercise any measure of self-control. He who does not practise non-violence, is incapable of practising goodwill towards others. Nor without the practice of non-violence can there be any freedom from reaction. A man divorced from non-violence cannot properly live in the present. Such a person is everlastingly caught in like and dislike, in pleasure and pain. The whole practice of meditation is in essence the practice of non-violence. Hence it is absolutely necessary to understand non-violence in the context of meditation, to analyse it psychologically, and to constantly examine one's conduct and behaviour in relation thereto.

Let us also fully appreciate the fact that the practice of *Preksha Meditation* strengthens our faith in non-violence and adds a new dimension to our life.

CHANGE OF HEART: THE BASIS AND THE TECHNIQUE THEREOF

X. CIRCUMSTANCES AND CHANGE OF HEART

We live between the known and the unknown. There is the conscious mind and the unconscious. We know a little and there is a great deal which we do not know.

A king fell ill. Physicians were called and the treatment began, but the king felt no relief. Then came a new physician who correctly diagnosed the king's disease and cured him. But one article of food was forbidden to the king; he was asked to abjure mangoes for ever. The day he took a mango, the disease would reappear with fatal consequences, he was warned.

Sometime later, the king, accompanied by his ministers and staff went for a stroll in the palace garden. It was the mango season. All the trees were laden with fruit. The air was redolent with the sweet smell of brightly-coloured mangoes. The king's mouth watered. His mind was divided: one part of it said, "I must get to the fruit!", but another part said, "No, this is forbidden fruit!" He was caught between attraction and repulsion. He went another way but after some time was again tempted to go and lie down under the cool shade of a mango tree. Still the inner voice counselled "No!"

Every man's mind is like that. Is there a man who is never caught in contradictory desires? To eat or not to eat, to do this or that? A part of the mind says, "I want to live in peace. I don't want to be embroiled in any quarrel." Yet, another part says, "When confronted with an evil-minded person, I cannot sit still. If a man calls me names, why should I not retort? Will it be right for me to allow the other person to indulge in all sorts of nonsense without any protest on my part? Am I made of clay or wax? I want to be left alone! But if the other person is out to tease me unnecessarily, I shan't spare him."

Such contradictory thoughts possess every man. To do or not to do? To eat or not to eat? A man has not one but a thousand minds. A devotee of non-violence is sometimes possessed by violent thoughts, and a man given to violence is sometimes assailed by doubt and refrains from committing a violent deed. Similarly, a man committed to celibacy dreams of sensualities and an ardent voluptuary thinks of embracing continence. What contradictory thoughts possess us! How many minds does a man have?

Lord Mahavir said, "Man has more than one *chitt*"—chitt meaning a fleeting disposition. In fact, there can be only one mind.

It is our vehicle, our tool, our means for action. The mind is one but the states of mind can be many. All kinds of tendencies rise in the mind, each tendency termed as one mind. Hence the concept of many minds. The mind in itself is one entity. However, because of different mental dispositions, it looks as if there are many minds. Freud rightly compared the human mind to an iceberg. The greater part of the iceberg, lying under the surface of the sea, is invisible. Only a small part of it is visible. The visible part is small but the invisible is very large. The known is limited, but the unknown is vast, unlimited.

Jung has compared the mind to a vast ocean. The conscious mind is just like an island in the vast ocean of unconsciousness, for it is the unconscious mind that constitutes the greater part. We analyse our conduct and behaviour with the conscious mind, which is for ever partial and therefore false. Only the collective mind, the conscious and the unconscious constituting one whole, can offer a complete exposition. Freud used depth psychology for interpreting the unconsious mind; not the conscious but the unconscious mind is the subject of depth psychology. Every action is explained in terms of the unconscious; it is the unconscious that dictates man's conduct, not the conscious mind. The exposition of the sub-conscious mind as given in modern psychology was undertaken in Indian philosophy on the basis of the *karma-doctrine*, consciousness and *chitt*. In modern psychology no distinction is made between the *chitt* and the mind, but in Jain philosophy, the *chitt* is clearly distinguished from the mind. The term 'mind' connotes the conscious mind, whereas the '*chitt*' stands for the sub-conscious. The 'mind' constitutes the upper layer which, touched by the *chitt* is generally taken for consciousness. It is, however, the *chitt* which represents the whole of consciousness, the conscious as well as the sub-conscious mind. The unconscious or the sub-conscious may be called *chitt*; the 'mind' stands for the conscious mind.

The king was caught in contradiction; a part of his mind urged him to approach the mango tree; another part counselled abstinence. When two contradictory desires simultaneously assail a man, he stands puzzled and does not know what to do. One part of the mind says one thing, the second counsels something else, and the third still another. The conscious mind alone cannot comprehend such a situation. Deep in the sub-conscious mind of the king, there was attachment, desire, which made him long for the sight of the mango tree, to inhale its fragrance, to eat the fruit thereof. This longing originated from great depths. The conscious mind remembered the physician's injunction and said to itself, "No mango-eating for me! No point in approaching the tree!" The struggle continued for a long time. At last the unconscious won.

The king advanced towards the mango grove. His minister objected, "Sir, where are you going? You mustn't. It would not be for your good. There is no point in seeking a place you don't have to go to. Come away, Sir, to that yonder grove. There shall we rest under the cool shadow of the trees."

The king said, "My good minister, you are agitating yourself quite unnecessarily, running to an extreme. Excess of everything is bad. Let's adopt the golden mean. The physician only said, no mango-eating. Well, I'm not going to eat the fruit. Merely standing or sitting under the mango-tree is not forbidden, is it? Then why do you object to my walking towards the mango grove?"

The minister could do no more. It was his office to proffer right advice. But if the king would not listen to him, if he continued adamant, he (the minister) could do nothing. After all, the king was his master. So, the king went ahead and seated himself under a large mango tree, and said, "Come, dear minister, make yourself comfortable. How pleasant it is to sit here! How cool! The shade here is so thick; no other tree affords greater shelter. The leaves of the mango tree are so broad! Could the short-leafed *neem* tree give out such a deep shade? Never!" After a little while, the king said, "O minister, look at the fruit above. What ripeness! What colour! How very gratifying to the eyes!"

The minister said, "Sir, why look at it at all? Why praise the fruit? You've done away with mango-eating. It is not for you. Come away!"

The king said in a huff, "What an extremist you are grown into! The so-called wise people often spoil all the fun! They bind you hand and foot — allow you no liberty whatsoever! Don't I know that mango-eating is forbidden to me? Mustn't I, on that account, even praise the fruit? Can't I even mention the fruit? Mustn't I bestow praise where it is due? Am I to be denied even that much freedom?"

Imagine the king lost in contemplation! His mind is sorely divided. The internal dialogue is on, one part of the mind saying, "Woe is me! Such delectable fruit and I can't come to it! How richly gratifying it would have been to eat mangoes to my heart's content! But no, something inside me tells me I mustn't." The king found himself in a dilemma. Just then a fully-ripened mango fell down from the tree plump into his lap. The king picked it up and began to survey it. The minister warned, "Your Majesty! What are you doing?"

The king retorted, "I haven't partaken of it, have I? I didn't pluck it; it fell down into my lap by chance. You are a witness to that. I have done nothing. The mango came down of itself. Mango-eating is not forbidden to you and yet the mango did not fall into your lap; instead it has come to me. What an irony of fate! What a man cares for, often recedes from him; and the unwanted thing follows him like a shadow. I had no intention of plucking the mango and mango-eating is forbidden to me, and yet this mango has landed into my lap. Now, I'm not going to eat it. But may I not look at it even? Am I to be denied the luxury of smelling it? O how delectable, how delicious!" The king handled the fruit most tenderly. So many eyes on him! Blast them!

When the urge within grows dominant, all restraint falls away. The king kissed the mango-piece in his hand almost transfixed. Then his hand gradually moved towards his mouth. The minister withheld it instantly, saying, "Your Majesty! You don't know what you are doing! The physician has forbidden it. No mango-eating for you. A little bite would spell your doom; you'll die." And thus we find the king standing nonplussed, caught between two minds, one urging him to eat, the other to heed his minister's injunction not to eat. But let us not get involved too much with the story; we are only concerned with its moral.

The mind is full of contradictory ideas and desires, giving rise to confusion and disorder. A man finds himself in a dilemma. "What idea to follow, which desire to pursue?" he asks himself and there does not seem to be any clear answer.

There are several minds at work, not one; the mind at dawn, the mind at noon, and at evenfall. The mind at the midnight hour, the mind during sleep, the mind on waking are all different. Early in the morning, a man may say to himself, "I'm going to fast today." But as the lunch hour approaches and pungent smells from the kitchen greet one's nose, one finds oneself quietly sitting down to eat! "Fasting is good, but I'll fast tomorrow." How swiftly does the mind change!

The lack of an integrated mind, its continual restlessness and changeability could serve for us as a turning point, from which we could directly proceed to the exploration of the unconscious. The problem posed by the conscious mind can be resolved by the unconscious. If the mind were wholly conscious, it would not be so changeable. The known has limits, but the unknown is unlimited. Our conduct can be fully explained and understood only in the perspective of the vast unknown. Modern psychology has explored the unconscious and revealed how it functions. Thus modern psychology may be said to have moved from the gross everyday world into a subtler one. Without the concept of depth psychology, we would be limited by the known, palpable world of everyday living—only whatever is known, whatever is perceptible, whatever is audible, would have been the centre of our activity. However, the analysis of the unconscious mind takes a man to a much deeper level. The visible part of the iceberg alone does not constitute the whole. The island is not all; it is only a little piece of ground surrounded by the vast ocean. After one has entered the ocean, after one has established contact with the deep lying iceberg, one's ideas undergo a complete transformation.

Take for instance the idea that circumstances determine a man's character. In himself a man is nothing; he is merely a product of his circumstances and can only be described in terms of his background. Without the concept of the unconscious, man's slavery to circumstance would have been absolute. Thanks to the concept of the unconscious, the notion of circumstances alone determining everything loses its validity.

A man learns a great deal from circumstanes. Indeed his whole development is based upon experience. Akbar the Great built a palace. He called it "Shish Mahal". The palace was built in a forest with a view to making an experiment. About 5 to 10 pregnant women were kept there. They were instructed to observe rigorous silence, to abjure all verbal communication with their colleagues. It was a severe command, no one could indulge in speech. The children were born in due course. Not one of them could speak. One month elapsed, then a year, two years, three years, five years. No speech could be heard. Mere moans and murmurs! No language! No gestures! Even if they grew to be fifty, none of the children would speak in that wordless atmosphere, would die indeed without uttering a word.

Occasionally we hear of a child stolen by a wolf or some other animal. Human children brought up by and among wolves begin to behave like them. They go on all fours; their arms and hands acting as legs and feet. They run and eat as wolves do and speak the language of their foster-parents.

Without human society, without the human environment, no child can learn to speak or use the language, which virtually means that he cannot do any thinking. Deprived of thinking, he is incapable of refined conduct. No thinking, no morality, no change of heart, no possibility of transformation in behaviour. For the transformation of the individual and his daily conduct can take place only on the basis of thinking and language. If language were possible in the animal kingdom, the cow and the buffalo or a lion would in no way have lagged behind man. The oxen and the buffalos possess tremendous physical strength, far exceeding man's. But they do not command language, have little capacity for thought, hence are incapable of any further development. But a man can learn from experience, from his environment. He owns the gift of speech. A child living in the midst of human beings, sees his mother and other elders talking and makes an effort to speak. Although he cannot yet properly speak, he is eager to make sounds like his elders. His whole mind is in it. Until the larynx is fully developed, he cannot speak well. But as the child grows up, he starts picking up each and every word and gradually learns to speak clearly. He achieves a command over the language. Impelled by circumstances, by the social environment, the individual soon grasps the language; words come to him easily and he wields them with ease, achieving mastery over them. There are two kinds of men—those who have language and those who have not. Devoid of language, a man cannot speak. But endowed with language, he experiences sensations, knowledge and speech.

An animal, if hurt, would squeal or squeak, but it cannot speak. Take for example a very tiny creature like the ant. However much you might vex it, it just cannot talk back; it can only move this way or that to avoid calamity. A tiny plant cannot even do that; it cannot evade the onslaught by moving away. It would of course display some sensation which we might not even grasp. But if you slap a child, he would scream, he would cry. He might even react by saying, "Don't do it! Why do you hit me for nothing?" The child would be able to say all these things because he possesses language. Because he is endowed with the faculty of speech, he can think. The first thing that he gets from his environment is language. There can be no language without society. It is only through the social environment that language develops.

Man's conditioning by circumstance is not utterly without purpose. Human progress could be adequately described only in terms of man's reaction to his circumstances. In fact circumstances play a significant role in the development of human civilization, knowledge and education. There are two things vital to the development of any living creature—sensation and learning. Sensation occurs naturally; it is not something to be taught. A child is slapped and experiences pain, without anybody having taught him what pain is. The slapping and the pain caused by it go together. The human nervous system is so designed that any attack upon the physical frame from outside automatically causes the sensation of pain. Sensation indeed is our natural, in-built reaction against danger. One does not have to be taught to experience sensation. A child is taught to count one, two, three, four. He is taught how to write figures. But does he have to be taught that sugar is sweet? It is not necessary. The moment sugar touches his tongue, he would experience the sweetness of it. No, the experience of sensation is not to be taught. Information about outside objects can be imparted, but the reactions of various sense organs, the experiencing of pain or pleasure come of themselves. Effortlessly. Knowledge is impartable. Philosophy is taught, so are other subjects. All the schools and colleges are there to impart knowledge, information. But no institution exists for teaching men how to feel.

CIRCUMSTANCES AND CHANGE OF HEART

Two kinds of consciousness operate in our life: (1) consciousness of sensation, and (2) consciousness of knowledge — that is the consciousness of learning, of memory, of imagination, of receiving something from another. The two are quite distinct. Circumstances affect learning. All that pertains to knowledge is influenced by circumstances. But the field of sensation lies beyond circumstances and is not therefore influenced by these. A man learns a language, learns how to think. The technique of right thinking can be taught. Training is given in these matters. One learns the principles of administration—how to administer, how to manage things. How to teach. How to think. All this development is mainly based upon circumstances. One's conditioning determines what kind of knowledge one acquires. In the present-day world, a number of disciplines exist. Man today learns an infinite number of things. In the Middle Ages, there were not known so many branches of learning. A man soon mastered all that was to be learnt and was recognized as a scholar. One learnt how to speak Sanskrit and was recognised as a Sanskrit scholar. He might not even know how to write, might be utterly deficient in structure, not having learnt the technique of creative literature, but the mere capacity to speak entitled him to be called a scholar. In the olden days even a moderately educated man commanded great prestige.

One man in an illiterate village had a smattering of the alphabet and on that score earned quite a reputation for himself as the only man in the locality who could read. Whoever in the village received a letter or telegram came to him to seek his assistance. All this attention went to his head.

One day a villager approached him with a letter and asked him to read it for him. The letter-reader was in a fix. After all his knowledge of words was very superficial and he barely managed to carry on the task of interpreting the simplest possible letters for the villagers. The letter presented to him by his latest visitor was somewhat difficult, written in a literary fashion far beyond his comprehension. He could clearly make no head or tail of the letter. So he resorted to guess work and told his visitor all kinds of tales. The visitor was a poor, illiterate villager, who had no option but to accept what the letter-reader told him.

Five days later, his brother arrived. The brother was very much irritated at finding no one come to receive him. He said to himself, "I sent a letter, specially requesting conveyance since the railway station is situated at a distance of 15 miles from the village. But my brother has paid no heed. He has not cared to send the bullock-cart. Is it a brotherly act? Well, I'm going to have nothing to do with him any more. I'll ask for a separation. We cannot live together. He has not shown me even this much courtesy." And while trudging his way home, he brooded over the unseemly conduct of his brother and worked himself into a paroxysm of anger. When he entered the house, his eyes were blood-shot and his face was tense. The younger brother wondered what had happened. He said to himself, "Whenever my brother comes, he is full of love and laughter, but today he is inflamed with rage. Why?" He greeted him but the elder brother averted his face and did not acknowledge his greeting. At this, the younger brother said, "Respected brother, what's the matter with you? You have not even returned my greeting!" The elder one said, "And what do you care for me? I specially wrote to you, asking you to send the bullock-cart to the railway station, but you never sent it! I had to plod along all that distance on foot." The younger brother exclaimed in surprise "My God! But you never said anything about it in your letter!" The elder one said, "Get me the letter and I'll show you." The letter was brought and the elder brother who was literate, read out the relevant portion. The younger brother protested, "But the letter-reader never told me so. You know there is only one person in the entire village who can read. I took your letter to him. He never said anything about your coming. What could I do?" Both brothers went to the letter-reader and asked him why he had omitted to tell that the bullock-cart should be sent to the railway station for fetching the elder brother. The letter-reader kept mum. What could he say? The wretch did not know how to read despite his cursory knowledge of the alphabet.

Such things happen. Even a semi-literate man among the totally illiterate, comes to look upon himself as a V.I.P. But the whole scene stands transformed today. There has been great development in various fields. Man has progressed so much in different directions that he is quite distinguishable from his ancestors in the distant past. It must be readily admitted that man has learnt a great deal from his circumstances. From philosophy to manifold branches of various disciplines, man's study has been extensive and he has been very ardent in the accumulation of new knowledge.

Both points-of-view are valid. One relates to the conditioning background, the other to inner consciousness. There is the conscious mind as well as the unconscious; both influence our conduct. Our effort is to bring about a thorough change of heart through proper utilization of both these powers.

XI. ENVIRONMENTAL INFLUENCES AND CHANGE OF HEART

I have seen the light generated by electricity, but electricity itself I have never seen. In fact no one can see it. It is invisible. Even the scientist giving a definition of electricity has not seen it. I only perceive the current, the flow of electricity. The other day I pressed the button, but there was no light because there was no bulb. But even when there was a bulb and the switch was put on, there was no light because the flow of electricity had ceased. For light to be, both are indispensable — the electric current and the bulb. One of these by itself cannot give off light.

An exposition of individuality can also be given in terms of both consciousness and circumstances. A condition of living without consciousness, or consciousness without a particular background is rendered null and void; the simultaneous presence of the two — consciousness and background — is an essential pre-requisite for individuality. Without an understanding of these two factors, individuality itself cannot be understood.

Consciousness is subtle and impalpable. I have not seen it, nor have you. Old masters have given us an exposition of consciousness, and we too explain it in different ways. But nobody has seen consciousness; it is invisible.

On the other hand, the conditions of living, the human circumstances are something gross which can be perceived. I have perceived them and so have you. Consciousness is subtle; it cannot be grasped, but circumstances constitute a gross entity which can be apprehended. However, without the union of the two, individuality cannot be explained.

Environmentalists have arrived at three conclusions:
1) that the conditioning of a child begins right from the moment of conception;
2) that, as the child grows up, his conditioning also deepens; and
3) that twins, though born at the same moment of time, display different traits in accordance with the different environments in which they grow up.

A king went out for a stroll in the forest. He passed through a thieves' hamlet. Before a cottage hung a cage with a parrot in it. The moment the parrot saw the king, it blurted out, "A traveller! A traveller! Come and rob him. Come at once. He's going away. Be quick!" The king heard the parrot speak and was surprised. He accelerated his pace and got out of the thieving neighbourhood.

After traversing a long distance, he came to another settlement, containing many cottages. Before one cottage stood a cage with a parrot in it. No sooner did the parrot catch sight of the king, it burst into speech, "Welcome, welcome, most welcome! Pray, come and be seated, honoured guest!" The king was astounded. He went near the cage and said to the parrot, "O bird, you speak man's language! Please explain to me a mystery. Sometime ago I passed by a habitation. There, too, I found a parrot in a cage. The moment it saw me, it blurted out, 'A traveller, a traveller, come and rob him. Be quick!' Here, you uttered words of sweet welcome. What makes for such a difference? Both of you belong to the same species. Both of you are parrots speaking man's language. But your conduct is so divergent."

The parrot said, "Sir, excuse me. Both of us parrots not only belong to the same species, but also belong to the same family; We're blood-brothers, the offspring of the same parents. I am the elder one; the other parrot is younger, but he is my real brother."

The king's confusion was confounded all the more. He said, "What then makes for such a wide difference in the approach and the language used?"

The parrot explained to the king the mystery thereof. He said, "Your Majesty! My younger brother-parrot lives in the company of thieves and robbers. He has been brought up in a corrupt environment. Naturally, he hears continually of pillage and plunder and talks accordingly. I live in the company of saints, so I talk of the good things of life. Virtues and evils proceed from one's associations; these are determined by the environment in which an individual lives. Bad company generates evil, good company generates virtue."

A child brought up in a clean and pure atmosphere acts virtuously, whereas even a good child, subjected to a corrupt atmosphere, becomes tainted with evil.

The impact of the environment is deep indeed. Intelligent and thoughtful parents create for their children the right atmosphere, free from all evil, in which goodness and virtue flower. On the other hand, those parents who neglect their children and are not able to provide for them a good atmosphere, only serve to spoil them. We find even small children indulging in vulgar abuse. It is unimaginable! A small child was found uttering some vile abuse. When the fact was mentioned to the child's father, the latter said, "It's really sad! He always keeps company with the servants. The servants indulge in vulgar abuse and the child has picked up the bad habit from them."

All children are imitative. It is primarily by imitation that a child learns everything — the good as well as the bad. His intelligence is not so developed as to distinguish between the two. Two boys belonging to the same house sometimes develop altogether different traits because of the different company they keep. Sometimes their conduct is so very divergent that one could hardly fancy them being blood-brothers.

The king could never imagine that the two parrots were real brothers because one of them incited men to rob, the other bade them sweet welcome. There was an enormous difference between their mentality and conduct. All because of environment which made one parrot a collaborator of thieves and the other a devotee of saints.

There are three kinds of environment:
1) the outer;
2) the inner ; and
3) the innermost

For the realization of man's total personality, we need to study all the three. Without an understanding of these, the personality, conduct and behaviour of a man cannot be fully comprehended.

The social, material and geographical environments constitute the outer atmosphere. The personality of a man is determined by the social, material and geographical situations.

The inner environment is at play within the body, which constitutes the borderland between the outer and the inner. Sensations originating from outside the skin, from the material world surrounding the body, make us aware of the outer environment, and those arising from within the body, embracing all the senses indicate the inner atmosphere.

The subtle atmosphere which lies beyond the gross corporeal constitutes the innermost environment.

The spiritualist, believing in the spirit and the subtle world would explain individuality with reference to the three environments. Even an absolute materialist, one who does not believe in the subtle world, would have to interpret individuality in terms of at least two environments, the outer and the inner within and without.

The great law of spiritual science is: 'Evolution from the gross to the subtle,' a movement from the gross physical world to the subtle innermost world of the spirit. The breath is gross, easily apprehensible. The soul is subtle, not so easily grasped.

The milk and the curd are visible, not so the butter oil latent within. We know that the milk and the curd contain butter oil; the latter is extracted from the former. But looking at the milk and the curd we cannot directly see the butter oil. To extract butter oil from the milk and the curd we take recourse to a particular technique. Similarly, to grasp the spirit flowing in each breath, requires a precise technique. The breath goes in, goes out. Why? What makes for this inhalation and exhalation? It is the spirit that moves the breath inside and outside. The breath-conduit may subsist unimpaired, the atmosphere outside may contain the air, but in the absence of the vital spirit, there would be no movement of breath, no inhalation or exhalation. Breathing continues as long as there is life; with the going out of the vital breath of life, breathing also stops. It is the vital spirit that causes vibrations and sensations all over the body. Without the spirit, there can be no movement.

To begin with, breath is perceived, perception of consciousness comes later. The perception of consciousness requires twenty times more concentration than that required for perceiving the breath. The movement of consciousness is very subtle. It is the subtle stream of consciousness which moves the breath, the body and the senses. The breath, the senses and the body, each have their own vital spirit. Likewise, language and thought each have their own power. These different powers have different functions. Though the moving spirit, the consciousness, is one, we might differentiate its manifestations in accordance with various functions performed. When consciousness moves through the senses, it is known as consciousness of the senses, when allied with breathing, it is called breath-consciousness, when linked with language, it is known as word-consciousness, when it is joined with the mind, it is called mindfulness. All power and movement flows from consciousness.

Two important principles are active in the inner environment of the body — bioelectricity and biochemistry. For a thorough understanding of human behaviour and conduct, it is necessary to understand bioelectricity and biochemistry. Every cell in the human organism produces electricity; each cell is its own powerhouse. Indeed no part of the body, big or small, can function without electricity. Bioelectricity and biochemicals activate the human organism. Secretions from the endocrine glands, mixing with the blood, powerfully influence a man's conduct. Man's emotional and mental evolution, patterns of behaviour, his character and conduct are all influenced by inner chemistry. By observing a man's behaviour and conduct, we can tell what chemical activity is going on inside. When anger, pride or lust arises it indicates that the adrenal gland is very active; when the gonads and thyroid glands are overworked, man's behaviour is influenced by these. No thorough understanding of an individual is possible without first understanding his inner chemistry, without knowing what glands are most active at any particular time. The full development of individuality is very much affected by secretions from the endocrine glands. Ignorance of this fact leads to a great many contradictions. Sometimes the blame is laid on outer circumstances, at other times a particular individual is held responsible for one's ills.

A man went driving his bullock on whose back was spread a gunny bag. Since the man had put on his load on one side of the sack, the equilibrium was disturbed, and the sack continually slipped off the bullock's back. Balance could only be maintained by loading the sack equally on both sides. One-sided loading caused imbalance, hindering the smooth movement of the bullock, with the result that the bullock could not move properly and the sack too continually slipped off. The man had put all the load in one pannier, vainly trying to restore the balance by putting his hand in the other pannier, exerting all his strenth. He did make some tardy progress, but was soon exhausted and was breathing hard. A wayfarer saw him and said, "You fool! Is this the way to carry a load? You are sweating profusely, unnecessarily taxing yourself and the animal! What a simpleton you are!"

The man said, "Well, what am I to do? How am I to restore the equilibrium?"

The wayfarer said, "Put half of the load in the other pannier!"

The man did as he was told. The balance was restored. With no more useless expenditure of energy, he completed his journey comfortably.

Many a time a man overloads one pannier and destroys the equilibrium and all his efforts to restore the balance come to nothing.

A man wants to absolve himself from responsibility by leaving everything to circumstance. All other alternatives are left unexplored. And he tries to justify his inaction by reason and argument. But the imbalance and disorder continue. The proper thing for him to do would be to maintain a balanced approach. That the background and circumstances shape a man's destiny is only a partial truth. The whole truth includes this partial truth, but also recognizes that the inward impulse is no less important. A man is influenced by society, but he also influences society. In fact a man's life is influenced by the outer, the inner, and the subtle innermost environment. The blending of endocrine secretions with the blood influences conduct, and a man is sometimes found indulging in excesses. We find it hard to comprehend such a man's actions. At times the parents are puzzled by a child's extremities. Likewise *gurus* and other well-wishers find it hard to explain some dubious conduct on the part of a pupil. The atmosphere of the home may be clean and orderly and yet parents feel their ward is being spoiled.

Why? The outer circumstances may be quite propitious and may not contribute to the boy's deterioration, but something has certainly gone wrong. What can it be? We shall have to concentrate here on the inner climate of the boy's mind. We shall have to go into it deeply to find out whether it is the outer circumstances or the inner proclivities that are responsible for the present unsavoury situation. The enquiry would itself dictate the desired course of action, as to whether the outer environment needs to be changed or the inward state of the boy's mind must be more closely attended to.

A psychological disease called the tantrums is often found among children of 2-3 years. Because of it the child starts behaving in a strange manner. His conduct appears to be unnatural: He either has fits of furious rages, or he cries, becomes extremely violent, flings things about and easily gets cross or sulks. All this happens because of the malady of tantrums that he suffers from. If his disease is not properly diagnosed, the child gets spoiled. In such a case mere outside control would not improve matters. If the parents are intelligent, they would not resort to beating or harsh language.

There are some mothers who are always calling their children names; they are continually finding fault with them, or even administering corporeal punishment. Here is set the machinery for spoiling children. The process is calculated to mar their character, not mend it. The children are thus so corrupted as to pose a serious danger to their parents later when they grow up.

All this happens because of ignorance. Parents do not know how to bring about a change in the habits of children. The challenge demands a transformation in the parents themselves. This is possible only through the practice of meditation. Meditation enables a man to orientate his mind to meet any eventuality with equanimity. If the parents keep their balance, they can help their children to come out of an intricate situation. When the parents chide or beat a child suffering from the tantrums, it merely serves to intensify the disease. However, if the parents treat the child with affection, if they give him understanding, show great love and joy, the disease begins to dissolve of itself and the child soon behaves normally. If the parents react just as the child is reacting; if, when they see the child flinging things about, they become angry, give him a hiding, the child would not be cured. Indeed, when he grows up, he will treat the parents with contempt.

We must also not lose sight of the inner compulsions. When a man goes bad even in prosperous circumstances, we must try to fathom the real cause. We shall have to adopt a constructive approach, act with clearer vision. If we act in confusion, it is bound to make matters worse confounded. It might even lead to terrible

ENVIRONMENTAL INFLUENCES & CHANGE OF HEART

consequences. Generally a man's approach is reactionary and therefore the problem remains unresolved.

While embarking on the practice of *Preksha Meditation*, a *spiritual practitioner* takes a vow. He resolves "to shun reaction" at all costs. He says to himself, "Action by all means, but no reaction!" The cultivation of a non-reactionary approach is a most important undertaking.

To indulge in reaction, adopting the doctrine of 'tit for tat', straight leads to a man's deterioration, not reformation. Instead of helping in the evolution of a unique personality, it destroys all individuality. Let us not be swept away on the tide of reaction; rather we must move against the current and meet reaction with positive, creative action.

Lord Mahavir said:

> The whole world moves with the current. Most people today adopt the easier course and are swept on the tide of reaction. A true spiritual practitioner, however, moves against the current. If a man really wants to make progress in the path of self-realization, he cannot afford to be slack.

Let us learn how to withstand the current. Merely to react in the same way as our brother, son, friend or neighbour reacts, is to broaden the gorge of cleavage and division; it is to fritter away our energies in senseless opposition, which serves no purpose. If we wish to resolve our problems, we must cultivate the non-reactionary approach. To be free from reaction, and to act positively is rather arduous; it involves moving against the current. But if we want to create a peaceful society, that is the one and the only way.

A man was looking for a candle. The servant came in and said, "Master, what is it that you are looking for?" The master replied, "I'm looking for a candle." The servant said, "But sir, how can you find it in the dark? Why don't you switch on the electric light?" The master said, "O fool! If there were electricity, I would not need to search for a candle; I'm looking for the candle because of the power-failure."

Man is lost in the illusion of switching on the electric bulb outside, and stops searching for the candle within. Of course, if light were available, there would be no need for the candle. The main objective is to be in the light. But though a man longs for light, he is more often than not lost in darkness and whatever he does adds to the confusion. Sometimes it seems that man is more in love with darkness than with light. He says he wants light, but he continues in darkness. He wants forgiveness, but is easily swept away by anger; he believes more in violence than in peace. He wants to have his own way at all costs.

Man keeps before him the ideal of non-violence, of forgiveness and light, but his everyday living is wrapped in violence, anger and confusion. He seems to have a 'split personality'. There is an everlasting contradiction between the ideal and the reality. If we really believed more in charity than in anger, we would be more forgiving; if we believed more in peace than in war, we would be more non-violent. But the fact is that we are more violent than non-violent, more revengeful than forgiving. It is quite apparent where our inward inclinations lie.

We only talk about light, we do not really seek it. The true seeker after light will have to delve deep into himself. The man who is totally preoccupied with the outer material world, can never come to this light. If mere observation of the material world could lead to illumination, there would be no need to practise breath-perception or body-perception. One does get a kind of pleasure, some sort of gratification and entertainment from the observation of the material world; there is endless variety there. The practice of meditation does not perhaps offer such entertainment. Yet modern man is attracted by meditation. He is probably fed up with the mere observation of the material world, is so full of tension that he wants to get away from it and peep within. Superficial observation of the material world has made man so restless, so very confused, that he has an urge to look deep within. That is why he comes to meditation camps. Here he is made to practise breath-perception, body-perception and to observe the inward movement of consciousness. As he goes into these processes, he will make contact with that which is not found in the outer material world. He will witness colours which he never saw before in the outer world. He will see light that the sensual world can never offer. In that inner world he will see sights, fearful or pleasant, which are altogether different from those of the outer world.

I asked one lady spiritual practitioner to experiment with meditation on the tip of the nose, the centre of the vital life-force. She did it for 2-3 days and began to experience joy. One evening she was sitting in meditation and her meditation grew long. In the darkness of the night, some terrifying sights filled her with increasing fear. But she sat immovable. Gradually it grew tranquil again.

The inner world is vast and mysterious. A million impressions gathered inside reveal themselves one after another. It is an endless stream. Sometimes a spiritual practitioner is quite bewildered.

Indeed *preksha* means inner observation. It is the observation of the world within which gives out new light, a new direction, a new point-of-view, new conduct and behaviour. The solution to our various problems of daily living lies within. Those who have despaired of finding a solution outside, might try looking within. All their frustration would then vanish. No problem can defy a man who has learnt to look within. So we have to move from the outer to the inner world. We must seek a resolution to our problems in the context of inner chemistry and electricity, in the vital power of consciousness and in the secretions from the endocrine glands.

Those who practise *Preksha Meditation* must resolve to seek a solution to their problems not only in the outer environment, but also in the world within. Having adopted this approach, the first principle of problem-resolution is readily available to them. That man is caught in illusion who seeks a resolution only in the outer world. But the right-minded person explores both the worlds — the outer as well as the inner. This provides him with a new direction — from partial to the whole, from the gross to the subtle, from the limited to the limitless. An entirely new dimension opens out before him. He probes within and in the very probing, all problems dissolve.

But if both looking without and looking within fail and the problem still persists, one has to enter a third dimension for resolving it. After exploring the outer environment of the material world and the more subtle environment of electrical and chemical changes within, one proceeds to probe the inmost environment of the spirit.

The masters of *ayurved* recognised three kinds of diseases:
i) those emanating from outward surroundings;
ii) those emanating from the imbalance of the wind, the bile and the phlegm: and
iii) those emanating from mental impressions.

The third type of disease proceeds from a subtle body where there are neither germs nor insects, nor wind, nor bile, nor phlegm; where there is nothing except mental impressions. This disease is the result of past action that subsists in the brain in the form of memory.

This psychological world is the inmost environment, the third dimension. We have to explore all the three dimensions, the gross, the subtle, and the subtler one. We cannot afford to be stuck up with one. We must move away from the first into the second, and then into the third. Only then shall our whole individuality reveal itself, and in that revelation all problems shall dissolve.

XII. TRANSMUTATION OF THE MIND (1)

The evolution of the world, of culture and civilization may be said to be an evolution of change. If things remain static, no evolution is possible. The people sitting before me are wearing clothes. Now, cotton is obtained from the cotton plant. Raw cotton is changed into threads, from which cloth is woven, and out of that whole cloth people make garments for themselves. Garments could not be made out of raw cotton. Nor could one wear bare threads. It is only when threads are woven into cloth that garment-making becomes a possibility, affording protection to people from the cold, the heat and the hurricane and the rain. Behind it all is the story of eternal change. We eat *chappaties* but do not swallow unground wheat. Similarly we make *chappaties* from gram flour, not regularly masticate whole grams. A total change is involved. We have also to exert ourselves a great deal for obtaining *ghee* and butter from milk. Milk is coagulated into *dahi* (curd); curd is churned and out of that churning butter flows; *ghee* is made from butter. The whole course of our living is a process of change. Nothing remains static; everything is continually changing.

Man changes his circumstances; also his surroundings. He does not leave his environment, his situation untouched; rather he tries to mould it in a particular way. The whole of man's effort is directed towards bringing about a change and he has made a good deal of progress. Outer circumstances, if not properly moulded, create a lot of difficulties. Man has, therefore, tried to alter his outer environment. There can be no light if darkness continues. But if there is light, even night turns into day. Man can turn even a dark night into a splendid festival of lights. Behind this capacity lies an infinity of diligent effort. There was a time when man ignited light from stones, or by rubbing together two pieces of wood. Now he just presses a button and there is light. Because of the extraordinary changes wrought in the means of procuring light, he can now turn darkess into light. Living in darkness, man sought light and found it. Thanks to human efforts to change the outer environment, man can to-day provide a cool retreat in the midst of great heat. The coolers and the fans were specifically created to banish heat.

Likewise, electric heaters were created to banish cold by providing warmth. Air-conditioners were invented for the same purpose — to modify the atmosphere and make it conform to man's comfort. The whole of this process is a process of change. Man has laboured hard to change the outer environment and he has achieved remarkable success in moulding it to his heart's desire. Thanks to his perseverance, he has performed unimaginable feats in this direction and is still progressing ahead.

Man has also attempted to change the inner environment. However, unlike his achievements in the outer field, he has not been able to make much progress in the direction of inner change. The chemistry of the body can be altered. The secretions from the endocrine glands can also be changed though doctors have not yet succeeded in bringing it about. Medical science has not yet perfected the technique thereof. As a result, the character of endocrine secretions remains unchanged. Nor can one's inward feelings or thoughts be altered at will. A great many difficulties are encountered. Man finds himself incapable of changing the inner climate. He is puzzled by the fact, and does not know how to meet the challenge. Evil thoughts assail the mind and man finds himself utterly powerless to withstand them. He seeks consolation in fate. "One can do nothing," he says. It is not possible to keep the evil out. Man has no control over the mind. He feels helpless. And fatalism comes in very handy. "Whatever happens, happens because it is so destined. One can do nothing about it." Why then blame a poor thief, or a dacoit for his actions? He does what his inner voice prompts him to do. The chemistry of his body determines his behaviour and conduct. If so, why find fault with him? He is a helpless victim of his passion; he cannot control it! Man can coin innumerable excuses to justify his conduct.

A man sat watching the construction of the village temple. The village folk had decided to construct the temple themselves, without hiring any labourers from outside. The entire population of the village was at work while one man sat idle. Some folk approached him and said, "What a shame! All the people are working and you are sitting idle! Come, let's get busy with the construction of the temple!" He said, "What do you expect me to do? The stomachs of other people you see at work are full while my stomach is empty. How can a famished person work? How shall he get his energy without food?" Someone said, "He's right. We can't expect him to work on an empty stomach. A labouring person needs food, more not less." So they brought him plenty of food and he ate up everything they brought him. After he had finished, they asked him to accompany them to work. He replied, "Oh, how do you expect me to work now? My stomach is too full. I am not in a position to exert myself!"

Man is good at making excuses. He cannot work if his stomach is empty. He also cannot work when his stomach is too full. He is not at all interested in working, so he finds excuses right and left. The man who wants to evolve further, never resorts to excuses; he enjoys working and puts in his best effort. There are very few who are intent upon doing their best. A verse from the *Gita* reads, "Only one man in ten thousand really works for fulfilment." One must not, however, imagine that fulfilment is rare or difficult to attain. Each man can find fulfilment. We have the goal before us, and also the means to achieve that goal. Success is certain. The end, the means, and fulfilment are inevitably linked together. Any man who chooses a particular goal and acquires the right means thereto, is bound to succeed. One does not have to bother about success. What one must attend to is the right end and the right means. Fulfilment comes of itself. It is foolish to be preoccupied with the result. We need not bother about it at all. Only a little while ago, a man came and said, "I'm suffering from a particular disease. Is it possible to get rid of the disease through meditation?" This sort of question invariably crops up. I feel and often declare openly that the place you have come to is no hospital. Still, I concede that most diseases get cured here of themselves. If the mind is healthy and in order, the process of healing is set in motion. Diseases start losing their virulence, and often get cured. All this is possible. The first essential is to bring order in the mind, to change the inner environment. If the inner environment undergoes a transformation, the atoms of the outer environment also begin to change. The real problem is to change the inner condition, where the cause often lies buried. The inner overcomes the outer.

A man saw a dog and fled from it in fear. He went running and the dog chased him. On investigation it has been found that the man flees in fear. He is afraid of the dog. When in a state of fear, the adrenal gland becomes very active. Profuse secretions from the adrenal gland fill the air with their odour. The dog's sense of smell being very acute, it smells the adrenal from far. It is because of its acute sense of smell that a dog is used in chasing murderers and other criminals. A dog does what a man cannot do. It can take hold of the scent of a man and pursue this smell for miles together, till it apprehends the man himself and starts circling round him. As a man flees, his adrenal gland becomes very active and secretes more profusely. The more profuse the secretion, the intenser the smell it gives off, and the dog takes hold of this smell. Outwardly it may appear that the dog chases a man to bite him, but the real cause is the dog's attraction for the smell. The man is running because of fear; the dog runs for the sake of the smell which it finds very pleasant. One is in the grip of fear, the other simply allured.

Indeed, allurement and fear are the two basic offences. One man acts out of fear, the other out of temptation. All our urges, all our social motivations, lie within the orbit of fear and temptation. There is the action of fear and there is the action of greed. If fear and greed come to an end, human action, as it is at present, will also come to an end.

We shall have to explore the hidden causes behind appearances. The real cause of all human action lies within. One man is swayed by anger, the other by love. Still another is dominated by fear. Someone indulges in back-biting or abuse. Still another is utterly restless — restless without a cause; he finds himself in the grip of a strange melancholy and despair. All these various moods cannot be adequately explained in terms of the external situation alone; it is also necessary to delve deeper and be fully acquainted with the inner condition of a man's mind. If anything, it is even much more important, for the inner overcomes the outer. Every man longs for a change; he wants to get rid of his restlessness. He wants to be happy; to free himself from all kinds of tensions and frustration. Nobody wants to live in fear. A man confided to me that when he was in a state of fear, all his dreams were coloured by fear. He saw a leopard or a lion, or a wild bear. Or he would find himself near the edge of a stream and see himself drowning in it. He had such terrible dreams that he did not know what to do with himself. He wanted to get rid of fear altogether. It was not at all a very pleasant state to be in. He wanted to get rid of his deficiencies. He wanted his morale to be high, and not so inhibited by fear as to imagine calamities everywhere. Even a little problem appeared to be very acute and irresolvable in a state of fear; one then created mountains out of mole hills. So to change oneself was a dire necessity. But how to change? The first essential is to comprehend the inner compulsions. What motives are at work inside, creating a particular situation. Only then something could be done. First insight, then action.

Change in attitude, change in thinking, change in the body chemistry — these are the three inner changes. First of all there has to be a change in attitude. When the attitude undergoes a change, thinking, too, is transformed. Thought does not create attitude; it is the other way round — it is attitude that shapes thought. Some people give out wrong interpretations. Even today I came across an exegesis that what arises first is thought and that in turn creates attitude. It is like saying that the son is born first and then the father! How can thought create attitude? It is always attitude first and then thought. Attitude is the fountain that springs from the inmost recesses of our being; it springs from within. Good attitude, bad attitude, attitude springing from dark *leshya* (psychic colour); it all comes from within. The mind receives what comes from within and thought is moulded accordingly. Attitude is the creator of thought. A change in attitude is a precursor of change in the inmost being, then thought, too, changes, the mind is transformed, and the inner chemistry of the body too alters. For a change in the body-chemistry, a change in attitude and thought is a must. The three are inevitably linked with one another. The pineal gland and the pitutary gland give out particular kinds of secretions. With a change in attitude and thought, the nature of the secretions also changes. It is not that the secretions from all the glands are of the same character. The secretions change from individual to individual. All human organisms are equipped with glands—there are five to seven predominant glands in each human being—the adrenals, the thyroid, the pituitary, the pineal, the gonads, etc. There are different kinds of glands and the secretions therefrom are different too. Each person gives out individual secretions which mould his attitude and thought. The secretions taking place in one man are different from those in another. Not only are the secretions of two individuals different, but the secretions of the same person vary from time to time. Lord Mahavir, in an important exposition of the doctrine of *leshya* * says, "*Leshya's* origination is legion!" Not one, not two, not a thousand, not a million or trillion, but *legion,* beyond count, innumerable. An interminable rise and fall! Our secretions vary in accordance with our diverse attitudes. Doctors have tried to classify these. They have even laid down the precise number of secretions from the pituitary gland. The enumeration is of course incomplete. Medical science also recognizes the inadequacy thereof—the secretions are much more. In Lord Mahavir's exposition, the number of these secretions is given out as 'legion'. The chemical secretions in the body conform to and are determined by changes in attitude. A change in the body-chemicals requires a change in thinking and a change in thinking requires a change in attitude. Once we have acquired the key to the change in attitude, we may be said to have embarked upon a rapid inner change.

The important question is : How to bring about an attitudinal change? It is easy to talk about the necessity of change, but how

---

* the individual light, the particular state of a living creature which binds him to a particular kind of action,

is one to accomplish it? Every body says one should be good, honest, authentic; that one should uphold the truth, be happy. The exposition of good principles is the easiest thing in the world—easier than cooking food. In the cooking of food, one may still encounter various difficulties. But in laying down a doctrine, in repeating it endlessly, there is no difficulty whatsoever. A computer or a tape-recorder can do it as well. Nothing is required but reiteration. It is the easiest thing in the world. But the accomplishment of a change is no easy task. It is a very complicated problem. To effect inner change, one has to delve deep into the mind. For changing the chemical composition of the hormones from the endocrine glands (which influence our conduct), we shall have to undergo a definite course, a whole series of precise actions. In the ancient language it was called the method of 'purifying the stream'. Without purifying the stream of life, there could be no change in attitude. The vocabulary of the ancient language has undergone a complete change during the course of two to three thousand years, so that it is not easily intelligible. Man is very well acquainted with the modern language; he understands the modern vocabulary quite well. But the old texts are not so amenable to his understanding. Through meditation one must explore the truth hidden in the ancient texts, and to present it in a form accessible to the modern reader. It is very clear that meditation is one powerful medium of research, of inner exploration, so as to bring the hidden elements to light. Whatever remains hidden, becomes intricate, gets lost. To unravel the hidden truth requires a serious effort. The truth that has been lost has to be rediscovered. How? Through the body, the tongue and the mind, a body that is still and steady, a tongue that is still and silent, a mind that is still, emptied of the noise of thought—all three divested of restlessness, and in a state of alertness, fully concentrated. No truth can be found by an unsteady body, tongue or mind. It is only when all wavering has come to an end and the body, the tongue and the mind are still and receptive that truth is revealed. It may be the scientific or the philosophic truth, or it may relate to the world of business. Whoever has discovered the truth, experienced reality, has done so in a state of aloneness, in a state of mind where thought has come to an end, in perfect silence. The great scientific truths have been all discovered in a state of total concentration.

Einstein was asked, "How did you discover the theory of relativity?" He said, "I don't know. One day I was strolling in the garden. All of a sudden I felt something descending upon my mind." Did Newton discover the theory of gravitation through exercising his intellect? It was certinaly not the result of an intellectual exercise! It was a case of direct vision. He was just watching—he saw the apple fall and instantly conceived the theory of gravitation. The great truths come upon a man when least looked for, never through thought. Too much thinking tires the brain, puzzles the mind. All thought creates tension and a man who is full of tension can never find the truth. Only when a man is totally free from tension, there is a sudden awakening of inner consciousness and the great truths are effortlessly perceived.

The first principle of changing the inner environment is: Do away with restlessness! It is an inveterate defect of far-reaching consequences. An illusion might dissolve in the course of time, furious passions recede, like and dislike disappear, yet the fickleness of the mind remains.

Gautam put a very interesting question to Lord Mahavir. He asked: "Sir, the man on his way to salvation, who is fully awake, has freed himself from passions, from like and dislike, who knows everything—can he place his hand on the same spot twice?"

The Lord answered, "No".

How strange! The man who is familiar with each tiny bit of the courtyard, not an atom of whose own hand is hidden from him, who is fully awake—such a man places his hand on a particular spot, but he cannot touch that point again! A stupendous question calls forth an equally stupendous answer. Lord Mahavir said, "No, he cannot touch that point again!"

Gautam said, "How is it, Sir? Why cannot an awakened person touch the same point again? A pseudo-saint. the one who does not know, who is not dispassionate, who has not been able to free himself from passions and affections, one caught in illusion, will certainly go wrong; he is not fully alert, he cannot remember; due to ignorance and negligence, he cannot find the spot. But why can't the awakened one do it?"

Lord Mahavir said, "He knows it all right, but he has not yet attained perfect tranquillity; he is not totally free from restlessness. There is the body, and it is fickle; it wavers. There is unsteadiness. Therefore, though he is wide awake and knows everything, yet he cannot touch the same point again."

Movement remains with us till the very last. All conditions pass away. All obstacles are removed. The right approach replaces the false one. Dissatisfactions cease, attachment dissolves, no more passion, no more like and dislike, no more good or bad. And yet until the restlessness of the body ends, the goal is not reached, there is no fulfilment The goal may be clearly outlined, the means thereto readily available, but as long as movement persists, the highest achievement is not possible.

If we want to change the inner environment, we shall have to clearly determine our aim, and the means that we are going to adopt. There is no need to worry about fulfilment; it will come of itself. Our aim is transformation—that is, changing the circumstances, the inner environment and consciousness. With a change of circumstances consciousness already stands modified. All imperfections of consciousness are the result of outward circumstances. With a change in the outer situation, consciousness is established in its perfection. As a matter of fact, there is nothing which requires to be changed. Consciousness remains what it is. However, whatever came to pass because of a particular motive stands altered. Without cause, there is no effect. If the motive changes, the state of mind resulting from the original motive also undergoes a change.

Our aim is the transformation of consciousness, of inner motives. That means: freedom from fickleness. The first move is the establishment of steadiness, of full concentration. One starts practising *Preksha Meditation,* but if the body is unsteady, the tongue wavers and the mind is restless as before, if there is absolutely no change there, it would mean that the reality of meditation has not yet been fully grasped. If at all there had been true meditation, a change would have occurred. Not that one would attain full composure just in a day, yet a slight change should be discernible. The mind that was totally incapable of concentration before, should be able to concentrate at least for 5-10 seconds. After ten days, it should be able to keep steady for a minute or two at least. Likewise, there should be a corresponding change in the tongue; it was continually wagging before, now it is comparatively quieter. The uncomfortable feeling experienced before when confronted by silence, the restlessness of unaccustomed quietness, should grow less acute.

The second step is to lessen the frequency of sensations of like and dislike. It is a very important step. Is it possible to undergo an experience, whether it is eating, or sleeping, in all its purity, without attachment, without identification? One may relish sugar, or salt too much; one may derive a vast, secret satisfaction from quarrels and excitements of all sorts. The man who is seeking gratification will find meditation a bore; he would be all for eating, drinking, sleeping, quarrelling and fighting. He would find immense gratification in sensation. All this has to be changed. To keep indifferent in the face of sensual gratification, and to awaken interest in the hitherto ungratifying practice of meditation, to change the very pivot of mental attraction, is an extremely important step.

Two men were quarrelling. People gathered round them. They enquired as to what the matter was. One of them said he had been cheated by the other of a penny. The other asserted he had paid back the full amount. It was incredible—this quarrel over a penny! The close combat, the bad language, the beating, hundreds of onlookers gathered around them. A sensible man advanced towards one of the brawlers and said, "Good man, why fight so furiously just for a penny?" The brawler replied, "You don't understand! It's not really the question of a penny or two; rather of gratification. Of the immense satisfaction I derive from owning a penny and the excitement of the scuffle. It requires a connoisseur to fully appreciate the irresistible flavour of identification with an object!".

The question is how much attached a man is to an object and what gratification he derives therefrom. Unless we fully understand this phenomenon of identification, no progress towards equanimity is possible.

XIII. TRANSMUTATION OF THE MIND (2)

As we were sitting in meditation in the courtyard a short while ago, a question arose in my mind: Why all this effort? Why devote so much time? What for? There is only one objective — to set the mind in order. There are many problems. Indeed, in our everyday world, there are innumerable problems and we are here merely chasing the mind! What do we hope to gain, after all? Suddenly, it became clear to me that unsteadiness, lack of equanimity, constituted our biggest problem. A mother complained to me of her son's skittishness. A restless child becomes a problem to the mother, causes her endless worry. Naturally, she wants her child to be cured of that defect. But restlessness is not always bad. Some kind of movement is also a necessity. If the tree remains perfectly stationary, if the leaves do not move at all, the traveller would be subjected to the torture of intolerable heat. The leaves flutter as the wind blows and it gives the traveller a pleasant feeling of coolness. Similarly, a stilled mind becomes a problem. Silence is good but if a child does not start speaking, its parents begin to worry about it, "The child is two years old and yet cannot speak!" They begin a round of visits to the doctor.

Constant movement has its own use. If the body does not move, it becomes a problem. If a finger or a foot does not move, a man is rightly worried. "Has it been paralysed?", he wonders. One woman spiritual practitioner went into deep meditation. At the end of her meditation-period, her hands and feet would not disentangle. People sitting near her got worried at her immobility. Actually, there was nothing to worry about. The point is that movement, constant movement, is necessary; it has its own utility. But there is a point beyond which it must not go. Restlessness, in the sense of constant movement, is necessary to a certain extent, but if it exceeds its bounds, it becomes harmful. We are trying here to lessen the mind's restlessness in order to find our fulfilment. A restless mind cannot achieve anything. Our goal is mind-transformation. We want to change the mind. As long as fickleness continues, there can be no transformation. Something is said. You are told to do or not to do something. You hear the words, but the mind is so restless, so much caught up in the vibrations of its own thought, as to completely ignore the direction. No theory can be put into practice if the mind remains unsteady. No problem can be resolved as long as we continue to be fickle. We are not right now talking of a point where perfect equanimity is attained—to be without any kind of movement for a year! Like a statue, just as Bahubali stood in *kayotsarg* for one year in one posture. No storm or hurricane, no furious downpour, neither heat nor cold, not even if creepers were to sprout all around in which birds made nests—nothing whatever would shake us out of our resolve! We would be steadfast like a rock! We are not at the moment talking of that, since it would be for us, as we are, an impossible undertaking. Every man cannot be Bahubali, cannot continue in one posture for long. Our effort just now is not aimed at dissolving the mind altogether, arriving at a state of non-mind. Non-mind, freedom from the tyranny of thought, is good. But it might immediately create a good many problems. Without the mind, one will not be able to think or imagine or remember anything. All memories dissolved!—to be in a state of non-mind is not easy; it demands concentrated work on oneself. If one achieves it, the whole of one's life stands transformed. However, an average householder might experience a lot of difficulty in essaying it. The mind, with its memories, stands dissolved! What shall we do now? If the memory weakens a little, we become greatly solicitous about ourselves. "Can't remember things! What's going to happen to me?" For the average householder, the state of non-mind, non-speech, non-body is impossible. And yet we are working just for that. What an effort! An effort aimed at acquiring effortlessness! All our endeavour is bent to that end. Disassociating ourselves from everything else, we engage in a process calculated to lessen the tension of the mind, body and tongue. The practice of *kayotsarg*, of silence, of concentration—this is the first step towards mind-transformation.

We all talk about the desirability of a mutation in the mind. We want to dispense altogether with the use of force; a real change of heart is what we desire. Without such a change, no human problem can be resolved. We talk about it endlessly; we indulge too often in theoretical discussion. But is this desired change of heart really possible, without experimentation, without practical work on oneself? People agree that violence serves no purpose. That violence is undesirable, that we must always practise non-violence. That the mind-heart should change. But how is this change to be accomplished? How is a new mind to come into being? You have not done anything to lessen or dissolve your restlessness! How then are you going to bring about a mutation in the mind? If mere theoretical discussion, endless talk, could change one's heart, the whole world would be non-violent and all problems would have been resolved. But it does not work like that. It is an illusion and self-deception that the mind-heart transformation can be achieved through theoretical discussion and analysis. To try to establish non-violence through violence is altogether vain. Non-violence cannot be established until a serious effort is made to dissolve the inner restlessness of the mind.

There are many who are concerned with the propagation of non-violence. They sincerely want that non-violence should spread everywhere, that self-discipline should be the order of the day, that the whole world should tread the path of non-violence and self-discipline. It is a laudable wish. Every sensible person will approve of it. However, it should be very clear by now that nothing is accomplished by wishful thinking; theory without practice is absolutely futile. It was so in the past, it is so now and it will be so in the future. We all have to seriously follow one course—that of lessening tension and restlessness. The first thing to be done is to obviate all perturbation.

Some people decry meditation. They assert that nothing is gained thereby. They would rather do something 'practical and useful'. No purpose is served by sitting idle—that is what meditation appears to be to them—losing oneself in abstraction. And truly meditation, if it be nothing but losing oneself in abstraction, is a futile undertaking. According to such critics, those practising meditation do no productive work. They do not cook, nor do they weave cloth, nor do anything useful. They do not labour at all! Just sitting cross-legged with closed eyes serves little purpose. The poor labourers breaking stones in the hot sun are real workers. Office workers too, moving their pens from 10 A.M. to 5 P.M. accomplish something. What do those sitting in meditation achieve? Nothing whatever! According to these critics of meditation, action, movement is work, and inaction, tranquillity, sitting without any movement, mere idleness. As long as this false approach continues, no social transformation is possible. We must seek the truth. Without seeking the truth, without coming to know it, our problems will never be resolved. The truth is that in our life, action and inaction must be finely balanced. Sitting still, without any movement in so far as it reduces tension and restlessness, is the first step towards accomplishing useful work. Indeed, inaction is the highest form of action.

After having crossed the stream by boat, two travellers came to the roadhead and inquired of the people there what distance they had as yet to cover to reach the village. Four miles, they were told. One of the travellers further asked, "Shall we be able to reach the village by evenfall?" "Oh, yes. Slow and steady wins the race," a wise old man answered. Now one of the travellers rode a horse and saw little point in going slow. The other, a pedestrian, moved slow and went at a steady pace. The four-mile track was uneven, stony, interspersed with thorny bushes and in parts marshy. The pedestrian trod carefully, avoilding all the pitfalls. The rider went galloping without a thought. As he approached a marshy patch, his horse slipped and both the rider and the horse found themselves rolling helplessly in the swamp. The steady walker reached his destination by evenfall, but the horseman could not make it.

Logic of course says that the man who rides a swift horse will cover four miles within ten to twenty minutes, or say half an hour. Whereas the man who walks on foot might take an hour. Arithmetically, the horseman would reach his destination earlier than the pedestrian. But in life logic and arithmetic are not everything. What seems logical, mathematical, does not sometimes come to pass. In real life, the slow and steady goer reaches his desitnation while a swift runner staggers to a halt midway. Everything revolves around practical work, it is a matter of maintaining one's balance, doing away with one's restlessness. The man who has not been able to transcend his impatience, who is not steady, experiences such difficulties that he is often bogged down in the morass of endless new problems. Not to be fickle, appears to be inaction, though such inaction is the highest form of action and a sure guarantee of success. He who has been able to end restlessness is better able to achieve his goal. He finds himself capable of accomplishing 10 hours' work within five hours because of greater concentration. In the absence of single-minded concentration, one finds that a mere two hours' work is not accomplished even in eight hours, and sometimes even in eight days. One loses oneself in endless gossip, the mind keeps flitting from one thing to another, and no work is accomplished. The man who has not learnt to end restlessness, to be fully integrated, can never attain a real change of heart because he has not done any groundwork in this direction.

Another important principle is that of rising above like and dislike. Which means, the evolution of equanimity, of what is right and proper. The capacity to do the right thing at the right time does not come easily. One has to excercise a great deal of restraint. On the right hand flows the stream of 'like', on the left flows that of 'dislike'. Our right eye views the pleasant; our left eye views the unpleasant. To adopt a middle course between these two streams and steer clear of each, to be fully aware of the right as well as the left, but not to be influenced by them, is rather arduous. The cultivation of equanimity requires austerity. To keep a fast is not so difficult, nor is it so difficult to abstain from drink; but to steer clear of like and dislike is a formidable undertaking. The mind gets badly involved. When through the practice of meditation, through *kayotsarg*, equanimity develops, the consciousness of equableness is awakened, and by keeping indifferent towards the pleasant and unpleasant sensations, one directly experiences tranquillity, one has already advanced towards the mind-heart transformation. It is, however, not easy to be free of like and dislike. The problem crops up time and again. Someone dear to us comes, and we are inclined to oblige him at all costs. If necessary, we even ignore justice and act so partially that everything gets muddled. All reason, intellect, is engaged in upholding what we approve of. Naturally, propriety is adversely affected and equanimity destroyed. Similarly when reason, intellect and power are used for downgrading or destroying what we disapprove of, propriety once again suffers. Under the circumstances, the question of heart-mind transformation is simply thrown into the background.

Non-violence can be an active principle in everyday living. It is not at all impossible. But one has to practise non-violence regularly. Without practising equableness, one can never bring about a radical change in the mind. The practice of meditation is indeed the practice of equanimity. The man who practises meditation, moves towards equanimity almost effortlessly. People generally believe that it is not right to waste time in idle meditation, and yet without practising meditation, without sitting quietly, no man can attain a just and equable temper of mind; no man can be really impartial. If people have a feeling that a particular person is being partial, they will come to have little faith in him. Whenever there is talk of appointing an arbitrator for resolving a problem, the first consideration is whether the arbitrator-designate is really objective and impartial. No one would accept a partisan as an arbitrator. Even a person given to partiality and nepotism will not take an unjust man for a mediator. It sounds rather strange. I am partial and yet if I want a mediator, I would look for a man who is not partial. Unless I am certain of the man's impartiality, I would not accept him as an arbitrator.

Equanimity, we said, is the second important means for bringing about a transformation of the mind. And equanimity springs from inaction, that is meditation, which is commonly taken for 'idleness'. Without meditation, without experiencing freedom from like and dislike, no man can be really objective or impartial. During breath-perception you are advised again and again to feel the breath only, which means, to feel it without any attachment, without approbation or disapprobation. There is no question of approval or disapproval. The mind is clear, altogether unclogged, without any identification whatsoever. To be thus unidentified is to live in a moment of pure perception. It is to be totally free from like and dislike. This freedom from like and dislike is most opportune. Indeed it is in itself equanimity and impartiality. The inaction of meditation ensures deliverance from many complicated problems.

The third step in the transformation of the mind is alert awareness. Lack of alertness creates fear. All fear in the world is the result of negligence. In the words of Lord Mahavir, "Fear surrounds the negligent on all sides—above, below, on the right, and the left, before and behind." The man who is awake has no fear.

In *Mandal Brahmanopnishad*, it is mentioned that the body is liable to five faults—lust, anger, short-breathing, fear and sleep. The way to keep away from these faults is also suggested.

Firstly lust. Freedom from lust lies in not willing it. Not to will it is the surest way to conquer lust. The important passage in *Agastsya Churni* reads:

> Lust, I know thy character. Out of will art thou born.
> I shall not will, I shall make no images. So you will never
> be born. I shall not sow the seed; so it will never sprout.

The second fault is anger. To root out anger one must cultivate forgiveness, toleration. If you quarrel, you are liable to grow more angry still. The more you quarrel, the greater your indignation. So stop quarrelling. Be tolerant. Do not adopt a negative approach, cultivate a constructive point-of-view. With the cultivation of tolerance, anger would disappear of itself.

The third fault is short-breathing. That is, to take short breaths — the number of breaths taken is consequently more. The remedy lies in moderate eating. You might wonder what moderate eating has to do with short breaths. But the fact is that the gluttons are often panting; they breathe heavily and hard, which means taking short breaths. The cure lies in eating less. Moderate intake of food is conducive to free regular breathing. The heavy eaters' breathing is ever short; the light eaters' long. One who takes short breaths expends greater energy; while the long-breather conserves energy and his whole being is filled with power.

The fourth failing is fear. Its cure lies in fearlessness. Inattention creates fear and fear in turn aggravates negligence. The remedy is to be without fear. The man who is awake is never afraid. It is a matter of common experience that one is more subject to fear at night. One is assailed by fear during sleep. When one is alert and attentive, fear does not arise. It arises only in sleep. If man did not sleep, there would be no need to lock doors. When one goes to sleep, one seeks security in locking the door. One is at that time more subject to fear. The enlightened person, who has seen the truth, is ever wakeful and attentive. Fear cannot touch him.

The king of Greece was once displeased with his minister. A king's pleasure and his anger are both dangerous; his high position makes it so. The prudent, therefore, keep away from these. "Keeping away" here means keeping indifferent, in the middle course, not to be swayed by extremes. The minister had been all in all. He had immense authority and supervised the entire kingdom. The king got so displeased with him as to pronounce for him the death penalty by hanging. The whole town was in turmoil at this turn of events. The day fixed for hanging happened to be the minister's birthday. People were celebrating it with song and dance. Trumpets were being sounded. Hundreds of relatives, friends and well-wishers had gathered at the minister's house. The atmosphere was like that of a grand fair. In the midst of these celebrations arrived the royal decree announcing that the minister would be hanged in the evening. All singing and dancing and trumpeting came to a sudden halt. All joy and merry-making as suddenly ended. Sorrow pervaded everywhere. People became sad. The minister saw it all and exclaimed, "Why? What's the matter? Why have they stopped playing on the trumpets and the timbrels? Who has put an end to singing and dancing?" His friends replied, "Sir, you are going to be hanged in the evening. Our hearts are full of sorrow. How can we dance and make merry?" The minister said, "Nonsense! Why can't one die with a song on one's lips? Why drown oneself in sorrow? What for? Go ahead with the festivities please!" So the dancing and singing and the merry-making recommenced, and all went on as before. The minister displayed not the slightest worry, and no fear at all. Not a wrinkle on his merry face! The king came to know of it. He learnt that the minister's birthday was being celebrated with elan. Dancing and singing and joy-making were in progress. His messengers told him, "Your Majesty! It is as if there were no cause for gloom. Instead there is wild merry-making, as if a son had been born — a son whose arrival had been long wished for. There is not a trace of sorrow anywhere!" On hearing this, the king became thoughtful. He said, "Why kill a man who knows how to live?" There did not seem to be any point in hanging the minister. The order for his death was revoked.

He who is established in fearlessness, becomes fully conscious and alert. Such a man is not afraid of anything. Only such a man can practise non-violence; his mind may be said to have been completely transformed. In the practice of non-violence, Lord Mahavir places the greatest emphasis on freedom from fear. According to him, a man who is not utterly fearless could never be non-violent. The man who is not free from fear could not practise heart-purification; the fearful man could never effect mind-transformation. The great reward of wakefulness is total absence of fear. Freedom from fear is the greatest means of obliterating langour and negligence.

We have briefly discussed the three means of heart-purification. All these have to be practised in right earnest for inward flowering. Wakefulness cannot be aroused in a moment; it does not descend from heaven for nothing — it has to be worked for. Likewise, equanimity and integration evolve through work. Outwardly, a meditator appears to be engaged in a useless pursuit; outwardly, he appears to be inert, but a great light is burning inside him. There is a good deal of inner exertion. Inner effort and inner light go together. Through constant practice, equanimity is aroused; wakefulness and concentration increase.

The meditators were out for *gaman-yoga*. Some outsiders saw them and said, "These people are having their constitutional; they are having a stroll so as to digest their food." I said, "They've eaten little and need no stroll to digest their food. In fact they are practising meditation even while strolling. So that they are fully aware of the act of walking, directly experiencing the movements involved. No thinking, no choice, no memory; nothing but walking! The feet lift of themselves. Now the right foot, now the left. There is only the awareness of walking; all other memories stand dissolved. This is *gaman-yoga*, i.e., the practice of *yoga* in walking. Here is an experiment in wakefulness. Action and awareness merged into one whole. It is totality of being to experience a movement in the very act of moving, to experience speech in the act of speaking, to experience sitting in the act of sitting, to know fully when the hand is lifted up or brought down, to be conscious during sleep that one is sleeping, to be aware of eating while at table. When such wakefulness is aroused, there is no room for any fear to creep in. Fear creeps in the mind only when one is in a state of unconsciousness. When one is asleep, one is assailed by fear. It is in that state of sleep that ghosts trouble one. A spectre is frightening only to the fearful; it shies away from him who knows no fear. In the fearless man a ghost cannot abide; it has no business to be there. The spectre needs protection, an atmosphere of fear in which to subsist. Fearlessness drives it away. It is an affrighted man who is tormented by spectres; a fearless man is beyond their reach. With increasing consciousness, we become aware of every movement of thought, body or tongue, and in that state of alertness, no evil thought dare enter our mind. The moment an evil thought starts in the mind, the sensation aroused thereby is immediately perceived. Which means that the master of the house is awake and the thief has no option but to depart. The moment anger or pride arises, you, being fully conscious, are on you guard against it, and the evil vibration soon dies down. If we are vigilant, no evil speech, vulgar abuse or improper word dare escape from our lips. There would be effortless restraint. Similarly watchfulness about the body would render impossible any unjust action. The hand, for example, has its utility; likewise the foot. But the hand can be used for slapping someone, the foot can be used for kicking, but if we are fully awake to our body, all these wrong uses end of themselves. Only that happens which is right and just.

If we are really keen on transforming ourselves, if we want to get firmly established in non-violence, we must practise meditation. Without practising meditation, there can be no full awareness, no evolution of equanimity, no integration. Religion today has become void, because it has degenerated into mere theory, without practice. There is no direct experiencing of it. Mere argumentation without experience! If religion is to recapture its power and glory and regain its utility, theory and practice must go hand in hand. Only then will people have faith in religion, and the life of religious men be established in truth.

XIV. TRANSMUTATION OF THE MIND (3)

When a child is born, its first contact is with the material world. Our whole life is based upon materiality; it cannot be adequately explained without reference to matter. Food, water, clothes, shelter, all visible things, all serviceable articles which we use. Gradually man becomes materialistic. He is so deeply attached to matter as to lose sight of consciousness altogether. Matter is visible; consciousness is not. The utility of matter is obvious; the utility of consciousness is only comparative. It is natural to be attracted by matter. Indeed, material objects constitute the prime centres of our attention. This has also created an impediment. Our aim is to bring about a change of heart. That aim becomes somewhat blurred. We want that man's heart should change and that there should be revolution in the psyche. We want all violence to come to an end, all aggressive feelings to dissolve, no mischief whatsoever, no untruth, only the authentic; no stealing, no robbery, no selfish hoarding, only chastity and purity. We want all that. All men, irrespective of their communal affiliations, want that. The social reformers also want that. Nobody wants exploitation, untruth or dishonesty to prevail. Social ethics demand it. No civilization can progress on the basis of violence, rioting, aggression and plunder, pilferage and dishonesty. Freedom from all these evils can alone form the basis of a truly civilized, cultured and progressive society. All religious values are social values too. They are also spiritual. But we do not see them flourishing. People are not very much interested in them. We are trying to find out why.

Why modern man is not interested in truth and honesty is because he is much more interested in material objects. If the two were balanced—interest in matter and interest in spirit, interest in the outer and the inner, there would be no chaos in society; there would be no disorder, corruption and immorality then. But the imbalance is there and it is there because of man's preoccupation with material things. Too much attachment to anything creates disequilibrium. The biggest impediment to spiritual progress is man's fascination with materialism, with the outer. In the language of spirituality it is called "attachment". Man of course desires change. He also wants to get rid of his preoccupation with material objects. But the path of desire is a strange one. There is the tradition, now part of every religion, that the root of attachment lies deep inside, whereas man tries to free himself from desire outwardly. He repudiates desire verbally, even forsakes it, but inner attachment continues. That is man's difficulty.

A man was smoking a cigarette. The cigarette was mounted on a long pipe, nearly a foot long. Someone asked, "Why do you use such a long pipe for smoking?" He replied, "I read in *Health Care* that one should keep away from narcotics. So I do as far as possible; I dare not keep the cigarette too near."

Similarly, a man wants to keep away from attachment. But he would use a pipe. There are innumerable pipes available, diverse ways of escape. When the inner attachment continues unchanged, one deceives oneself by outward denial. What is required is inner transformation. When there is an inward awakening, outer attractions would lose their appeal. Only this morning, after meditating on the psychic centres, a meditator approached me at the conclusion of the session. He said, "I'm experiencing great happiness. Words cannot contain it. I feel as if my whole being is inundated by bliss; every atom of my body is radiating a mighty sense of wellbeing." And as he said this, I saw his eyes filled with tears of joy. When delight awakens insight, when the throbbings of roused consciousness and the ecstatic pulsations of inner felicity are felt, man comes to know for himself that our material world is not everything, that there are within our bodies such elements and powers and they afford us such heavenly joys before which the pleasures of the material world pale into utter insignificance. However, this realization cannot be achieved without practice. One may spend a thousand years expatiating on the beauty of meditation, and yet never experience real joy. Only practice, and nothing but practice, may yield this invaluable treasure. Only that man who actually practises meditation, who has dived deep into the mysteries of the inner world, can know what rapture, what ineffable joy lies inside.

Until there is a revolution in the psyche, restlessness would continue. Why is there restlessness at all? Because of inner impulsions. The fan cannot but revolve as long as the current is there and the switch is on. The mind is a whirl, in great agitation. Material temptations are so strong that the mind cannot withstand them. The attraction of material objects is great. Now the mind craves this, now that. Such powerful allurements surround it that it stands quite bewildered, and knows not what to do.

There is an old tale about an acrobat called Ilaichi Kumar. He was very talented. Originally he came of a rich, aristocratic family, but allurement can do wonders. This young and rich aristocrat became fatally enamoured of a maid, the daughter of a performing acrobat. For her sake he gave up everything — his house, his family, and his fortune. He began to live with the acrobats, became an expert acrobat himself. Once he went to perform before the king. All the court was there. Ilaichi Kumar climbed a bamboo pole and performed such acrobatics that his spectators were all spellbound. Not the king, however. He did not witness the performance at all because his attention was arrested by the beautiful maid who stood by the acrobat. The king was fascinated by her. The spectators were clapping like mad and shouted themselves hoarse, saying, "Ah! wonderful! Bravo! Remarkable! May you live long!" All were fascinated by Ilaichi Kumar's skill, but the king himself was carried away by the maid. He bethought to himself: "As long as this acrobat lives, I cannot get her. He must die."

For three hours, Ilaichi Kumar performed to the delight of the crowd. With his bamboo stick, he performed upon the ropes, such marvellous tricks that made their hair stand on end. He was a great acrobat, his body perfectly trained. After the performance, he came down his pole and saluted the king, thinking the king would be mightily pleased and would give him a handsome reward. But to his great disappointment, the king said, "Have you not anything more wonderful to show?" Ilaichi Kumar wondered why the king did not appreciate the remarkable feats he had performed and which had fascinated all and sundry. But how could the king appreciate anything? His preoccupation lay elsewhere! The acrobat once again mounted his pole and displayed his skill in surprising acrobatics for another spell of three hours. But when he came down and approached the king, he found the latter still not pleased. His colleagues counselled him to re-do his feats, excel himself so as to please the king. If the king was not pleased, they said, he would give no reward, and unless the king was satisfied first, nobody else would give them anything. All their labour would be wasted. So Ilaichi Kumar went up for the third time and once again delighted the assemblage with his skill and yet the king was not pleased! The acrobat was greatly disheartened. He said, "No more attempts shall I make to please him. Let this day's labour be lost." At this the acrobat's wife came forward and strongly urged him to make just one attempt more. The poor fellow was utterly exhausted but at his wife's instance once again mounted the pole. He began to perform. Then in the middle of a feat, his mood changed. A strong feeling of disenchantment overtook him. He realised all of a sudden that the king's attention was fastened elsewhere and there was no point in his continuing to perform. He came down, sorely disillusioned and did not once look in the direction of the king. His whole approach towards his wife and his profession underwent a change. He renounced everything then and there and started on a spiritual pilgrimage.

Desires create a lot of difficulties in our life. Every desire poses a danger. The counsel that all desires be ended will not be universally acceptable. For an average man, a life without desire would be terribly dull. To do away with all kinds of entertainments would be a most unattractive proposition. However, this may be said without any fear of contradiction that unless gratification is kept in check, no wholesome living would be possible. Preoccupation with the outer must be counterbalanced by interest in what goes on within. This would put a stop to all unnecessary violence, which constitutes the greatest problem of the day. Some sort of violence is implicit in living. But is modern man only engaged in necessary violence? And is he never guilty of unnecessary, inessential use of brute force? An impartial enquiry would reveal that man's resort to force may be appropriate in only 25 per cent of the cases, in the remaining 75 per cent of cases, violence is totally unnecessary. This unnecessary violence owes its origin to man's restlessness, to his deep sense of approbation and condemnation, to sheer negligence and to his preoccupation with the outer. It is certainly on account of these four causes that unnecessary violence prevails in everyday living. If a proper balance is maintained, if integration supplants restlessness, if equanimity dispels like and dislike, if wakefulness replaces langour, and the inner is given as much attention as the outer, all unnecessary violence would cease. All aggression and dishonesty would come to an end. It is often said, "Be honest and fair! Do nothing which is base; no adulteration, no counterfeiting, no deception!" Man hears the words—they sound good. And yet in everyday action, man resorts to lying, dishonesty and fraud. He even commits murder unhesitatingly. He causes endless pain to others and seldom shows compassion. One wonders why. What is it that makes him court evil deliberately? Is it not because of his excessive attachment to material things? Caught in craving, the mind loses its equilibrium. The man whose mind is unbalanced, may indulge in abuse, in violence, in rowdyism. Such a man can do anything, because his mind is in disorder, because he is in fact mad. He is so much attached to material things that he must have them at all costs. To gratify his desire, he would stop at nothing. And if he cannot have his own way, he goes mad. Under the circumstances, no change of heart is possible. For such a transformation to be possible, communion with truth, with what is real is the first essential.

One man lit a lantern to dispel darkness. A blind man came and stumbled against it, and kicked it off, breaking its chimney. Now what is the use of lighting a lantern, if one has no eyes to see and cannot, therefore, utilize it? Without the ability to see, the lantern serves no purpose.

The light comes from the lantern, from the fire, from the lamp, from the electric bulb, from the sun and the moon. All give out light, but if there is no light in the eye, all other lights turn into darkness. The greatest light is that of our eyes with which we take in other lights. When the light in which other lights are comprehended fails, everything turns into darkness. Without the awakening of inner consciousness, of the consciousness of meditation, of the light emanating therefrom, all outer lights, all doctrines of enlightenment, become darkened—they only serve to confuse. It may be the word of the most enlightened person—the word of Buddha or Mahavir or that of Krishna—without inner awakening, it only leads one to darkness. Chanakya has rightly observed, "What can scriptures do for one whose wisdom is not awakened?" Great truths are revealed in religious books and if man had lived in accordance with those truths, the world today would have been entirely different — man would have presented quite another picture—not a confused mass of distorted lines but a resplendent figure of great beauty. But man's image today is not at all gratifying. Because man's wisdom lies dormant, all the great truths of religion are of little use to him. Chanakya's description is most apt. A man stands before the mirror to descry his face. But if the man is blind, the mirror will not show him his face. For a sightless person, the mirror is of little use. You must possess sight to see your reflection in the mirror.

What is urgently needed is the seeing eye—right perception. The order of our discussion stands reversed. We have discussed the role of restlessness, passions, negligence and attachment; now we start from right perception, which brings about a total change in one's vital interests. One is not then so deeply attached to the material world as is a person caught in illusion. One whose approach is faulty is bound to be excessively preoccupied with material objects in which alone he seems to find security. It appears to him that security lies in money, a big bank balance. He says to himself, "I'll get old, I might fall ill, there would not be anyone to tend me in that time of extremity, money alone will stand me in good stead. The riches alone will then avail." But sometimes wealth leads to self-destruction or becomes the cause of murder. When it becomes known that a man is old and blind and has plenty of money, some people are tempted to murder him for his wealth. The poor fellow is afflicted with a multitude of troubles. A great many difficulties arise. This search for security in material objects undergoes a complete transformation with the arising of right perception. A man then begins to perceive that true security lies within, not in outer things. As long as one is caught in material objects, finding in them great pleasure, one would never be secure. One certainly derives much gratification from attachment, but this very gratification becomes a hurdle in one's path to salvation, and to civilized living. The man who has experienced the bliss of non-gratification and non-attachment, has already triumphed over many difficulties. Out of 12 vows prescribed by Mahatma Gandhi, one was specially concerned with indifference towards taste. The word 'indifference' here does not apply to food alone, it includes all gratifications. Where there is a desire for satisfaction, search for pleasure, it is an indication that inner attachment has not diminished, has not undergone any transformation.

There was a monk out for begging alms. He happened to reach an acrobat's house. The daughter of the house gave him a sweetmeat-ball. It had been finely prepared, and it spread its fragrance all around. It was quite a big ball too. The monk was fascinated by the fragrance. "It smells so sweet!" he thought, "How delicious would it be in eating!" The desire for gratification had taken hold of him.

This desire for gratification is found in everyone. Just by becoming a monk, you do not get rid of it. However, the keener one's quest of truth, the greater one's spiritual endeavour, the less prone is one to desire for gratification. Mere renouncing the world and becoming a monk is not enough. One has to accomplish a lot of groundwork. One has accepted asceticism. But there are the passions, the laziness and langour to be conquered. There is noble dispassion to be achieved. A lot requires to be done. Gratification dies hard.

So the desire for gratification awoke in the monk. "What wonderfully pleasant smell this sweetmeat ball gives out! The very sight of it is most gratifying to the eye; how very delicious will it be in eating! But I've got only one. How can one ball suffice? There is the master, there is my teacher and there are my co-monks. There's also the very old monk, my care. All these have to be fed first. Courtesy demands it. Until I can procure at least six sweetmeat balls, there is little prospect of getting one for myself."

The cycle of gratification had started, and the poor monk was caught in it. Now, through devotion and ceaseless endeavour, he had acquired a great many powers. Immediately he assumed the appearance of a young hermit. Not that he put on the garb of a hermit. Oh, no, thanks to the great mystical powers he had, he simply transformed himself into one by changing the shape and structure of his body. So it was quite a different monk who approached the acrobat's house for alms. Thus he received another sweetmeat ball. But again, two balls would not suffice, he thought. He wanted six. So, one after the other, he assumed the shape of still another monk, and collected six balls. Now at least one would fall to his share. The master-acrobat, from his high perch above, observed all this and thought, "Here's a remarkable putter-on, a grand magician! If only we can get this man, we would make a fortune. Our troupe would become famous all over the world. We acrobats and actors also change garbs, but this man needs no outer paraphernalia; he can change his appearance anywhere, and at any time, right in front of the spectators, to their mounting wonder. We must procure him." So he came down and told his daughter, "If the monk who came this morning revisits our house tomorrow, offer him the most delicious dishes." He rightly concluded that the monk was a gourmand, a covetous eater who sought pleasure in food. Once you get hold of the pulse of a man, there is not much difficulty in treating him right. The difficulty lies, not in treatment, but in making a diagnosis. If the diagnosis is correct, right treatment follows naturally. If the diagnosis is not correct, even the most renowned doctors get confused.

The master-acrobat said to his daughter, "See to it that the monk is handsomely treated. Prepare for him the most delicious dishes." The monk came and was immensely gratified by his reception. He came the next day. And the next. He came daily, till at last, he gave up monkhood and joined the company of the acrobats.

The search for gratification, for enjoyment, constitutes the first hurdle. It is what creates restlessness. It makes a man fall from high to the lowest depths. It makes him lose his balance altogether. Behind a man's restlessness lies his desire for sensual pleasure — of taste, touch, sight, hearing and smell — all these pleasures make a man restless. Powerful currents from the five senses are continually flowing. A shock from one sense staggers the mind; a blow from another makes the mind yet more unsteady. One scorpion's sting unsettles a man quite and it would be hard to imagine his plight if five scorpions were to sting him together. The mind by itself is not fickle, but five scropion-stings would madden any man. The effort to decrease restlessness is inevitably linked with that of controlling desire for gratification. The practice of *Preksha Meditation* is designed to bring about an integrated mind, to promote stability, to lessen restlessness with a view to removing it altogether. However, the mind's restlessness cannot be done away with until desire for gratification comes to an end. The less the desire for gratification, the lesser is man's restlessness.

Another factor behind the growth of restlessness is inattention, that is lack of awareness. Attachment, illusory thinking, attraction and repulsion, are various forms thereof. Sleep, idle gossip and sloth — all produce restlessness, destroy stability.

The third factor is pleasant and unpleasant sensations. Impulses, emotions, passions — all these increase restlessness. How terribly restless one becomes when caught in a paroxysm of rage.

One's whole frame shivers, the lips tremble, the mouth quakes! A verse from Acharya Bhikshu is most apt here:

> While in rage, the mouth quakes
> Like grams being parched in an oven!

I myself witnessed the truth of it once at Gangapur in Mewar. There was a terrace in front of the house where we stayed. The street that passed before was narrow. A bullock-cart entered the street. The man sitting on the terrace said, "Don't go this way! The street is narrow. The bullock-cart in passing would damage the terrace." The bullock-cart-man said. "How can you prevent my using this thoroughfare? It is not your personal property." The bullock-cart advanced into the street. The man sitting on the terrace flared up and actually jumped into the cart. He was white with rage. This reminded me of the Acharya's verse. Not only does anger make a person talk loud, it also makes him leap and vault.

For three days now we have been discussing principles underlying a change of heart. In this context, we have enumerated five causes of restlessness: wrong perception, attachemnt, inattention, strong passions and carnal disposition. These must be controlled. To decrease restlessness, let passions languish,. inattention fall away and let attachment subside. This leads to the dissolution of false impressions and augments the possibility of heart-purification. Those who want a real change of heart and wish to do away with violence altogether, should not rest content with mere theoretical discussion, but must take practical steps in this direction.

XV. EXPERIMENTS IN HEART-PURIFICATION

A man went to the provision merchant and asked, "Have you got flour?" The shopkeeper said, "Yes." The man asked, "And sugar?" The shopkeeper said, "Yes." The man asked, "And butter-oil?" The shopkeeeper once again replied in the affirmative. The man said, "Well, you've got all the ingredients, why don't you prepare sweet pudding to sell?"

The shopkeeper said, "Brother! All the ingredients for preparing sweet pudding I have, but I don't know how to prepare it. I have not the skill. If I start preparing the pudding without first acquiring the skill, all the ingredients will be spoiled. There would be no pudding, nor would their remain flour, sugar and butter-oil! It would all end in a mess."

All production requires skill. Without skill nothing can be produced.

We have been talking about a change of heart. A change of heart is eminently desirable, but if we do not know how to go about it, if we are not acquainted with the process thereof, we shall never be able to achieve it.

Transformation of consciousness is not an easy task; it is the most important task though. A change in the psyche is in fact what we mean by a change of heart. When consciousness changes, a change of heart takes place of itself. If consciousness remains untransformed, nothing is changed. And no change in consciousness is possible without first mastering the technique thereof.

Two big tasks confront us—firstly to transform general consciousness and secondly to change human consciousness. Both are important. A number of laws have been discovered to govern the functioning of the material world, but to find out universal laws governing the world of consciousness is much more difficult. A material object has no consciousness. To discover the laws of the unconscious is easier, because an inert object does not change. However, the conscious is eternally changing, and it changes so fast that no one rule applies. All the rules framed go by the board because consciousness is never still. The smallest living creature makes use of its volition; it makes a leap and the rule is overthrown. There is no leap in the inanimate world; it is possible only in the animate. The former has no will; the latter has it. This freedom to act is a living being's most characteristic virtue. To find out laws governing conscious living beings is therefore a most difficult undertaking.

To change a living creature, which is possessed of an independent consciousness, is a complicated task. And to transform human consciousness is still more intricate, because a man is possessed of logic, intellect, and all other qualities of consciousness in their most developed form. To transform man is really a very complex affair. The transformation of human consciousness is just not possible without first learning the technique thereof. After all it is not a matter of merely changing one's circumstances. A man thinks in terms of changing his circumstances, he works for that, finds the right means and possibly does succeed in his aim. But to change one's consciousness which is inseparably connected with memory, with one's impressions, one's virtues and faults, is very difficult. One's mental impressions are deep-rooted; impressions from the distant past arise and infect the whole of one's life. To change all that is not easy.

Strange things happen in life. Quite inscrutable! We were told of a nun haunted by a phantom. Her agony was great; it continued for months. All remedies failed. Charms, iteration of the deity's name, and reverent worship were of no avail. Something would take hold of the nun and make her say, "We are taking revenge. In the last birth but two, she misappropriated our money. We kept this money with her as a pledge. When we demanded it back, she clean denied it. We are now avenging that lie. We shall make her suffer yet." When the apparition would go away for some time and the nun felt a little better, she would say, "Never should one purloin another's property. The consequences thereof are terrible."

For a few months, the nun suffered greatly. The phantom gave her no rest. One day, the phantom spoke thus: "We could have killed her. Our appetite for revenge is most keen. But this woman is continually praying to God and is very regular in her devotion. We couldn't kill her. But we have made her suffer greatly. Now we depart."

After the apparition left, the nun became perfectly normal.

We may explain this incident psychologically and dismiss it as an illustration of a feeble mind. But this is one aspect of the matter. There is another way of looking at it. Every living being reaps what he sows. All that one has accumulated — good or bad — yields fruit. Accumulations are also of two kinds—natural accumulation and acquired accumulation. Acquired accumulation of mental impressions goes on yielding fruit for a long time. One's hereditary acquisition of character and impressions over a thousand years matures in time and yields fruit and a man sometimes changes beyond recognition. He reveals hitherto unsuspected possibilities.

That is why it is said that the transformation of man's consciousness is not an easy task. Many restraining influences come

EXPERIMENTS IN HEART-PURIFICATION

to the fore. Even a passing acquaintance with truth leads some people to full realization. And in consequence they stand transformed. On the other hand, there are people who, despite repeated efforts, cannot accomplish any change. One naturally asks, "Why?" We find one man simple, straightforward and kindly. He avoids evil like the plague. Another man is crooked, cunning and cruel. He is such a hardened sinner that no evil, however great, can make him pause. To kill becomes an instinctive act for him.

Why are there such differences between man and man? Between one man's conduct and behaviour and that of another? These differences cannot be explained in terms of circumstances alone. If the outer situation were responsible for these differences, then people belonging to the same background would all behave in the same way. But it does not happen so; people living in similar circumstances do not behave uniformly. There are differences between them too. We are thus compelled to look at things from an entirely different angle. We have to acknowledge that our circumstances are not everything; inner environment is also an important cause of differences between men. Perhaps more so, for the inner always overcomes the outer.

Karkandu was a prince. He is counted among the "Specially Enlightened Ones", i.e., those who are enlightened spontaneously at the sight of a specific object, whose consciousness is awakened under special circumstances. In time Karkandu ascended the throne. He was specially interested in cows. Once on a visit to the cow-asylum, he saw a very frail calf. His heart melted at the sight and he gave orders that the calf should be properly fed with the whole of his mother-cow's milk. And when it grew up, he should be fed with other cows' milk. The incharge of the cow-asylum did as instructed by the king.

The calf began to fill up. It grew up into a stout bull with mighty limbs. His horns were beautiful and all his limbs authentic and well-proportioned. He appeared to be the very image of energy. The king was greatly pleased at the sight. Every day he went to the cow-asylum and sat with the bull.

Thereafter, the king went on an expedition and was absent for a number of years. On his return to the capital, he remembered the bull and went to the cow-asylum to see how it was doing. He said to the manager of the cow-asylum,"Where is my bull?" He replied, "Sir, there, right in front of you!" The king was stunned, for the animal sitting in front of him was a lean, old creature, whose eyes had receded far into the sockets, whose gait was staggering and who cowered abjectly behind a host of other animals. The king said, "How robust was this bull once! Its shoulders were so powerful, its horns a'beauty! Where are gone the power and the glory? Am too subject to such decay? Shall I too become old and weak?" The king was sorely disenchanted. He straight went to his palace, renounced his kingdom, and became a monk.

Old bulls are a common sight. But does everyone who sees them renounce the world? If the mere sight of an old bull awakened in men the desire for renunciation, all would become monks and there would not be left any householders. An old bull became the means for bringing about a change in the consciousness of King Karkandu; it cannot become a factor for change in everybody's consciousness. Some people are transformed by some happening which does not move others at all.

Thavachaputra was sitting beside his mother. A band was playing in the neighbourhood. He said, "Mother! Why are these bandmen playing? The mother said, "A son is born in the neighbour's house. They are celebrating the birth."

The next morning, a great hue and cry was on in the neighbour's house. Thavachaputra said, "Mother! yesterday they were singing songs which sounded pleasant. Today's songs are unpleasant. Why so?"

The mother said, "Son! This is no paean but an elegy. Yesterday, a son was born in the house. All were jubilant and celebrating. Today that son is dead. They are now lamenting his passing away."

Thavachaputra said: "Mother! What's it you're saying? A son was born yesterday and today he is no more! Shall I too die?"

The mother said, "Son! That's the universal law. He who is born must someday die. Nobody lives for ever.,"

Thavachaputra said ,"Is it so mother? Well, I don't want to live in a world haunted by death. I'd rather find immortality."

Thavachaputra renounced the world then and there and set forth in search of eternal life.

Not all people would be moved by songs of jubilation and mourning to set forth in search of immortality.

What is sought to be made clear here is that one man's inner state of mind may be different from another's and despite similarity in their outer circumstances. The inner climate is the chief differentiator among men and it is what makes them take to different paths. Some people turn towards violence, others take to non-violence. Those brought up in an atmosphere of non-violence become violent, and those bred in an atmosphere of extreme violence sometimes move towards non-violence.

Similarity of outer circumstances and dissimilarity of inner response — it is possible on that basis to move towards a complete psychological change. In *ayurved* are found two kinds of medicine: purificatory and suppressive. A disorder appears. It is cleaned out

EXPERIMENTS IN HEART-PURIFICATION

of the system. There is a definite process of purification which cures many diseases. This process is divided into three parts — vomiting, purgation, sweating — all serving to remove the disorder. The process of purification is an important process designed to uproot the disease altogether without any danger of a relapse.

The second process is that of suppression. In case of certain diseases it is not necessary to go in for a complete overhauling. These diseases are cured by sedatives. The intensity of the bile, for example, is diminished by the application of butter-oil. 'Giloi', 'gaduchi' are sedatives. Nothing is cleaned out of the system, but the disease stands allayed.

There are three kinds of bodily disorders caused by the excess of wind, of bile and of phlegm respectively. Similarly, the mind has its own disorders. According to Sankhya philosophy, *Rajogun* (luxuriousness, merry-making, exhibitionism, etc.) and *Tamogun* (darkness and ignorance) are two qualities of the mind which lead to a number of disorders.

These diseases of the mind are cured through purgation as well as sedation. To these two processes may be added that of dissolution. So, from the spiritual point-of-view, three things are possible: cure by purgation or purification, by sedation or suppression, and by dissolution or decay. Diseases which are suppressed may re-emerge, but those dissolved are gone for ever.

Thus, the process of bringing about a change of heart may be divided into three parts. The first part is purgation or purification. We must learn how to purge our system of mental perversions. Let us learn the technique thereof. We want to change the mentality of violence. How do we go about it? We are convinced that the process of obviating restlessness leads to a transformation of consciousness. Yet the question remains as to how to end restlessness. What is the process, the precise method, the technique of it? When we talk of the technique, we have to go into the matter more deeply. There are innumerable truths around us, but we do not see any of them and we cannot even explain our conduct at any particular time.

A wife sat down to write a letter to her husband. She was completely fed up with being alone. Her husband had been away now for six months. She grew sentimental. Her eyes were filled with tears. She sat down to write. She had the pen in her hand and was writing on the pad. Tears were falling on the page. All her attention was fully concentrated on her writing. She was translating her feelings into words. It so happened that her husband returned just then. He saw his wife totally absorbed in writing and stood aside, watching silently. The wife went on writing, and the beloved whom she wrote to was standing near her. At last she finished writing, stitched the pages together and put them in an envelope. Then she put the address on the envelope and lifted her face in elation at having completed the task. It was only then that she saw her husband standing near her.

It happens like that quite often. The truths lie scattered all around, but man is so blurred in his vision that he sees nothing. He does not realise that the truth he is seeking, lies right in front of him.

Some men get their ears pierced. Women get ears and nose pierced. But they do not really know why. Getting the ears and the nose pierced is a common practice, but the background thereof is not known to many. The main reason behind getting women's ears and nose pierced was to control lust. So that desire might not become licentiousness. It is all very scientific. At the points where piercing is done in the ear and the nose are situated subtle glands and these glands excite desire. The piercings serve to lessen the keenness of desire so as to keep it under control. But this scientific fact was quite lost sight of and it was commonly accepted that the ears are pierced for wearing tops, the nose is pierced to wear the nose-ring. The real purpose was forgotten.

A man's ears were pierced so as to restrain the activity of the testicles and that of the intestines. That was the main reason behind the custom of ear-piercing. But this was lost sight of and many men started getting their ears pierced so that they could wear ear-rings. Now-a-days of course men generally have dispensed with ear-piercing altogether.

A man follows a particular trend without understanding the reality behind it. There is a truth behind every custom and when that truth goes unperceived, the custom degenerates into a meaningless ritual.

All human beings breathe. Some take short breaths, others long. Some others' breath is even. These are three different situations. Long breath suggests one thing, short breath suggests something else, and even breathing something still different. We take breaths but we do not understand the significance thereof. So we never come to realize the truth about breathing. Breathing does not mean only sustaining life. Breath of course is life — but there is something more to it. The real significance of breath is that it serves as a means for establishing contact with both the outer and the inner world. The breath goes in, it also comes out. It is thus a part of the outer world, also a part of the inner world. Indeed, breath is probably the only thing in our make-up which is connected with both the inner and the outer world.

We want to do away with restlessness. The method thereof and the means lie before us. We need not look for these elsewhere. Let us learn the right technique of breathing. As we proceed with perception of breath, we shall find our restlessness on the wane. Restlessness can thus be decreased by means of breath-perception. The man who starts observing his breath, gradually gets rid of restlessness altogether. As the practice of breath-perception grows more perfect, concentration increases. To say that one could completely get rid of one's disquiet by practising breath-perception for 4-5 days would be an idle exaggeration. But this can be truly asserted that breath-perception leads to greater control. About this there can be no doubt.

In the meditation camps various methods of breath-perception are practised; the meditators practise these whole-heartedly. But if their practice is limited only to the duration of the camp, whatever gain they might have acquired during that period is soon lost. But if the practice is continued at home after the camp is over, self-realization is gradually attained until the devotee can rightly claim that he has full control over his restless mind, and that thought comes to him only if he invites it; it does not pester him otherwise. He is then able to utilize memory and imagination to good purpose in perfect freedom, without being in any way used by them. He enters a state of mind which transcends thought.

Breath-perception is one infallible method of ending the mind's restlessness.

I have no faith in mere doctrine. A doctrine without the technique of practising it is of little use. To talk about change without suggesting how to bring it about would be utterly futile. The man who does not want to be caught in futility has to discover the way. We talk about the necessity of change and we also suggest a method.

A saint delivered a long discourse on bringing about transformation in oneself. He said, "We must speak the truth, we must shun anger, we must cultivate forgiveness, and we must be simple and non-acquisitive, etc." One of the audience said, "Sir! What you say is all very good. But how do we go about achieving it?" To this the saint had no answer. An uneasy silence prevailed.

There is a good deal of talk about changing oneself, but no method is suggested. It merely leads to hopelessness. I have no faith in such useless talk. Only when the path is clearly indicated, does the talk of bringing about a change become useful. Mere theory without practice leads nowhere.

We find ourselves in a muddle. But there is a way out of it. We must discover it and make use of it.

The question arises as to how we can diminish the effects of 'like and dislike' in everyday living. Our living is made up of these two elements — like and dislike — either we approve of a situation and want it to continue or we disapprove of it and want it to end. Each person is bound by this principle of pleasure and pain. It is not easy to get rid of it. But it is certainly not impossible. There is a way out.

He who wants to be free from both pleasant and unpleasant sensations, should concentrate on *Jyoti Kendra* (The Centre of Enlightenment). This is an important and well-tried device. The individual who has concentrated on *Jyoti Kendra*, with white, red or other colours as directed, invariably finds himself free from anger, pride, love and hate. He triumphs over the passions. Concentration on *Prana Kendra* (The Centre of Vitality) helps conquer negligence. Negligence leads to lack of enthusiasm, it deadens consciousness and renders it completely inactive. A panacea for all these ills is concentration on *Prana Kendra*. The man who achieves mastery over *Prana Kendra* through concentrated attention, becomes free from negligence. His mind is peaceful and free from restlessness. For him the materialistic impulses lose their vigour. Only that remains which is essential for life.

A meditator does not deny himself the necessities of life, but he steers clear of all superfluities. Let each one of us closely examine our life to find how much useful work we accomplish and how much time we spend in futilities. Let alone our whole lifetime, or even a year, let us take each day as it comes and note precisely how much work of real utility is done, and how much of our activity is utterly useless. It would not be an exaggeration to say that about 70 to 80 per cent of an average person's time is spent in doing things which are quite unnecessary.

To practise *meditation* does not mean that one becomes inactive and indolent — rather it means freedom from all that is futile and unnecessary, so that one can devote oneself to that which is essential with all one's energy unimpaired; so that the work in hand is accomplished more efficiently and with greater finesse and each succeeding work with still greater skill. Freedom from the unnecessary and concentration on the necessary is the way to increasing dexterity. It is an indication of our proficiency, a sign of mental health.

The one important means of rooting out negligence and of achieving success is to concentrate one's attention on *Prana Kendra* (The Centre of Vitality) or *Darshan Kendra* (The Centre of Intuition).

There is still another problem—that of outward attraction, of temptation. Control of this is necessary and desirable. Attachment with material things must be counterbalanced with concern for inner development. What is required is a balanced approach, so that outward life proceeds smoothly without any inner turbulence. Man must not progress along a path which leads to certain destruction. An achievement which threatens to annihilate mankind itself, cannot be said to be good or desirable. The capacity to control destructive power is a must for the survival of mankind. The best means for restraining outward ambition, temptation and dissatisfaction is to concentrate on *Vishuddhi Kendra* (The Centre of Purity) and *Anand Kendra* (The Centre of Joy). Concentration on these two centres helps in the development of inner vision and in decreasing the force of outward temptation. *Anand Kendra* is the great door to inner felicity. The man who succeeds in activating this centre of joy, experiences for himself the great virtue of this centre as a powerful means of establishing contact between the outer and the inner world. By these means it becomes easier to enter the subtle world of the spirit.

I should like to conclude by re-emphasizing that to practise *Preksha Meditation* is not to become inert or futile. On the contrary, you will find at your disposal two swift horses—the truth of the doctrine and the truth of the practice. While expounding the doctrine, we also point out well-tried means towards mastering the truth thereof.

XVI. NEGATIVE THINKING

There is a mythological tale about an ascetic who led a life of devout austerity. The extremity of his penance made Lord Indra's throne oscillate. Lord Indra became apprehensive; his position was endangered, his splendour dimmed. He might be supplanted. So the threatened god descended to the earth, where he saw a devout monk practising great self-mortification. Lord Indra thought of a stratagem by which he could defeat the monk's growing power, and thereby preserve his throne. He approached the ascetic and placing before him a beautiful sword made of gold, said, "Sir, I'm going to town. Will you kindly take care of my sword for some time. I'll collect it from you on my return from town,"

The ascetic said, "All right. But you must return soon." Indra went away. Two hours passed. A whole night. But Indra did not come back. The sword was made of gold. The devout man had to keep an eye on it, lest someone should steal it. He kept waiting for Indra, but the god never returned. The care of the golden sword diverted the ascetic's attention from his devoted task. His meditation was disturbed. His power decreased. The threat to Indra's position receded.

It may be said that whenever someone practises meditation, Indra's throne oscillates. There abides an Indra in each one of us and his throne within us is endangered by penance. So Indra dangles before the meditator a golden sword, diverting his attention and making a mockery of his meditation, so that the meditator's virtue stands diminished.

Those who practise meditation know how destructive thoughts, some of which they never entertain even in a dream, come to the surface during meditation. It happens so because Indra's seat within us wavers and to protect it many golden swords in the form of negative thoughts appear. As a spiritual practitioner goes further into the depths of meditation and as his virtue grows, the Indra seated within him gets frightened. Indra here means craving for glory and power, the desire to be on the top. At the centre of our life-cycle is ensconced a most powerful element which dictates our everyday living. This element — avarice — occupies Lord Indra's throne. At the centre is the greed, with other elements on the periphery. The centre, Indra's seat, is possessed by greed. It is greed that dictates every action; it is invested with the greatest power and glory. It is the strongest force and everything else is subservient to it. Theoretically we might say that even when anger, pride and illusion are destroyed, avarice remains. Even when other elements on the periphery are no more, that at the centre persists. It is only after every passion stands annihilated that greed is destroyed.

At the centre stands avarice and it gives rise to attachment. That is why negative, destructive thoughts rule man's life. Postitive, constructive thinking is rare. Fear afflicts every mind. Evil imaginings and apprehensions predominate. Fear of what might or might not happen worries a man endlessly. If each man goes into himself and does some introspection, he will find that 90 per cent of his thinking is negative and destructive with hardly 10 per cent of it constructive. In the state of meditation, all these negative, destructive thoughts rise to the surface, and we have a kind of network in which man is entangled.

In ancient literature we come across an abundance of tales and legends connected with the gods. In the context of meditational practice, all these gods and demons and ruthless monsters could be interpreted as negative, destructive thoughts.

There is a tale of the times of Lord Mahavir about a lay-follower called Chulnipita who lived in Varanasi. He solemnly declared his faith in Lord Mahavir's teachings and was very much alive to religious inspiration. One day he sat meditating in his penance-retreat. The day passed. Night came. It grew to be midnight. He was totally awake, meditating. All around him was darkness. But inside him burned the flame of meditation.

It was the midnight hour. Perfect silence reigned; quiet solitude. Chulnipita sat totally absorbed in meditation. All of a sudden a demon appeared before him. The demon said, "O beloved of the gods! What are you doing? Give up meditation. It is not going to do you any good." Chulnipita sat calm and immovable. The demon urged him twice or thrice to give up meditation. But Chulnipita kept silent. At this, the demon said, "Do you hear me or not? I say, give up meditation. Buzz off! If you disobey me, you are in for trouble. Dreadful consequences would follow. So better get going. Back home!" But Chulnipita continued unperturbed, unmoved, indifferent. Thereupon the demon said, "You aren't heeding me! Well, I'll fetch your eldest son and cut him into pieces and roast him in a boiling cauldron and the blood thereof I'd sprinkle on your body." But Chulnipita continued steadfast, fearless and immovable. The demon dragged forth Chulnipita's eldest son from his house and right before Chulnipita he killed him, cut him into bits and fried those pieces in a boiling cauldron and with his son's blood he smeared Chulnipita's body.

Chulnipita remained unperturbed and went on with his meditation.

The demon said: "You are very stubborn, utterly heartless and cruel. Here you seem to be engaged in religious meditation, and the springs of love are drying up in your heart. He alone may be said to be religious whose heart is full of compassion. But your son is being tortured to death and you are so pitiless that you wouldn't move your little finger to save him. Better give up your obstinacy even now or your remaining two sons will meet the same fate as your eldest son. Away with hypocrisy! Better save your sons!"

All this had no effect whatsoever on Chulnipita. The demon killed the middle son, cut him into pieces, and fried him in scalding oil and smeared Chulnipita with his son's blood.

Chulnipita continued unswerving. The demon did with the youngest son as he had done with the elder ones. But Chulnipita continued in religious meditation as before.

All Chulnipita's sons were killed. But Chulnipita continued firm. The demon was crestfallen, filled with despair. Yet he would make one more attempt, without hope. He said, "Chunipita! You're very obstinate. I'm now going to kill your mother Bhadra and I'll cut her into pieces, and fry her in the cauldron."

This threat Chulnipita duly registered. He thought: "This vile savage will stop at nothing. He can do anything. He has killed my sons. And now he is going to kill my mother." Chulnipita's affection for his mother overwhelmed him quite. His firm resolve melted into thin air, and he rose up to chase the wicked personage before him. The evil spirit rose into the sky and disappeared. Chulnipita happened to catch hold of a pole and he started hurling curses on it. Thereupon all the members of his family came running to him. None of his sons had been killed. Nor had any harm been done to his mother. There was no cauldron and no bodies quartered into bits. All was illusion, the demon's trick.

This myth may be interpreted to mean that an evil sprit appeared and perpetrated atrocities. However, in the context of meditation or *yoga*, it might be interpreted in a different way altogether. There was no spectre; there was nothing. The negative, destructive thoughts of the individual rose to the surface and these wove a net of illusion in which the individual was badly caught and he imagined his sons killed and his mother threatened with death. When the cycle of negative thoughts came to a close and his meditation ended, everything vanished; nothing was left.

Every man living in this world of ours is acquainted with violence, murder and suicide. He knows that there exists in this world, theft and pillage and all sorts of crime. He is acquainted well enough with the prevalent disorder and criminal mentality. All these are imprinted on his mind. There are many things which he experiences for himself, and others which he hears happening to others. All these are stored in memory. Not the accumulated experience of one life, but of many previous lives as well. All these leave their mark on the mind. When a man, freeing himself from outer interests and inclinations, sits in concentrated attention, the inner memories rise and manifest themselves. Is there a man who has never perpetrated violence, never killed anything, never told a lie, never indulged in deceit and illusion, never committed thefts, robberies and plunder or other crimes? Each of us is guilty of these crimes, if not in this life, in innumerable previous lives at least. These proclivities in subtle forms cling to our emotional being for ever. These are not visible. When a man is in a state of meditation, inner warmth increases. Under the pressure of this inward heat, the subtle imprints on the mind soften and appear in gross forms. It seems then that some demon is causing harassment, creating endless trouble. Strange visions arise and a man is quite perplexed.

According to an *ayurvedic* doctrine, one should start one's day at dawn with the incantation of 'Om'. Every religious community holds that one should remember God immediately on getting up in the morning. Spiritualistic philosophies recommend self-contemplation or self-perception as the first activity of the day. All these serve as a means of awakening constructive thought. If the wheel of constructive thinking is set in motion at the very beginning of the day, all actions thereafter are likely to be performed with full awareness. On the other hand, if the wheel of negative thinking is set in motion at matin, the whole day is engulfed by the destructive aura thereof.

Modern man's mode of living is somewhat different. Nowadays, a man likes to begin his morning with a cup of tea and a perusal of the newspaper or by listening to the radio. The newspaper is full of material for rousing negative tendencies, enough to vitiate the quality of the entire day. The daily newspaper is mostly full of news of violence of various kinds, murder, rape, theft, robbery, pillage or accidents; it is largely filled with romantic incidents, all of which are expressions of negative and destructive thinking and which nourish morbid thoughts and feelings in the reader's mind. A man spends the entire day under their domination. That is what constitutes modern man's worship of God, his act of self-observation, his cherished substitute for the incantation of the sacred word Om', with which he begins his day!

All this shows that man's approach in determining the course of his everyday living is not scientific; rather it is most unscientific. What to speak of meditation and practice thereof, even his daily routine (which is of foremost importance) is not properly chalked out.

How to start the day? What kind of routine must one follow? What is the right beginning and the right ending? It is but proper that a man should carefully consider these details. In ancient times people gave much thought to these. They underlined the importance of maintaining good health, but also emphasized at the same time the necessity of working out a healthy routine. A proper beginning and ending of the day was necessary for the maintenance of physical, mental and emotional health.

Our day should begin with a glimpse of that which is all-powerful, omniscient and full of joy. In other words, one must begin one's day with full consciousness and observation. The moment of awakening is the moment of meeting the beloved—the beloved being an entity charged with power, consciousness and joy. That which is divested of power, that which is unconscious and ignorant of bliss, can never be good; it can only be productive of evil.

One's palms and fingers constitute a symbol of the good. The first thing many people do on getting up in the morning is to look at their palms and fingers. They do so because they know that the goddess of wealth abides in their fingers. Prosperity is a good thing, not at all bad. It is a symbol of power, of consciousness, of joy. Without prosperity, all our power is lost, our consciousness dwindles and our joy turns to nothing. Symbolizing this trinity of power, consciousness and joy is prosperity, our deity. Of course it is a symbol — it may symbolize God, or enlightenment or the soul — all these may be looked upon as symbols of what is good and desirable, which destitution can never be.

Prosperity and poverty respectively symbolize good and bad fortune. All divine powers, self-realization and virtues are symbolized by prosperity; all misfortunes, negative emotions and destructive thoughts are likewise symbolized by poverty.

A scholar approached the king for a gift of money. He thought out a plan for accomplishing his purpose. The moment he saw the king, he made a deep bow and said, "Sir! I'm your brother and have come to see you from far." The king looked at him from top to toe. He was clad in rags — a very picture of misery, his face unfamiliar. The king was all astonishment. The scholar said, "Sir! Why don't you say something? Do you not recognize me? I am your younger brother and come to visit you after a long time." Ignoring the scholar's impertinence for a while, the king said, "Tell me how you claim to be my brother; if you were my brother, should I not recognize you? How is it possible?" The scholar said, "Sir, I'm speaking the truth. I *am* your brother." The king persisted, "How?" Thereupon the scholar recited a verse:

O King!
My Mother's name is Adversity.
Your mother, all know, is called Prosperity.
Both are sisters.
Being the son of your mother's sister
Aren't I your brother?
Do you recognize me now?

The king said, "Yes! I know thee now."

Adversity and prosperity, poverty and wealth, misery and joy are real sisters — both live together. It may be said that the right and the left sides of the body symbolize these two: prosperity abides on this side and adversity on the other. The right side belongs to the goddess of wealth, the left to the spectre of misery and want.

There are only two ways, wherever you might roam in this world — the right and the left. Even in the field of religion we have people traversing two paths — the rightists and the leftists. The Tantrists may be called leftists, while the followers of other religions are often termed rightists. Likewise in the field of politics. Our bodies, thoughts and emotions are no strangers to these two paths—the right and the left. The two paths, in fact, run together: the path of prosperity and that of adversity; the path of positive and constructive thinking and that of negative destructive thinking. The latter is very much crowded. It is the most frequented path—a busy thoroughfare. On the other hand, the positive and constructive path lies almost deserted. It is a wide path, but not much frequented. Never crowded. Rarely is a traveller seen traversing it. It is for ever vacant. When we sit in meditation, we try to impart some order to the left and make an attempt to cross over to the right. And as we do so, we are confronted by unruly crowds on the left, who often get out of bounds and violate the sanctity of the right.

Had not the ascetic involved himself with the security of the golden sword, his meditation would have continued undisturbed, the path to salvation would never have been obstructed.

Many a temptation crosses the mind during meditation. If the meditator allows himself to be tempted, his meditation fails; all his effort goes waste.

A good many tales are told about ancient sages. It is said that many temptations assailed them. Some yielded to these while others withstood them and remained unaffected. Yama, the God of Death, offered many temptations to Nachiketa.

"Nachiketa", said the Lord of Death, "Give up your resolve to know the Truth. Don't be obstinate. I'm ready to give you anything you like — wealth, family, kingdom or glory. But you must give up your search for truth." Nachiketa said, "O God, I want to find Life Eternal. I long for Truth and desire nothing else."

Similarly, the dialogue between Maitreyi and Gargi in the *Upanishads* and Kamlavati's message in the *Uttaradhyan* highlight this very truth — that nothing avails but the Truth. All temptations lead astray. The man who, freeing himself from greed and fear, succeeds in evolving a positive and constructive approach, continues steadfast in his resolve. He progresses by leaps and bounds; on the other hand, the man who is caught in the cycle of negative and destructive thinking is overthrown.

Let us concentrate on the fundamentals. The question then arises as to what force directs our life. What is the central fact within whose periphery our life moves? Let us explore it, calmly and wholeheartedly. If we persevere we shall see that greed is what actuates our life. Let us concentrate on that. Greed has given rise to attachment and ignorance. It has created an illusion which haunts man everywhere, and in which he is eternally caught. One wonders sometimes why man, like a bullock working a crusher, going round and round everlastingly, should condemn himself to be a galley slave. What is at the bottom of it all? The poor bullock has been labouring hard from time immemorial. There seems to be no end to its drudgery. It appears to be a short distance to cover but the journey is never done. There is one small mercy shown to the bullock — its eyes are muffled with blinkers. If its eyes had been left uncovered, there could be trouble. The bullock-driver is clever. He muffles its sight, so that the bullock never knows where it is going. Does it say to itself, "I'm ever moving, without a pause. I must have covered a lot of distance!" The poor thing does not know it is merely going round and round, without making progress in any direction. The bullock working a mill goes round and round all its life. If, at the close of its life, it is asked, how much distance it had covered, what could it say? Nothing at all. It had been only treading a beaten track!

Let us concentrate on the centre, get hold of the fundamental urge. If the spiritual practitioner practising meditation does not get hold of the basic urge, the central inclination, if he does not explore it to the full, his meditation would not be very successful. He has to explore the central motive to find out what element is responsible for the creation of negative emotions, wherefrom these negative emotions arise. If he can grasp the root thereof, his meditation is bound to be successful. He will know then where anger comes from, where pride and fear originate. He will know the root cause of all the negative emotions.

A thief was looking out of the iron bars of his cell in jail. Someone said, "Are you expecting a visitor from outside?" The thief in said, "Who will pay me a visit? All the members of my family are here in jail. There is no one outside."

All the negative emotions abide within. There is no destructive thought outside of ourselves. When the central fact of greed is grasped, one shall know that pride, fear, envy, etc., also abide within, not outside. The whole thing will become crystal clear. The truth will stand revealed. After one has explored the negative emotions to their root, one could then address oneself to the task of changing these destructive emotions into constructive ones.

XVII. POSITIVE THINKING

Hitherto we have been discussing ways and means of bringing about a complete change of heart. There is nothing in this world which is constant; everything is liable to change. The heart also undergoes a transformation. The question arises as to the validity of a long discussion on the subject. However, intelligent discussion has its own significance. "Change of heart!"—we are here conducting an experiment with a particular end in view. By "change of heart" we do not mean mere replacement of one heart by another. This transplanting is the surgeon's job. They transplant an artificial heart in place of the defective organ and help a man live longer.

A man and his wife paid a visit to the doctor. The husband suffered from heart disease; he had strokes from time to time. After examination, the doctor said, "The heart will have to be operated upon. I'll put a strong heart in place of the damaged one."

The operation was performed. The diseased heart was replaced. The man was restored to health.

After some days, the wife visited the doctor again. The doctor asked, "How is your husband? Quite well, I hope? The heart is working smoothly, is it?" The wife said, "Doctor! My husband is in good health. The heart is functioning all right. But he is certainly somewhat changed. He makes false promises, which he never keeps. He never did so before!" The doctor exclaimed, "Oh, I'm sorry I acted in a hurry. After taking out your husband's heart I replaced it with that of a politician!—the one that was immediately available."

Mere replacement of one organ by another is not what we mean by heart-change. By change of heart here, we mean the ending of negative emotions and awakening of positive thinking. Inside every man flow two streams of thought—negative-destructive and positive-constructive. Hatred, envy, malice and attachment are all negative emotions. A stream of these emotions is flowing within. Friendship, non-violence, tolerance, straightforwardness and compassion are all positive feelings and a stream of these emotions also flows within. Both these streams are to be found in every man. However, in the world as it is, negative emotions have more opportunities to manifest themselves than the positive ones. Having innumerable contributory factors, negative emotions arise almost effortlessly. Our actions are not casual or abrupt. If someone is assailed by anger, we think it is a mere accident. But no emotion descends upon us suddenly. If someone is consumed by hatred, it cannot be said to be accidental. All these emotions abide within us constantly. A stream of these emotions is flowing within us for ever. As soon as an occasion offers itself, these emotions manifest themselves. It is not a question of fresh creation; only a manifestation of something which is already there. There is manifestation, no origination. Negative emotions already exist within, though they manifest themselves only when some occasion offers itself.

Everything is invested with two meanings—express and ineffable; the obvious and the occult. The ineffable becomes effable and what is obvious is sometimes not manifested. The stream of passions is invisible, subtle. But when an occasion offers itself, it stands manifested. This manifestation we call conduct. No conduct or behaviour can be fully explained in terms of its manifestation. It can be adequately explained only on the basis of feeling underlying it. One's conduct indicates what kind of feeling is flowing within. A person who flares up every minute, who becomes easily excited, is fearful or ridden by pride, may be said to be dominated by negative thinking. Another person who is tolerant, forgiving and humble, who is disciplined and free from pride, who is full of affection and goodwill, is clearly impelled by positive, constructive thinking. It is no mere accident. Behind each positive, constructive approach there is conscious and creative effort. It is surprising how different manifestations occur sometimes in total disregard of the occasion. Manifestations conforming to a prevailing occasion cause no surprise. But manifestations incompatible with and even contrary to the occasion do. For example, the arising of anger in the context of forgiveness or the manifestation of forgiveness when confronted with anger. It does indeed cause surprise.

There is a tale relating to the temple of Goddess Sheetla. A crow alighted on the temple and settled down. The Goddess said, "How are you, friend? What brings you here?" The crow cantankerously rejoined, "Why, can't one come and sit here? Is this ground your sole property?" A little later the crow started filling the spot with dung. The Goddess said, "Friend crow, your dung drops today are rather cold." The crow instantly flared up and said, "You befriend a bird that sheds warm dung. I've no wish to stay here any longer." And the crow flew away.

There is absolutely no offence in Goddess Sheetla's talk. She was perfectly tranquil. But the crow was full of offence and felt affronted for no cause whatsoever. Even when addressed affably, he flared up. Thus we see forgiveness and charity giving rise to anger. We also witness at times forgiveness welling up in the face of growing indignation. Efforts are made to excite anger, but no anger manifests itself. There are numerous instances of sages and seers keeping their balance and meeting gross anger and insult with perfect grace and forgiveness. They never react or display anger despite repeated provocation.

A great saint of Maharashtra called Eknath went to take his bath in the stream. As he came out of the stream, a miscreant spat on him. The saint went back for a dip in the stream to wash off the defilement. But as soon as he started on his way back home, the miscreant repeated his act of desecration and the saint was obliged to have a bath again. This went on for a while. For twentyone times, the man spat on the saint as soon as the latter came out of the stream and each time the saint went back for a purificatory bath. At last the man gave up in despair and prostrated himself before the saint, seeking forgiveness for his misconduct. The saint took him up in his arms and embraced him and said, "Brother! You are a great friend of mine. Usually I have a dip in the bosom of Mother Godavari once a day, but today with your cooperation, I had the good fortune to renew myself in the sacred waters twentyone times. I feel blessed. You are my benefactor!"

How is it that certain things come to pass despite factors which are not conducive to them? That certain things happen despite apparently unfavourable circumstances only goes to prove that irresistible inward feeling manifests itself in outside behaviour. Other factors become secondary and ineffective. The first cause reigns supreme. Inward feeling is the primary thing, the first cause. As long as the individual does not get within himself through meditation, as long as he does not delve deep so as to touch his innermost being, the outer influences play a disproportionate role and the man is dominated by these. But the man who, through meditation, comes to know his inner being, who is intimately acquainted with the moving spirit within, transcends outside influences.

In ancient literature are mentioned ten kinds of *dharma*, four or twelve kinds of concentrated observation and countless ways of enlightenment. These multiple expositions serve to help the seeker to establish direct contact with the inner spirit, the inmost being, so as to awaken pure and concentrated consciousness.

What distinguishes a meditator from a non-meditator, the man of religion from the non-religious, is the fact that a meditator, through self-observation, is ever activating and intensifying his constructive vision. The one who does not do so and instead wallows in the stream of negative emotions is rightly called irreligious. That is the only distinction between the religious and the non-religious, between a meditator and a non-meditator. Only on that basis can a man's behaviour and conduct be truly explained.

Thoughtful people all over the world are concerned over the incidents of growing violence, untruth, envy and malice and continual increase in the number of thefts and dacoities, rapes and debaucheries. Crime is increasing day by day, lawlessness and aggression grow unchecked, imperialistic mentality is spreading far and wide. They wonder what is behind it all. Considering the prevailing mentality, it can be safely asserted that man's life today is more dominated by negative emotions. Within each individual two streams flow for ever—positive-constructive and negative-destructive. However, if negative emotions are more active, it leads to greater violence in society, and the question arises as to what is more predominant in man—the positive approach or the negative one, constructive or destructive feeling. It is a complex problem requiring a patient enquiry.

There is the story of Shukraj (the Parrot-Chief) going to meet the King. The two held a dialogue, and the King was greatly awed by Shukraj's wisdom. On the King's enquiring about the reason for his late arrival, Shukraj told him how he had got involved in a case brought before him by two members of his race.

Two parrots had approached Shukraj with a problem. One of them held that there were more anuses than mouths in the world, while the other asserted that there were as many anuses as mouths — neither more nor less. What was the truth? Shukraj argued all those who have mouths have also anuses, and vice versa. However, there are men who go back on their word, deny what they themselves have uttered with their own tongue. Such people cannot be said to have a tongue or a mouth at all; they have only an anus; they have no virtue in them, only vile refuse. So one might affirm there are more anuses in the world than mouths.

Similarly there are more negative emotions prevailing in the world today. Actually it should have been the other way round. The more desirable thing would have been to have more of positive and constructive thinking or at least some worthwhile equation between the positive and the negative approach. However, the stream of negative emotions is more powerful and more active. Consequently, we find in the world a great deal of incongruity of speech, feeling and conduct. In the face of strong negative emotions, constructive feelings cannot survive. That is precisely man's great problem. It requires a serious effort on the part of each individual to bring about a complete change of heart. That effort implies a willing acceptance of beliefs and practices which further the development of a constructive outlook before which negative emotions pale into insignificance.

Nothing can be abruptly wiped out. It is not easy to root out what has become long established. We see this principle in operation in everyday life. Gazetted officers cannot be retired before their tenure is over. If the government attempts to do so, the law courts come to the rescue of the affected officer. The service of a suspended officer is restored. The government is bound by the decision of the court. The government cannot suspend an officer arbitrarily; it can only transfer a person to a place where, without being actually suspended, he strongly feels the taste of suspension.

Similar is the condition of negative emotions. These have been so long established that it is not easy to dislodge them or suspend them altogether. However, these can be deprived of their primacy and relegated to a subordinate position. When the positive vision is strong, the negative approach loses its potency. The only way to strengthen the constructive approach is through impartial observation, by seeing things as they are. In calm observation, the stream of positive thinking regains its primacy of itself and negative thinking becomes a thing of little importance.

Acharya Vagbhat defined health and illness as follows: "The evenness of humours constitutes health whereas their incongruity makes for ill-health." There are three humours in the body: the wind, the bile and the phlegm. The mind has two flaws — intemperance and ignorance. To annihilate them altogether is to court death itself. Generally, a man thinks in terms of annihilation. One who suffers from the wind, dreams of doing away with the wind altogether; likewise the man suffering from the bile or the phlegm. However, divested of the wind, the bile and the phlegm, the body cannot survive. All the three humours are necessary for life. There is no need to work for the removal of any one of them. What is required is to maintain them in an even degree. The disparity between them is what constitutes disorder. The excess of wind gives rise to one kind of disease, and the excess of bile or phlegm produces another kind. Likewise their deficiency gives rise to a still another set of maladies. The excess or deficiency of any one of the humours leads to disorder. The disproportion between these humours constitutes disease, but their existence in the body in right proportion, their equilibrium, is health itself. Health means, perfect balance — nothing in excess or deficient, the maintenance of all that is necessary for life. According to Acharya Sri Tulsi, life is nothing but humours in perfect equilibrium.

Regarding psychological disorders, one might safely assert that as we are constituted today, the state of complete detachment is for the time being unimaginable. If attachment goes, life would not be as we live it now; it would be a different kind of life altogether. Life, as we know it, cannot go on without attachment. And with 'attachment', with 'like', goes 'dislike' and 'aversion'. Like and dislike, love and hatred may be described in the language of Charak or in terms of Sankhya philosophy as *rajas*[1] and *tamas*[2]. The attribute of *rajas* is equivalent to 'like', and that of *tamas* to 'dislike'. These two attributes are the motivating principles of our life; without these, life would be impossible. A person totally free from the passions and affections will never be able to run a shop. Whether the goods are pilfered from the shop or duly sold to the customer is all the same to him. In course of time, the business will have to be wound up.

If a *kevali* (a person freed from passions) becomes the leader of the government, that government would pass into other hands in no time. The kevali is impartial—he is not attached; nor does he entertain any malice towards any person. He is above like and dislike. Such a person cannot run the government. He is not troubled by thoughts of foreign aggression, nor is he worried about the territorial rights. If someone occupies the Himalayas, he is not disturbed, and the usurpation of whole parts by someone leaves him indifferent. He transcends all limitations. The whole of life on earth and in society is directed by two humours — like and dislike. It might surprise you to hear me declare a *kevali* unfit to govern a state. But I am presenting before you a bare fact. Recognising this fact, the Jain Masters coined phrases such as 'auspicious attachment' and 'inauspicious attachment', 'auspicious aversion' and 'inauspicious aversion'. Gautam was greatly attached to Mahavir. Who could find fault with such attachment? Where the object of attachment is a person like Mahavir, it could not be called bad. So the Acharya called it 'auspicious or purified attachment'. This would be acceptable; it could not be repudiated, for without it life could not go on. Devotion is essential for life to be meaningful. Love and attachment are a source of inspiration. These must not be denied. So the *agamas* lay down that the mind of a religious person is imbued with love and devotion. A person so attached cannot be said to be a *kevali*. But such attachment has been recognized as 'auspicious attachment'.

So both attachment and aversion can be auspicious. A master was reprimanding his disciple. The disciple had done something wrong. And the master scowled at him, his eyes red with anger. The disciple was trembling. Here is a condition of 'auspicious aversion'.

Thus both attachment and aversion can be auspicious or inauspicious. Someone imbued by hatred or contempt administers a reproof. Another's love is totally dominated by lust. There are

---

1. *rajas* : One of the three attributes of nature which manifests itself in luxuriousness, merry making, exhibitionism, etc.
2. *tamas*: One of the the three attributes of nature which manifests itself in darkness or ignorance.

innumerable ways in which love and hatred, like and dislike reflect themselves. It is difficult to give up auspicious attachment or auspicious aversion; almost impossible. I am not here talking of making possible the impossible. I am not asking you to evolve a different kind of consciousness through meditation, in which all like and dislike is dissolved. Such dissolution is possible; but only at a very advanced stage., Total freedom from like and dislike is possible in due course, but we are talking of the present. At present, constituted as we are, it is not possible to be totally free from attachment or aversion.

Many people wonder if all became emancipated through meditation, how could life go on? I say, don't worry about that right now. The more important thing at the moment is to observe how the wind and the bile and the phlegm have grown out of proportion and our malady has become acute.. How to control it? How to restore the balance? How to keep the humours in a state of equilibrium so as to maintain good health? That is the challenge of the moment. Because of attachment, all our psychological problems are multiplying. How to get rid of them should be our chief concern. There are two kinds of diseases: physical and psychological Physical diseases flow from the incongruity of the wind, the bile and the phlegm in the organism. There are other diseases whose source is the psyche. Lust, anger, envy, etc. are psychological perversions that cause much harm.

We talk of spiritual practices of meditation, the transformation of the mind and evolution of a positive and constructive approach, because the human mind today is in a state of disequilibrium, oppressed by countless problems. There is the imbalance caused by attachment and aversion—we are too much attached to certain things, and too much repelled by others. There are impurities caused by attachment and those caused by aversion. The imbalance thereof is the root cause of psychological fear and mental perversions. It is essential to restore equilibrium here. This is possible through meditation.

Let us make use of the above-mentioned ways to bring about an equation between attachment and aversion, so as to maintain good health; so that we may attain mental peace at least. We may or may not become *kevalis*—full freedom from passions is just not possible under the present circumstances; it requires an altogether different background—let us forget complete emancipation for the moment. A spiritual practitioner has to procure sustenance for himself and to ensure the welfare of society and the nation. He is attached to himself, to society and the country at large. And as long as he is so attached, there is no possibility of freedom from passions.

This is also true that people who come here for meditation have no intention whatsoever of becoming *kevalis* though salvation continues to be the ultimate goal. But we are just now going through the initial stage.

If all those attending *Preksha meditation* camps come here with the intention of becoming *Veetarags* (sages who have subdued their passions), it might produce a stalemate. The entire organisation of society will be upset. Parents would hesitate to send their sons and daughters to *Preksha Meditation* camps. If their wards returned home as *Veetarags*, indifferent to participation in the activities of everyday life, attending camps would be a profitless undertaking. The husband, the wife, mothers and fathers, and sons and daughters would be of no use to the family. People would stop attending *Preksha Meditation* camps. Those who attend these camps have no intention of becoming *Veetarags*. They are primarily interested in getting rid of their physical and mental diseases, so as to maintain themselves in perfect health. Let all incongruity dissolve, let there be balance, let diseases fly, let there be perfect health—that is the only objective of the practitioners of *Preksha Meditation*.

What is called health, or freedom from diseases, in the language of *ayurved* is known as equanimity in the language of spirituality. They are one and the same. The masters of *ayurved* have given a beautiful definition of health: 'The equilibrium of humours is good health', they say. But how to achieve equableness? The only means lies through ceaseless attention, through the evolution of a mind given for ever to positive and constructive thinking. The elements of positive and constructive approach are — truth, forgiveness, tenderness and sincerity. But these are mere aphorisms, words. Will mere reiteration of these words make a man tender or sincere? Will cruelty or illusion vanish of itself? Such an expectation is bound to fail. The word is a convenient symbol for the thing, not the thing itself. The right choice of words has great psychological significance. The words no longer remain words but represent a positive and constructive vision. Positive attitudes which lie buried deep in the subconscious are not palpable; they cannot be known. Words like truth, forgiveness, etc. serve as a link to establish contact with the reality within. The Master's expositions are perfectly valid. If one gets down to the feeling inherent in the word 'truth', it would awaken in one the constructive vision. Similarly, a descent into the depths of words like 'sweetness' and 'sincerity' will help awaken the positive attitudes latent therein. Here let me share with you an important fact. The Master's saying is for ever a kind of spell, an incantation. An Acharya is a magician. He initiates his followers into an eternal secret. A spell is something occult, mysterious.

Something about it remains hidden, unrevealed. It is never wholly clear. The whole truth about it is known by the Master alone. He alone may communicate the whole truth to another. At times it seems everything has been revealed, but later one finds that nothing is really intelligible. The key to the secret remains with the Master.

We learn about the attitudes. We also know the words representing those attitudes, but we do not know how to establish contact between the two. One who practises *Preksha Meditation* becomes acquainted with this secret—which is wakefulness, an emotional rapport, unceasing awareness, constant mindfulness. The manifestation of a particular quality or humour demands constant practice, eternal vigilance. Working by fits and starts, remembering it now and letting it slumber for long periods, would not be conducive to its manifestation.

Ceaseless and total attention is important. A drop here and there would not do, what is required is an unceasing flow. Generally a spiritual practitioner would practise meditation spasmodically, devoting himself to it now and then, sitting down to meditation when the mood takes him, and abstaining from it for months together. Such intermittent practice yields no fruit. For success, continuity of practice is essential. Whatever quality we wish to manifest, or develop, we must give it our alert and incessant attention. Only constant endeavour will bring about the needed transformation.

Incessant awareness, eternal wakefulness is the spell that takes us directly to the inner world of the spirit.

A word is like a spell. Every word is a charm. To negate fate, the Jain Masters have spelled out different kinds of charms. For weakening the effect of actions hindering full knowledge, they have given us the incantation *anantgianibhyonam* (i.e. Obeisance to the possessors of infinite knowledge!), for actions hindering direct experiencing, the incantation, *anantdarshanibhyonam* (Obeisance to endless experiencing!) and for the removal of all kinds of obstacles, the incantation, *anantviryabhyonam* (Obeisance to inexhaustible power!). There does not seem to be any mystery in these maxims, yet all these reperesent knowledge, direct experience and power. If we can be, at all times, open to limitless knowledge, endless experience and inexhaustible power, the resulting spell would become so powerful as to inculcate all these qualities within us.

Today hypnotherapists and psychiatrists give some words to the patient for continuous reiteration. The patient is required to repeat those words at all times, awake and asleep, eating and drinking. The idea behind it is that by constant repetition, you are ever mindful and the disease is likely to reach its culmination sooner and dissolve, thus marking the beginning of freedom from disease, and of good health. One ayurvedic aphorism runs as follows: "Time gradually reaches its point of culmination." That marks the beginning of a timeless state.

In order to evolve a constructive approach, ceaseless awareness is essential. By observing continually, by constant watchfulness, we can strengthen the positive and constructive urges within us and reduce the force of negative and destructive thinking.

XVIII. TRAINING IN METHODS OF MIND-TRANSFORMATION

Two men were travelling together. They came to a stream. The stream was full and deep. One of them stood at the bank, the other descended into the water and soon crossed over to the other bank. Crossing the stream presented a problem. One man stood helplessly on the bank, while his companion crossed over to the other bank. The one who knew how to swim, crossed over; the other, who had not been so trained, stood helplessly—purely a matter of training!

Life too presents us with many problems, much more intricate and serious than crossing a stream. It is easier to cross a stream, but to meet adequately life's challenges is harder. However, a man trained in the science of living overcomes all problems. One whose mind and heart are not so disciplined, stands helplessly and cannot resolve a thing. He never reaches the other shore. So proper training is of great importance in life. A task which may be beyond the capacity of an average person, is easily accomplished by a trained person. Skill in drama, sculpture and other arts comes through training. It is through training that all works are properly performed. Without training and practice, even passing the thread through the needle becomes a problem. Every man cannot do it. Thus, without training everything becomes a problem. It is only through proper instruction that one acquires the ability to meet all kinds of problems, big and small. If the kitchen is assigned to a person who does not know how to cook, the boarders are likely to go hungry.

Not only man, but animals too — the elephant, the monkey, the horse and the dog — require to be trained. Feats performed by many animals are truly astonishing. It cannot be gainsaid that training plays a very important role in life. A person who has not been disciplined or trained cannot be truly religious. A man requires no qualifications to become a minister. Likewise, a man who takes to the religious life is not commonly supposed to require any training. But this is an illusion; an untrained disciple cannot be of much use to himself or others.

There can be no radical transformation of the mind without proper training. Training is likely to be hard and long. Without it, there is no possibility of transformation. Training is essential for the flowering of non-violence in life.

One spiritual practitioner said, "Non-violence fails in war. One who is vowed to non-violence has no utility whatsoever in wartime."

I said, non-violence never fails, nor one who is given to non-violence. What makes for failure is deficient effort. The fault lies with us who provide no training in non-violence. We have made no headway in that direction. With proper training in non-violence, an individual develops in himself a great capacity for death. Whether on the war-front, or in any other battle of life, a person endowed with the capacity to die—one who has no fear of death—can never fail. The root cause of failure is love of life and fear of death. The man who is attached to life and fears death can never succeed, particularly on the battle-front. Only the man who has ended all attachments and knows no fear of death, can be truly non-violent. Such a person never fails.

Does the soldier going to the battle-front proceed with the assurance that he will not die? Actually he knows that death is most probable, and it would be a great thing if he escapes. He is prepared for death at all times. It is his good luck if he escapes unhurt. What accounts for such an attitude on the part of the soldier? His training, the discipline he has undergone. From the day he enlists, his training starts and it continues for ever. Daily practice, theoretical instruction and training courses make him a fit soldier. A great deal of effort is devoted to training in violence. If even a half of that effort were devoted to training in non-violence, then these non-violent gallants could fight any war with perfect fearlessness. But today no training is imparted in non-violence, nor is there visible any concern for the proper training of persons embracing non-violence. It is generally believed that no such training is required. For proficiency in violence which is imposed from outside, some training is considered necessary; not for non-violence. This is obviously a delusion. For lack of training, truth is failing; likewise are failing the non-acquisitive spirit and *brahmcharya*. It may be said that all the truths, the realities of life, are rendered futile for lack of proper instruction and training.

A *Preksha Meditation* camp provides training in spiritual development. There are three essential elements:
   (1) the evolution of faith;
   (2) comprehension of the means thereto, and
   (3 regular practice

Whatever work a man undertakes to accomplish, if he has no faith in it, he can never succeed. The first condition of success is faith in the work being accomplished. If we have faith in whatever we propose to do, we succeed; if we work without faith, we are bound to fail. Lack of faith in the thing to be done prognosticates failure.

TRAINING IN METHODS OF MIND-TRANSFORMATION

The second principle of training is full understanding of the means to be employed. It is an essential requirement for success. There may be faith, but if the right means is not available, if one does not possess the necessary know-how, the work will never be accomplished. Most people are not even conscious of what they are doing, or what they really want to do. They are totally engrossed in futile worries.

A man kept standing in the bus. People close to him said, "Why don't you sit down? Your destination is yet far off." He said, "I can't sit down. I must be up and doing. I have to reach my place at the earliest possible."

Man is lost in ignorance and problems. He is caught in an illusion and his vision is distorted so that he can never grasp the truth.

No training course can be successful without a comprehension of the means to be employed. The importance of methodology cannot be too much emphasized.

Shreinik, the emperor of Magadh, had a powerful elephant called Sechanak, whose very odour made other elephants lose their nerve. Once, while crossing a stream, this elephant was caught by a crocodile. It was a very powerful elephant, but the crocodile was in its element and therefore no less powerful. The elephant stood helpless in its grip.

The emperor came to know of it. But all his efforts to free the elephant from the clutches of the crocodile failed. The emperor asked his chief minister, Abhay Kumar, to suggest a remedy. Abhay Kumar said, "Sir! if we can procure the water-sucking jewel, it might be possible to free the elephant—that jewel has the virtue of drying up water and making a solid path thereon." The emperor issued a proclamation saying that he would be prepared to marry the princess, his daughter to anyone who procures the water-sucking jewel.

It so happened that that very day a sweetmeat-seller received a *laddu* (a sweetmeat ball) which contained a jewel. The confectioner put that jewel into water to clean it. The water instantly evaporated. On hearing the emperor's proclamation, he at once took the jewel to the king. Abhay Kumar recognized the jewel; it was the genuine article. He took the jewel to the stream and downed it into the flowing water. The water gave way to-land. Deprived of its element, the crocodile lost vitality; its grip loosened and the elephant got away.

However tight the grip of the problem in which our life's Sechanak is caught, however complex the situation, however monstrous the crocodile that holds our *Gandhhasti* (the elephant with a powerful smell), if a suitable means is found, the problem stands resolved.

The mind is very complex. Its restlessness poses an extreme problem. Even great men of action, doers of formidable deeds, have little control over their mind. The fickleness of the mind is one of the biggest problems facing mankind. To evolve a stable mind, capable of concentration, to enter a condition of living in which the mind becomes non-existent, a state of mind in which all thought, all duality come to an end, is the biggest problem — the problem of problems indeed. But given the right means, even this problem is capable of being resolved.

In *Preksha Meditation* camps we work for the evolution of faith. We cultivate faith and an awareness of the right means. We practise meditation for an hour. At the end of the meditation period, some meditators say, "Has it not ended rather abruptly? Did we practise meditation today only for 10 minutes?" While practising meditation, all sense of time is dissolved. It is only a restless, disintegrated mind that experiences space and time. In a state of complete integration, all such distinctions vanish of themselves.

Leshya meditation, perception of psychic colours, is a very important means of transforming the mind. It affects the whole of the inner self. After passing through the experience of *leshya meditation* many men and women meditators said, "Today the mind was so concentrated that we did not want to come out of meditation at all!" I thought, on the one hand there is the problem of the mind that is incapable of concentration, on the other hand, there is the mind that is too much concentrated and it does not want to move away from a particular centre. In the formation of curds, no coagulation of milk, or too much coagulation, both constitute problems.

We live in a world of constant change. There is nothing fixed, eternal. Innumerable series of events confront us without beginning or ending. One is quite lost. One development follows another. Milk forms into curd; curd yields butter. Gas becomes liquified and liquids form into solids. There is endless development. But all changes have a cause. They occur through a means, there is behind it all a methodology.

We gain a knowledge of the right means through *Preksha Meditation*. We know of the device which makes the mind capable of concentration. How to steady the mind? How to end its fickleness? There are many ways to achieve this. *Leshya meditation* (perception of psychic colours) is one of them. *Chaitanaya-Kendra Preksha* (perception of psychic centres) is another. Perception of body is still another. To observe, to see, is a great device. Thinking has not as much utility as seeing. Thinking is a function of the mind.

To think means to reflect, to deliberate, and all thought is fickle. Fickleness and thinking go together. There is no thought which is not fickle, and there is no fickleness in the absence of thought. Thinking is one alternative. Another is seeing in which all fickleness ends of itself. To observe and to know are to be free from sensation. Sensation is ever fickle, changeable. Knowledge and awareness, knowing and seeing, end fickleness.

Darshan (philosophy) is an important element. But today's philosophy is the outcome of intellect; logic and argument play a great part in it. Such philosophy is highly misleading; it does not bring about wisdom. The root meaning of *darshan* is direct perception. where there is direct experiencing, all illusion and hindrances come to an end. The distance between the knower and the known disappears. The knower experiences the known without any mediation. There is then direct knowledge; perfect identification. This is ancient philosophy, the starting point.

I am using the word '*darshan*' in that sense. *Preksha Meditation* is an experiment in *darshan;* a process of direct experiencing. In *leshya meditation* (perception of psychic colours), we offer suggestions—perceive the white colour on *Jyoti Kendra* (the Centre of Enlightenment); perceive the green colour on *Anand Kendra* (the Centre of Bliss); perceive the blue on the *Vishuddhi Kendra* (the Centre of Purity) and so on. You might wonder how you are going to perceive the white or the green or any other colour with your eyes closed. Our faith is usually based upon the senses. It is, however, necessary to enter a newer and a much more comprehensive dimension. What we see with our eyes is very limited. Man's capacity is far greater. We can perceive something even without the eyes. The whole of space is full of colours. Whatever colours we see on earth, the atoms thereof are diffused in the whole of space. Keeping our eyes closed, when we experience reality with complete identification and total concentration, we begin to perceive a variety of colours around us. Even with eyes closed, we perceive such a variety of sparkling colours, such beautiful and attractive hues, that are never seen by the eye open. All those colours are the outcome of extrasensory perception.

Direct perception lays bare that which is hidden and unrevealed. Thereby starts a process by which all things become apparent. The phenomena of the material world as well as those of the inner world — both are directly experienced. With a fully integrated mind and with eyes closed, we perceive all that is happening within, which we never witnessed before. All that remained hitherto unexperienced, now manifests itself. The phenomena of the material world too pass before one even though one's eyes be closed.

We can see for ourselves that our consciousness is not confined to the five senses. That is, whatever we perceive through the senses, does not constitute the whole of consciousness. Our consciousness is vast, beyond measure; it has no ending, and it knows no limit. By limiting this infinite and boundless consciousness man is leading a life of ignorance. *Preksha meditation* is a process for putting an end to this ignorance. With the dissolution of ignorance, a new dimension of consciousness manifests itself and evolves. There is a technique for the evolution of consciousness.

Still another factor in education is practice. One may have faith, one may also have a technique, but if one does not practise it, no significant development is possible. Regular practice is a must for the confirmation of knowledge gained. People who abjure practice fail to make any headway. The knowledge of the right means and its practice are inseparably connected with each other. Without the means, no practice is possible. And without practice, no means can succeed.

A villager set out to purchase a cow. He rested for a while in a shop dealing in bicycles. The shopkeeper said, "Why not purchase a bicycle, instead? By riding the bicycle you will reach your village soon and comfortably. If you ride a cow, people would ridicule you. You've got the money, I have a bicycle ready for you. Take it.". The villager said, "You're quite right, Sir. But when I reach the village and begin to milk the bicycle, people would ridicule me much more!"

It is important to find the right means. If you want milk, you cannot get it from a bicycle. You can get milk only from a cow. Again, you may have a cow, but if you don't milk it you would have no milk. For obtaining milk, you must have a cow, and you must also know how to milk it and do it. Both are necessary. In the absence of either, you get no milk. The means and the practice of it go together.

Education may be said to be successful only when it is linked with practice. This has become very clear today. During the Middle Ages, the greatest stress was laid on the training of the intellect. Teaching was wholly knowledge-oriented, not action-oriented. However, after the development of modern science, education today combines both theory and practice—both go together. Nothing succeeds without practice. Students today are encouraged to experience the truth for themselves. Both theory and practice are important if a student is to become perfect.

Ancient masters have emphasized both these aspects of education — theoretical and practical. Theoretical education is knowledge-oriented and practical training is action-oriented. It is also called practical or experimental education. Mere theoretical education without practice loses half its value. In the beginning, the theory and the practical were combined. Later, however, mere theory, divorced from practice, continued. So one's education remained incomplete and became a burden.

Practical work is an important part of education. Many things become clear through practice. A doctrine, unintelligible in theory, is easily grasped when put into practice.

One starts with theory, and then moves on to practice. A master taught his pupil the following maxim: "A disciple should never take ill the *guru's* disciplining." That was the lesson. If merely memorising this maxim were enough, all would have learnt the lesson easily. If mere theory could work, none in the world would fail; all would be successful. But without practice, the maxim does not flower.

The master propounded the lesson. The disciple who learnt it was Koorgaru who had a weakness for eating. He could never keep a fast. Early in the morning he would grow restless for food. However, he started practising the lesson taught by the master. He was steadfast in his practice. Sometimes his mind would react against the master's admonishment, his heart filled with anger or some other contrary feeling, but he would keep vigilant and not allow his conduct to be affected by a passing mood. In time, practice matured. Whatever the occasion and whatever the disciplining, he discovered, it was possible to keep tranquil and unmoved.

Discipline is like fire. Only through practice can one endure its heat.

Koorgaru kept up his practice. On the occasion of a religious festival, all the monks observed a fast. The master too fasted. Koorgaru, however, got up early and stood before the master as usual, seeking his permission to go out for alms. The master expostulated, sermonized and later used hard words but Koorgaru kept calm. He brought his hands together in a gesture of humility and quietly said, "O Master, your teaching is infallible. But I'm really helpless." After taking the master's permission he went out. He returned with rice-porridge in his bowl. The master was still unpacified, flared up again at the sight of Koorgaru. In a harsh tone, the master said, "All the monks are fasting, but you must eat!" And the master uttered many a hard word. But Koorgaru was absolutely calm. Koorgaru's tranquillity inflamed the master even more and in great anger he spat into Koorgaru's bowl. Koorgaru, however, kept unperturbed. He went to his place and quietly took his meal. He never lost his equilibrium. He thought his *guru* was great since he had taught him to keep his balance under all circumstances. He never found fault with the master. He humbly realized the truth of the maxim which the master had taught him. It is said that while taking his meal, Koorgaru's equanimity grew to an extent that he attained omniscience; the *guru* remained unenlightened.

Fasting is no great achievement, nor eating something to be derided. Our yardstick is faulty. We accord honour to a man who fasts, and look down upon one who does not. But these are secondary considerations. What really matters is whether the practice of meditation has led to the growth of equanimity and how firmly is consciousness established in tranquillity, and whether consciousness has been awakened within. The thing to note is whether there has been some respite from like and dislike, from the extremes of heat and cold. Agreeability and disagreeability, approbation and condemnation constitute the summer and winter of life. The man who transcends these, experiences in himself the awakening of consciousness. But this is not possible without practice.

When all the three elements of education — the faith, the right understanding and the practice — are found together, it releases a force that sweeps aside all problems. Then there is no hurdle which cannot be crossed.

The spiritual practitioners who practise *preksha meditation* must deeply understand that their task is to evolve a powerful current. They must not be content with a mere drizzle; they must aim at a full-fledged flow. We must have faith, and grasp the means and regularly practise, practice being the key to success.

XIX. CHANGE OF HEART—A GREAT ACHIEVEMENT

Some time ago I happened to read a discussion on the subject, "Man's Greatest Achievement". Wherever there is a debate, different kinds of opinions are aired. In society are found people belonging to different traditions and owing allegiance to different beliefs. The ethnologists are of the view that the evolution of the family is the greatest accomplishment of human society. Man is the only intelligent animal that has continually developed. Many species of animals are today extinct, whereas human population has reached the five billion mark. The evolution of the race is man's greatest achievement, they say.

The social scientists are of the view that the commencement of agriculture is one of the greatest attainments of man. The day man sowed the first seed and cultivated the first field, he found a great solution to his problems. He has since steadily progressed.

The anthropologists believe that to be able to stand on two feet, so as to leave the hands complete freedom of movement, is man's greatest accomplishment, and undoubtedly it is a great achievement. To stand with one's spinal cord erect, to have the hands completely free to move, is a wonderful thing. If man were a quadruped, he would have been no better than cows or buffaloes.

According to still another belief, man's greatest achievement is the search for the species of man on other planets. Where else in this vast universe is the race of man to be found? If this search is successful, that would indeed be the greatest human accomplishment.

We began with a particular theme and in the consideration of that a great many thoughts, and different beliefs and conclusions came to the fore. In the context of these beliefs, I should like to state my own opinion that man's greatest achievement is 'change of heart'. With reference to man's image that has hitherto evolved, the line of distinction between man and beast, the most important concept is that of transformation of the human mind. No other living creature except man is capable of bringing about such a transformation. The biggest of the most intelligent beasts knows nothing about it. There is only one living being — that is man — who knows how to go about it. It is man who has established the doctrine of change of heart, and experimented with it. And he has succeeded.

Psychology admits of some basic human urges. Differences exist as regards the exact number of such urges, yet a few of these are acknowledged by all psychologists, for example search for food, sexual gratification, escape and bellicosity. These constitute the basic human traits.

Search for food is a basic urge. Its motive is hunger. Man feels hungry and looks about for food.

The second basic disposition is man's urge for sexual gratification, motivated by sexual passion.

Desire for escape is also a fundamental human trait. Its motive is fear. Man is afraid and seeks to avoid it.

Likewise bellicosity, motivated by pride, is a fundamental urge. Man revels in war.

These are some of the fundamental urges which can be sublimated by man alone, and which no other living creature can refine. Lust is sublimated into continence. No other living creature except man is capable of it. Fear is sublimated into fearlessness. No other living creature has evolved fearlessness. All the beasts are afflicted with fear today as much as before; invaded by lust, as much as a million years ago. Bellicosity is transformed by man into mutual tolerance; no other living creature has been able to transcend bellicosity; animals indulge in fighting as much as before. The dog still barks. There is no dog all over the world who has stopped barking, or stopped fighting with other dogs. As soon as a dog belonging to one locality goes to another locality, a fight with other dogs inevitably ensues. No change, no evolution has occurred in the dog's mentality over the ages. A dog may belong to India, America, or Russia, its basic disposition remains unchanged.

Man has been able to purify his primitive inclinations. In the psychological context, change of heart means purification of one's mental disposition. Refinement of one's fundamental nature amounts to a transformation of one's consciousness, a complete change of heart. A total change of direction is no simple accomplishment. A man going along a particular path conducts himself in a particular way. When the direction changes, there is a sea-change in circumstances, and a man's conduct and behaviour undergo a transformation.

Himmat Singh Patel was an inhabitant of Saurashtra. He was a very sturdy man, enormously proud of his physical strength. He believed that there was no task he could not accomplish. One day a friend said to him, "Himmat Singh! You are so powerful! You could do anything. I wonder if you can overtake your own shadow. Behold that rising sun. Get going. Accomplish the task set for you." Himmat singh said, "Well, this is no task really. I'll accomplish it in a jiffy!" And he ran after his own shadow. But the more he exerted, the farther the shadow got from him. In this race for getting hold of his own shadow, he was soon exhausted. He worked hard, but to no purpose. No matter how fast he ran, the shadow seemed to run faster. He was overwhelmed by fatigue and despair.

In this unenviable plight he saw a saint with whom he was acquainted coming towards him. The saint said, "Himmat! What is it you are doing? You look so perplexed!" Himmat said, "Sir, I've never failed to accomplish any task hitherto proposed to me. But today I seem destined to fail. I am therefore greatly upset. Kindly guide me! I have undertaken to overtake my own shadow, but I have not succeeded so far. What am I to do?" The saint said, "It's very simple. You just turn about!" The moment Himmat Singh turned his face, the direction changed. With the change of direction, he found himself at the head of the shadow that had eluded him before. His shadow lay behind him.

With a change in direction, the shadow can be overtaken. Man runs after shadows and pelf. Both elude him; they get farther and farther away—man finds himself caught in an illusion which never dissolves. However, when the direction changes, the shadow is overtaken; the riches too. Everything then becomes amenable.

Man is the only living creature who is capable of altering his direction, of purifying his fundamental nature, of effecting a complete change of heart by transforming his consciousness. In this context it can be safely averred that man's greatest achievement is his capacity for effecting a change of heart, a transformation of consciousness and a purification of his primal drives.

Moral values in society have evolved on the basis of heart-change. In no other society of living creatures except man exist anything like moral values. Nor are they necessary to other animals because their intelligence is not fully developed. Without the development of intelligence, moral values cannot exist. Immoral values also originate from intelligence. In the animal kingdom there is no intellectual developement; it also accounts for the absence of immorality there; other animals never violate decorum, never step outside their ambit. They always move about within prescribed limits. There is never any infringement. There exists neither morality nor immorality. Man alone, through his developed intellect, has produced values which are not beneficial to society; on the contrary which are positively detrimental. A change of direction takes place and man establishes moral values. The use of penal force and power is prevalent not only among men, but also in the animal kingdom. Not only man but even the smallest living creature uses force. And this use of force is confined not only to living creatures, it is also prevalent in the vegetable kingdom. The ants of course employ penal force, so do the bees. A careful enquiry makes it clear that all living beings use penal force. But there are also trees which employ force to embroil a man in their tentacles. There are trees whose leaves are at first open, but as soon as a man sits under these, the leaves close round him, and after extracting all sap out of him, fling off the empty shell of a carcass. And there are not one, but many such trees and plants which use violence, which suck the life out of living beings and exploit them. Likewise the ants maintain social order among themselves, the queen-ant directing the movement of the whole community. The ants which shirk work and become lazy, are excommunicated. Similar is the organisation of the bees, the bee-queen awarding punishment to and boycotting the shirkers.

In the whole world of living creatures, penal force and power is employed for maintaining order. But man has also developed self-discipline to replace brute force. It is his distinction to use the minimum of brute penal force, and to awaken self-discipline instead.

The first principle of effecting a revolution in the psyche, a complete change of heart, is self-discipline. Until self-discipline is evolved, one cannot be said to have revolutionised one's being. Change of heart is an imperceptible process of our consciousness; it cannot be seen. But the evolution of self-discipline in an individual is an indication that a change of heart has actually taken place.

The evolution of self-discipline is an important step in the establishment of society and social values. Non-violence is unimaginable without self-discipline. Self-discipline, in fact, is the basis for the full development of non-violence.

The second element of a psychic revolution is the development of fearlessness. Non-violence is unimaginable without fearlessness. Fear is one of the primal drives. Man is afraid. Fear informs the whole of human life. Man fears the past, the present and the future. He is cowed down by the past; the fear of something which happened and is now no more, is indelibly imprinted upon his mind and man continues in fear of that happening throughout his life.

Something happened in a man's life. He was terribly frightened and by no means he was able to get rid of his fear. Somebody suggested, "The simplest and an infallible way to get rid of your fear is to forget the incident that caused it. Erase it from your memory altogether." The man liked the idea. Now he grew extremely self-conscious and found himself constantly iterating, "I must forget that event. I must obliterate the past." However, the more he tried to forget it, the more strengthened in memory the event stood. Thus, through memory, the event was constantly rejuvenated. The fear of the past continued unabated.

Man is also oppressed by the fear of the present. He is afraid of this or that, afraid of a thief breaking into his house, afraid of his boss—the fear of the present is a permanent trait. Man is not without fear even for a single moment. At all times and on all occasions, sitting or standing, awake or asleep, eating and drinking, he is oppressed by an unknown fear.

Then there is the fear of the future—born of imagination. It is no less terrible. Man continually says to himself, "I'm getting older and feeble. Shall my children take care of me? Shall I get meals at regular hours? If I fall ill, who will look after me?" One thought after another keeps worrying him.

A man was greatly afflicted by fear. A sensible friend asked, "What is it that you are afraid of?" He replied, "A dark phantom follows me constantly. I perceive it at all times, waking or asleep, while moving about, eating or drinking, it is never absent, and I live in constant fear of it." The wise friend prepared an amulet and gave it to him. The man wound the amulet round his arm and his fear evaporated. The black phantom disappeared. But after two months the man again approached his friend. His friend asked, "You're not afflicted by fear any more, are you?" The man replied, "Well, the dark phantom worries me no more, but a new fear has taken its place. I am now continually afraid of losing my amulet!"

Man is afraid of the past. He is also afraid of the present, and of the future too. Memory persists, thought worries and imagination fills one with fear. Everything becomes frightening. Man walks in fear every moment of his life. But man is also responsible for developing fearlessness. He is also able to make such progress in this direction that neither time, nor place, nor death itself causes him any fear. He grows to be absolutely fearless. He transcends fear altogether.

Such a development takes place of itself while man is practising meditation. Fear comes to an end. Man has been able to live with snakes in amity, even with snakes whose very thought at first makes him tremble with fear. Likewise man has been able to establish friendship with ferocious beasts who kill man for food. Man has developed friendship; he has also developed fearlessness. As nonviolence, fearlessness and friendship evolve, all living beings grow friendly.

When one living being attacks another, it is mainly for two reasons—fear and hunger. The cow, the buffalo or the bullock assume a threatening posture towards man. Why? Chiefly due to fear. While travelling on the highway, we often witness the cows and the buffaloes start in fear at the sight of the multicoloured flag carried by the forerunners. An investigation revealed that the animals are not afraid of the cloth, but they are mightily affrighted by the colours. The beasts have little sense of colour. Whenever confronted with a coloured article, they imagine it to be some horrible monster and flee in fear. Fear is the chief factor behind their flight and the hideous features they assume. Another cause of their aggressive attitude is hunger; the beasts attack man when hungry.

Through the practice of meditation and the evolution of fearlessness, man gives rise to such vibrations in whose presence even hungry and frightened beasts forbear aggression and imbibing fearlessness become docile. The effulgence of meditation, the radiant beams of consciousness, freed from like and dislike, spread in the atmosphere, putting an end to fear in man and beast. We have all seen pictures of a tiger and a goat together on the same bank of the stream, peacefully slaking their thirst—here is a symbol of fearlessness, of the stream of purified consciousness. With purity of consciousness comes dispassion, total freedom from affections. In such a state of freedom, the lion and the goat may subsist in a cage together in perfect fearlessness. However, it belongs to another dimension altogether.

A man daily visited a zoo where he found a lion and a goat in one and the same cage. He said to one of the warders, "What good fellowship! The miracle of the lion and the goat together!" The warder said, "Sir, you are imagining things! There is no such fellowship. A new goat is tied to the stake in this cage everyday. As long as the lion is free from hunger, the goat is safe. The moment hunger afflicts the lion, the goat is devoured and has to be replaced."

This is no fellowship! Goodwill exists where the lion, even though hungry, does not pounce upon the goat, and the two coexist without violence. Two persons with contradictory natures living together in amity—that would be a sign of genuine goodwill. Man has been able to develop such a consciousness. Through heightened consciousness man is capable of sending forth vibrations of utter fearlessness. No longer is he afflicted by fear of place, time, person or thing, or passions arising in his own heart. The greatest fear is that of the passions arising in one's own heart. When these passions assume a monstrous form, a terrific storm arises in the mind, and the whole sea of consciousness becomes deeply agitated. At that time an individual is liable to lose his balance. Fear born of imagination is the most dreadful. However, a man who regularly practises meditation remains quiet and unperturbed in the midst of this turmoil. His developed consciousness enters a dimension of complete intrepidity. He becomes wholly fearless. Fear comes from all directions—from the east, the west, the north and the south—the whole country is pervaded by fear. However, a completely intrepid person knows no fear from any direction whatsoever. Neither from above, nor from below, neither the fear of the master, nor the fear of the operative. He enjoys complete intrepidity—total absence of fear. The whole atmosphere is charged with fearlessness.

The third principle of mind-transformation is tolerance. A woman said, "How can there be peace in family life?" I said, "Don't bother about peace for the time being. Think first of toleration. Peace is the by-product of toleration. In the absence of toleration, there can be no peace. Toleration means—to tolerate one another. Different ideas, different impressions, different ways of living, different interests—everything is different. Neither ideas, nor patterns of living, nor traditions, nor interests cohere. Notwithstanding all differences, however, peaceful coexistence is possible. There need be no difficulty about it. The hot and the cold, light and darkness, fire and water, may exist together. Contradictory elements may abide in the same person or place. The great virtue of the doctrine of non-exclusion is the coexistence of the contraries. The harmonization of the opposites is the foundation of the doctrine. If contrary elements can coexist in the material world, why may not rival thoughts or different patterns of behaviour coexist in society Such peaceful coexistence is certainly possible. But the secret of such coexistence lies in the evolution of tolerance, which means tolerance of one another, tolerance of different thoughts and ways of living, of different cultures and interests. Mutual tolerance obviates discord and strife and is consequently a great factor in the maintenance of peace. Each individual thinks in his own particular way. I think in my own way. Is my thought, my idea, the ultimate reality? does it wholly symbolize truth? Have I alone the monopoly of truth? Do I deny the other person the right to think in his own way? Can't the other person think straight? Is the other person wholly incapable of right thinking or conduct? Great masters have said that an old and very experienced person can make a mistake and even a child may sometimes offer a wholesome suggestion. Truth, irrespective o where it comes from, should be universally acceptable.

There is the story of an autocratic ruler asking the head of a family to provide him with a rope of sand or face death by hanging. It was an impossible demand! A rope of sand! Nothing could make the grains of sand stick together. How could one make a rope like that? The headman and all the members of his family were plunged into despair. Death stared them in the face. The elders could find no solution. But a child said, "I see a way out!" And immediately he wrote a missive to the king and sent it through a messenger. The missive read: "Sir! Your command is acceptable. We'll do as you please. Only we must respectfully submit that we live in a very small village far removed from civilization and without any educational facilities. In your great capital dwell artists and craftsmen of all sorts, highly skilled in various disciplines. If you kindly send us a pattern of the sand-rope you want, we shall certainly gratify your desire and send you back as large a quantity of rope as you wish."

A mere boy, through his intelligence, was able to rescue his family out of a very critical situation.

What right have we to claim infallibility for ourselves, while completely discrediting other people's beliefs? Let us give up this rank audacity and cultivate tolerance for others. When the head of a family monopolizes for himself the right to think correctly, he creates intolerance which gives rise to strife and stubbornness. Wisdom is no man's monopoly or personal property, and the moment we realize this truth, we create an atmosphere of tolerance. Then the chief motive is mutual understanding. I make an effort to understand what the other person is saying and likewise the other person is keen to understand me. I tolerate you and you tolerate me. With the evolution of mutual tolerance, peaceful co-existence becomes a reality. Man alone among animals has developed these concepts of mutual tolerance and peaceful co-existence.

The fourth factor in bringing about a complete change of heart is the evolution of compassion. Here and there in the animal kingdom we witness exhibition of pity, but not in all animals.

There is the story of a dog who was highly intelligent. Each day his master sent him to the bazar with a bag. The dog went to a particular shopkeeper and delivered back to his master a dozen pieces of bread everyday. One day, the master found only eleven pieces of bread in the bag. He said to himself, "The dog has dropped one piece somewhere." But when each day the dog brought eleven pieces, the master resolved to enquire into the matter. And he found that on the daily route taken by the dog sat a sick bitch, who could not move about. His dog daily threw one piece of bread before the bitch, and thus delivered to his master only eleven pieces out of twelve.

Such examples of commiseration in the animal kingdom are found here and there. Also there are to be found stories of tenderness for one's own offspring. We give below an outstanding tale of affectionate attachment on the part of an animal-mother.

A hunter was about to kill a she-deer. He bent his bow and was about to shoot the arrow when the she-deer spoke:

"O hunter!" she said, "You may take every bit of flesh of my body, but kindly spare the dugs." The hunter wondered, "Why?" The she-deer said, "My two calves are yet too young to eat grass. They can only suck milk from my udders to keep themselves alive. Without the milk from my dugs, they will not survive. So do me a kindness. Spare the dugs; take away every other bit of flesh."

It is a very moving tale — an excellent illustration of affectionate love. Without affection, without the tender feeling of love, the she-deer's outburst would not be possible. So the beasts too display affection; they too possess a feeling of tenderness, but this feeling remains individual, unsocialized; it has not developed into a social ethos. It is man's distinction to have developed his sense of pity, to have established compassion as a great humanistic ideal.

We have been talking about a complete "change of heart". We have touched upon various aspects of this question and have come to know and appreciate the factors involved. We have also acquainted ourselves with the results thereof. In view of all this, it may be safely concluded that "change of heart" is man's greatest accomplishment.

FREEDOM FROM FEAR

XX. FREEDOM FROM FEAR

> "I salute the great preceptors who, on their part, have bestowed upon all total freedom from fear."

The above salutation occurs in a paean to Indra in the *Namaskar Sutra*. The preceptors are revered because they offer protection to mankind by investing living beings with fearlessness. To be subject to fear or subject others to fear is a material process; both impede spiritual development.

We talk about religion, about spirituality, but we never experience the essence of either religion or spirituality. No man who is fearful can ever be spiritual. Fear and materialism are synonymous terms. He who calls himself a spiritualist and is yet fearful is a spiritualist only in name, externally as it were; in actual fact, internally, he is a materialist. On the other hand, the man who is fearless, who is not afraid of anything, may call himself a materialist, and yet he is a spiritualist in the true sense of the word.

Fear is inevitably linked with body-perception which has two aspects—perception of body and perception of something beyond the physical organism. He who perceives the body alone, creates fear; mere perception of body is the root of all fear. The man whose vision does not go beyond the body, will never know true fearlessness.

All unconsciousness proceeds from the body, and unawareness of this fact is the root cause of fear. Fear can only exist in a state of unawareness. In a state of full consciousness fear cannot exist.

From the psychological point of view, emotional conduct and behaviour arise from the hypothalamus—a part of the brain which makes up the floor and part of the lateral walls of the third ventricle. There are such centres in our body from where different kinds of inclinations flow. Passions flow from the body. All the emotions have their origin in the hypothalamus. The hypothalamus is the centre of fear.

The doctrine of *Karma* postulates unconsciousness. It is ignorance which gives rise to fear. Among the various states of unconsciousness, one is fear. It is because of fear that man cannot perceive the reality. Due to non-perception of the truth, he unwittingly passes into a state of fear. It seems to him that the body is everything, and if the body dissolves, everything else would come to an end. The beginning, the middle, and the end of his perception is the physical organism. Apart from that of the body, he does not recognize any other perception. Such deep attachment to the body is bound to give rise to great fear, especially of losing the body.

In today's society, particularly among the intelligentsia, a campaign is going on with the catchy slogan, "End poverty!" The slogan undoubtedly is very alluring. But if we examine it closely, we shall find that this campaign is likely to further complicate the problem of poverty; it is certainly not going to end it. There is the problem of providing food to the hungry; and providing food to the hungry is good. But the "End poverty" campaign is not going to accomplish it. It often happens that man is not able to grasp the whole; he gets involved in a mere part. But partial understanding is no understanding. It is in the understanding of the whole that a part reveals its true significance.

A case was in progress in a court of law. The thief's counsel argued thus before the judge: "Sir," said he, "the hand has committed the theft. Why punish the whole body for this crime? Punishment should be awarded to the real culprit, the hand, which has committed the deed, and not the whole body." The judge appreciated the advocate's plea and gave his verdict accordingly. "The plea of the counsel for the defence is accepted. The hand which has committed the theft is hereby sentenced to 10 years' rigorous imprisonment."

The thief immediately advanced and spoke thus: "I joyfully accept the verdict of the hon'ble judge. My left hand committed the theft. It must be punished." Saying so, he quietly severed his left hand (which was an artificial limb made of wood) and placed it on the judge's desk, and walked away. Everybody including the judge was stunned.

When we are preoccupied with the part, we are liable to ignore the whole, and everything gets topsy-turvy. The hand has committed the theft, we say, and punishment must be awarded to the hand. It sounds so plausible, but negates the larger truth and therefore serves only to complicate the issue.

Of similar nature is the slogan "End poverty!" Unless consciousness is awakened, how will poverty end? If the tremendous amount of effort hitherto spent on the campaign has not resolved the issue, it is because in our preoccupation with the part, we have neglected the whole. This is not the way to end hunger or poverty.

Consciousness is one and indivisible. All that happens, happens because of consciousness. A part of consciousness is busy creating the problem of poverty, and another part is preoccupied with its resolution. Thus consciousness is falsely divided. If we try to resolve the issue without reference to the whole, all our effort is wasted. The problem continues as before. Therefore the greatest problem facing mankind is the awakening of consciousness so that it is no longer divided but remains one and indivisible. The movement for the awakening of inner consciousness is gradual and slow, without any fuss, whereas the campaigns for ending poverty and providing food to the hungry are conducted with ostentatious fanfare and slogan-mongering, which ultimately resolve nothing.

Some people, believing in changing the system for resolving the problem of food, have actually introduced a new pattern. With the introduction of the socialistic or communistic pattern, it seems at first that the issue has been resolved but when we inquire into the matter more deeply, we find that the problem of food has been further complicated, that man has lost his humanity and freedom and has instead become a mere cog in a gigantic set-up. His consciousness has grown mechanical; his emotional responses stand dulled.

Emotional responses of a man who drinks become slackened, his whole body staggers and his sensory centres are rendered inactive. His capacity for action lapses. As long as the intoxication of liquor lasts, his capacity for action is either wholly stilled, or partially damped. All solutions that adversely affect the vigour of consciousness, however plausible and tempting, ultimately prove futile. They only serve to create suspicions all round and the whole atmosphere becomes charged with fear.

Fear is a great motivating force. In psychological terms, escape is a tendency whose mainspring is fear. Man fears and tries to escape from his fears. Escape and fear are inseparably linked. In a state of fear, one wants to run away, is reluctant to face facts. Sometimes in sleep a man has a frightening dream and he gets up in a state of fear and starts running.

I remember an incident of my childhood. I was a small boy when I became a monk. One evening I sat against a wall dozing. All of a sudden a senior monk came and woke me up. I started in fear and instantly escaped into the courtyard. I was not conscious at the time; I fled in a state of sleep.

Even during sleep man is assailed by fear and he wants to escape. No one wants to continue in a state of fear; everyone wants to escape from it. This is but natural. Often we hear of a son or a brother or a wife or a husband running away from home. Fear is the main reason for such escapes. It may be the fear of losing honour, or wealth, or the fear of disappointment in love.

To escape is a natural tendency. When a man sees a dog, he runs away from it, and likewise a dog flees from man. Both run in fear. The man is afraid of the dog and the dog is afraid of the man. Each one is afraid of the other. The dog bites because it fears man, and the man flees because he is afraid of the dog.

Fear inspires escape. In a state of fear, certain reactions take place. Resistance to fear calls for greater energy. As soon as the emotion of fear is aroused, the adrenal gland becomes very active; more energy must be provided. Such energy would not be forthcoming without the additional flow of adrenal secretion. As fear grows, the secretion of adrenal also grows providing additional energy to escape or to resist. It is a fact that a man in a state of fear is charged with greater power than otherwise. Sometimes in a state of deep fear unusual strength is awakened in the organism.

There was a man sitting at dusk in the growing darkness. Presently he fell asleep. In sleep he had a frightening dream, and started screaming in a fit of fear, "Look! I see a ghost in that corner! In this corner too! There is a spectre wherever I look and all these are advancing towards me!" People around him said, "There are no ghosts. Please be quiet!" But the man was in a daze; he saw and heard nothing and continued with his act. They tried to raise his hand, but such strength he had at the time that even ten men failed to lift it.

Wherefrom this sudden acquisition of power? There was no ghost, no spectre, nothing. Only the man's adrenal gland was greatly stimulated and secreted more than usual, filling his body with such strength that even ten men could not control him. When someone has an attack of hysteria and falls into a swoon, his body is charged with extra energy and people think it to be the work of some invisible spirit. "Some demon must have possessed him, or he could never display such strength," they say. As a matter of fact, however, there is no ghost or ghoul; only increased adrenal secretion, creating a superhuman effect. The adrenal is the ghost, the spectre, the phantom great. As long as it is under control, all goes smoothly; the moment, however, it gets out of control, it begins to secrete heavily and then becomes a monster indeed. The additional secretions which in the beginning fill the organism with extraordinary energy are also responsible for extreme exhaustion and weariness after the fit is over. When the adrenal is active, one feels in oneself an upsurge of energy, when it is inactive, one grows very lax and spiritless.

There are four main causes of fear:
    Ignorance of the laws of nature;
    Ignorance of the laws of physiology;
    Ignorance of the functioning of the mind;
    Ignorance of the nature of consciousness.

The man who acquaints himself with the laws of nature, and those governing the body, the mind and consciousness, is freed from fear. On the other hand, a person who lives in ignorance of these laws, is afflicted with fear. He is frightened of everything. A child fears many things which an adult does not, because the latter has come to know many laws. The more one knows, the less one fears.

The practice of meditation is a good way of knowing these laws. Through *preksha meditation*, we come to know the laws governing the body, the mind and consciousness.

In this context, the achievements of modern scientists are highly significant. Through their research, many complex laws of the body and the mind have been adequately explained. The expositions found in ancient texts are not so full and detailed. Thanks to modern scientists, our concept of every part of the body today is clear and elaborate as never before.

I look at materialism and spiritualism from a different angle, the traditional view of these being highly inadequate and unjust. One is often asked whether one believes in the existence of the soul or God. I am not interested in asking or answering such questions. I instead ask if you recognize the body. Do you know your own body or not? Leave alone God or the soul! Attend to your body first. Know it fully. If you do not know the body, how will you ever come to know the soul? If you remain unacquainted with the body, how will you ever find God? We have certain well-established notions. We use words mechanically and thus get ourselves confused, besides confusing others. I wish to ask if you have any means of knowing the soul. Do you hope to get acquainted with the soul or with God with the help of the senses? Where are the means? We seem to be living in a fool's paradise. Man's condition is really very pitiable — with feeble means he wants to fly high. First of all we must procure suitable means. As it is, our feet are not strong enough to tread the ground and we want to conquer the Himalayas. Our senses through which we gather knowledge are too weak for the task. Whatever we know about God or the soul is either based on ancient books, or is the result of mutual discussion, of argumentation. There are only two means at our disposal—scriptures or rationalisation. Without enquiring deep into the meaning of ancient texts, how can we say what we read is the truth? There is no way to measure truth. Secondly, the ancient authors are not unanimous. One says there is God, the other says there is none. There is no accord; no unanimity. How can we say that a particular book contains the truth while the other does not? Is there a dependable criterion? Reason is man's only measuring rod. And what is the basis of reason? Knowledge accumulates through sensory experience and from that the brain generalises. Generalisation and sensory perception provide the foundation for conjecture and argument. So weak is the foundation that one argument cuts another. Often a man finds himself lost in a process of self-contradiction. The mind presents one argument and instantly supplants it with another. All our knowledge is based on authority. Unless based on direct experience, all action flowing from some belief or tradition will be unreliable — like a house built on sand, without much substance.

Reason furnishes no reliable basis. *Preksha*, direct perception, is the only strong foundation. *Preksha* is the way of direct experience which is not vitiated by any argument. *Preksha* means, "know and see for yourself." Here there is no belief involved, no verbalisation, no choice—only perceiving and knowing. Whatever is known and seen is valid, the rest is unknown and dark. One knows and sees *what is*, the real. Acharya Bhikshu said, "If doubt arises in the mind, resolve it at once." Consult others and try to understand what they say. If what is said is logical, accept it; if not, forgo it, saying, "It is beyond me right now. I can't perceive the truth of it." After all no one man holds the monopoly of truth. You can't say, "Whatever I think is right." Such an assumption can never be valid, so abandon it. No stubbornness! Don't be too cocksure. At the most one can say, "I am not able to see what you mean. May be you are right, my understanding is at fault. But I cannot accept it until I see the truth of it." This is the straight and sole path to arrive at truth.

Let us tread the right path. The right path is to know the body, to learn the laws governing it, to perceive how ignorance prevails. Ignorance has two factors—a subtle body (in the terminology of the *Karma* doctrine) and a gross body with glands and glandular systems (in the terminology of science). In the subtle body are accumulated a multitude of impressions, elements of physical ignorance in such abundance that when these get activated, they give rise to a diversity of emotional situations. Now it is anger, now pride, or lust, or hatred, or envy or attachment, or it may be like, dislike, or fear — all these impulses and emotions are different forms of ignorance. And these emotional behaviours are continually coming into being. That is what the doctrine of *Karma* lays down.

The other view—that of physiology—traces the origin of emotions and impulses, of fear, anger, bellicosity, etc. to reactions caused in the body by outer stimuli.

We have to understand the gross body, also the subtle body. Without knowing both these bodies, the talk of knowing the soul appears to be meaningless. I am not saying that you should not believe in God or the soul. I only suggest that you need not confine yourself to merely believing — you need not get stuck up there but may forge ahead into the sphere of perceiving. In childhood one accepts what is given. But to be stuck up in childish mentality, never to outgrow it, cannot be right. If one remains a child for ever, never grows up to be an adult or a mature person, it would look odd. The child takes his mother's word for granted; he obeys his father and brother, and other elders of the family. But when he becomes mature, he no longer accepts things at second-hand, but wants to gain direct knowledge of them. Mere belief is supplanted by direct experience.

That should be the way in the sphere of religion and philosophy. At present, however, it is not so. Even in this field, people have taken to believing rather than knowing for themselves. And this passive acceptance lasts all through one's life. There is never any true knowing, which is on the face of it highly ridiculous. A man must progress from a state of believing to that of knowing.

The practice of *preksha* is a process of knowing, not merely believing. First of all one comes to know the laws governing the body; later laws governing the subtle body. A spiritual practitioner must be well-acquainted with the anatomy of the body; also he must study the doctrine of *Karma* and know the structure of the subtle body and the factors influencing it. When we come to know the laws governing the gross and the subtle bodies, when we understand the doctrine of *Karma*, we shall find ourselves entering into the realm of true seeking. Questions will then arise in the mind— Is there a soul? Is there something beyond the body? Does God exist? This basic enquiry will lead to still deeper secrets. The door to true knowledge is not opened till then. Merely to accept is to shut the door. Acceptance is easy; I tell you something and you accept it. But what do you really get? There is no effect whatsoever. To know, one has to work hard, sometimes for thousands of years. The path of acceptance is an easy path, that of knowing a very arduous one. To know, to find out, one has to put in a great deal of effort. Whereas mere acceptance demands no effort. You say something and I accept it. I don't have to do a thing. Nevertheless, those who merely accept the truth at second-hand, are stuck up in belief. It is only those pioneers who, laying aside all belief, have sought to know things for themselves that have proved to be the true benefactors of mankind. Here a difficulty arises. Those who have realised themselves find a great many believers. One man becomes enlightened; a million follow him, often blindly. The centre is a mere dot, but the periphery is large. All the problems arise on the periphery, not at the centre. If all became knowers, if all realized themselves, there would be no difficulty.

Lord Mahavir said, "He who is not a knower and a seer, faces obstructions time and again. He who does not know and see for himself is ever beset with obstacles. He who does not know from his own experience, does not see with his own eyes, is interrupted at every step." Opportunities offer themselves for knowing and seeing, but a man deliberately shuts his eyes to them. He deprives himself of vision and is consequently surrounded by impediments. Our effort is aimed at knowing and seeing — attainment of ultimate knowledge or vision is our goal. For this, one has to experience for oneself the supraphysical state.

The one great aim of spiritual endeavour is the experiencing of the supraphysical state. One has to go beyond mere body-perception. Two things are connected with body perception—life and death. Both are inseparably linked with each other. When we look at life, we experience attachment; when we look at death, we experience fear. Both these aspects of unconsciousness—attachment and fear—are connected with the body. The care of the body gives rise to attachment. We do not want to be unattached. The giving up of the body, on the other hand, causes fear. What is fear after all? A fable from *Uttaradhyana Sutra* will illustrate the point. King Samprati went out hunting. A deer came across his way. He shot the arrow and the deer was killed. The king drew near and presently he saw a monk sitting under the tree in *kayotsarg*. The king was filled with fear. He said to himself, " I have done a great wrong. The deer probably belongs to this monk. I have killed it. What will the monk say? He appears to be a great ascetic. If he lays a curse on me, I am undone!"

Even a killer is afraid of death. He does not want to die. He dishes out death to lots of people, but is reluctant to face death himself, and is terribly concerned with ensuring his own safety. His fear is so intense that he employs a great many people for his own protection. The killer is even more afraid of death than the killed.

So the king was gripped by fear. He alighted from his horse and prostrated at the feet of the monk. The monk completed his *kayotsarg* and motioned him to speak. The king, with folded hands, said, "Sir! pardon me! I did not know that that deer belonged to you. Not knowing this, I have killed the deer. Kindly pardon me!"

The monk sat still. Then he said in a quiet tone, "O King, I will pardon you, but then you must deserve it. You will deserve it only when you yourself accord protection to all and sundry. All fear you. Not only the deer that you have killed, but the whole kingdom fears you. You want to be free from fear. You must also learn to offer this freedom from fear to others. If you give protection to all and ensure for others full freedom from fear, you will enjoy this freedom for yourself. Tell me one thing, O King! Why in this short life of yours are you doing so much violence to others? Are you going to live here for ever? Are you immortal, will never die? Pause and consider! Nothing is immortal. Nothing is going to last for ever. Why do you then commit so much violence? What for?"

Only that man can give others freedom from fear who has attained such freedom for himself, and whose whole being is resonant with vibrations of fearlessness. These vibrations radiate fearlessness all around. Only that man has complete protection from fear who offers such protection to others. Only that man radiates fearlessness who is himself totally without fear.

It is necessary to be completely free from fear because only through fearlessness can fear be eliminated.

XXI. SOURCES OF FEAR

The world we live in is very dynamic — nothing but vibrations, eternal flux. Movement means change of place. We are at a particular spot. As we move, the place changes. Both the conscious and the unconscious world are subject to continual motion, constant change.

Our mind too is very dynamic. It is also running helter-skelter all the time. Now it is in one place, and a little later it moves to another place. The practice of *preksha meditation* is designed to stabilize the mind. As it is, the mind is in constant motion. It does not stay at one place. The famous psychologist Gland, after making many experiments, concluded that in one minute the mind changes fifteen times. Which means that thought changes its object after every four seconds. Another psychologist Willings also came to a similar conclusion. He found that every one to five seconds attention changed its object. Every spiritual practitioner practising meditation comes to realize that the mind is incapable of concentration on any subject for any considerable length of time. We sit down to concentrate on one object, but attention falters. The change of object or place is a natural process. Thought changes, the object changes, attention changes, everything undergoes a change. Our life is like a motion picture. All the pictures that we have seen on the screen pale into insignificance before the show going on in our mind. A movie lasts for two to three hours, but the cinema of our life goes on for ever. There is constant movement. The scene changes every second. And there is no end to it.

Two friends, both gossips, were engaged in conversation. One of them said, "My grandfather was so expert a swimmer that when he went for a bath to the village pool, he kept swimming there for three days and three nights together. What a remarkable swimmer!" The other said, "Is that all? Now listen! My grandfather went swimming in the sea. He never came back and is still there. He has been swimming for the last fifty years. What a remarkable swimmer!"

The cinema of our life goes on for ever. It never comes to an end.

Likewise the procession of our mind with its changing thoughts and passions is ever on the move. Now it is anger, now fear, now lust, or attachment, later hatred or malice, greed and ambition. Different emotions come to the fore one after another and present their image. Among these, fear occupies an important place. Some psychologists admit only three primary instincts — fear, anger and love. These are the great emotions that last all through life, that live with man for ever. It is these emotions that arise more often.

Fear is the greatest of them all. Man fears everything. One fear follows another; there is never an end to it. One tries to get rid of one fear and in the very attempt to do so another fear rises in its place. Such is man's nature. Fear is his constant companion; he never can get rid of it.

We are seeking to find the very mainspring of fear. Why is there fear at all? What is its root cause? Wherefrom does it arise? We know of provocative situations where excitement is the rule. When confronted with a fearful situation, man is afraid. A loud voice, an explosion, is enough to frighten him. The thunder-cloud in the sky makes men on earth contract with fear. Likewise, a flash of lightning in the heavens makes a man quiver while sitting in his own house. The thunder of lightning unnerves him quite. A loud noise provokes fear.

It was night. Two travellers were going together. One of them fell behind, the other went on, rapt in himself. After a while he became aware of his being left alone — his companion had lagged behind. Instantly he was filled with fear. His feet trembled. Loneliness provokes fear.

We have talked about certain situations which stimulate fear, but stimuli cannot be said to be the root cause thereof. We have to find what the root causes are.

There are said to be four sources of fear:
Lack of Vitality;
The Fear Complex;
Constant Thought of Fear; and
Stimulation of the Atoms of Fear

(1) Lack of Vitality

Some individuals have no courage, no strength, no power, no guts. In the absence of these, fear is born. Guts may be said to be inner heroism of the man who is constantly aware of himself, who has no inferiority complex, has a pure consciousness. The purity of consciousness thus implies constant self-awareness, an awareness of one's inner peculiarities. In the absence of self-knowledge, a man is frightened of others; he is easily influenced by others. To be influenced is also a kind of fear. Lack of inner vitality is the cause thereof. It is one's own feebleness that creates fear. The game of power versus powerlessness, weakness versus strength, goes on for ever. Nobody comes to the aid of the weak and the powerless whereas strength invites cooperation from unknown sources. A Sanskrit poet says:

Even the wind grows friendly to the strong.

When fire is kindled in the forest, it destroys the whole of the forest. And it is aided by the wind. Without the aid of the wind, the fire cannot spread. In spreading the fire the wind acts as a collaborator. Now, why should the wind support and cooperate with the fire. The two are contradictory in nature, and yet the wind acts as a collaborator. Why? Because the fire is powerful, and when the fire begins to spread, the wind comes to its aid uninvited. On the other hand, when the fire is weak, the wind only helps to extinguish it. When the lamp begins to flicker, a gust of wind puts it out. So the wind acts both ways. It helps to spread the fire; it also helps to extinguish it. The feebleness of the little lamp makes the wind extinguish it. The might of the forest conflagration instead makes the wind cooperate with it, enhancing it all the more, turning it into a blaze.

That is the universal law—all come to the aid of the strong. The man who is weak and without power, has no friends. The mind is ever afflicted with fear.

So, the foremost source of fear is lack of vitality, powerlessness.

(2) The Fear Complex

When the mind is filled with fear, everything becomes frightening. A house was declared to be haunted. People took it for granted that ghosts lived there. A spectre may be invisible, but the mind obsessed with the thought of the ghost is beside itself with fear. Nobody wants to buy a 'haunted' house, however beautiful or cheap; the main reason behind it being the mentality of fear. Once fear is entrenched in a man's heart, it abides there for ever and manifests itself in a variety of ways.

(3) Constant Thought of Fear

To indulge in fearful talk, to think of fear always, to read horror-thrillers, to hear and contemplate upon these, all help to create more and more fear. What is going to happen now? What will happen tomorrow? What will happen when I get old? Who will look after me then? Such waves and streams of fear get started that nothing is perceptible except fear. The thought of fear creates more fear.

There are many people who delight in reciting horror tales. They say, "My father once saw a witch. Her feet were turned backward." Or they say, "One day my father came across a ghost, or my friend met with a spectre, or a most terrible thing came to pass," etc. There is no end to such loose talk. Ghost stories are told one after another whether they are real or imaginary. Imagination, indeed, has a legitimate place in a fable. The tellers of ghost stories have their fun, but the listeners have a hard time later; they cannot sleep because of fear. All night they turn in their beds this way and that. They see ghosts and spectres on all sides. Their bodies tremble with fear. Whether the story was real or imaginary, the scenes thereof are recreated in the mind of the listener, making him restless.

(4) Stimulation of the Atoms of Fear.

This fourth source of fear is very important. No immediate provocative situation may exist, nor any thought of fear, nor any discussion thereof, nor may there be any fear in the mind and yet as soon as the atoms of fear become active, a grave misgiving takes hold of one. This apprehension is not due to any outside factors; it owes its origin mainly to inner disquiet. In the absence of any outside causes, it is also known as a causeless fear. It is produced by the activity of the atoms of fear accumulated inside. A situation of fear develops, apparently without any cause. Fear pervades the whole atmosphere without any reason.

We are well acquainted with the doctrine of circumstances. We know of the factors and circumstances influencing our conduct from the outside. However, we are not so well acquainted with the inner environment.

This aspect has certainly been considered by the psychologists. The objects of knowledge sometimes occupy our conscious mind, and at other times they occupy our sub-conscious or the unconscious mind. These objects have their movements in three mental spheres. Some thought comes to the conscious mind; after a while attention falters and that thought enters the sub-conscious mind. We know it from our daily experience that hundreds of thoughts come to the conscious mind and are soon forgotten. Where do these go? A little while ago we were discussing one thing. After two minutes, the subject is changed, and the mind is now concentrated on another object. Was the previous topic exhausted? Oh no, it was only relegated to the sub-conscious mind at a greater depth. The objects of the sub-conscious and the unconscious mind keep changing all the time. The cycle goes on. The thought occupying the sub-conscious mind moves to the conscious mind, and that possessed by the conscious mind goes back into the sub-conscious. The cycle never stops. That is why sometimes a particular memory fills a man with fear; at other times with anger or love.

What we receive from the sub-conscious is often not clear, but the intimations of the conscious are quite distinct. Thought which comes from the conscious mind is unambiguous; that which descends into the sub-conscious gets obscured. Conscious thought exists between certain limits, but on entering the sub-conscious mind, the same thought becomes diffused, expansive. Spiritual science has analysed this phenomenon much more carefully than psychology. The whole doctrine of *Karma* is founded on the fact that every happening in the conscious mind goes to the subtle body and leaves its impression there.

The subtle body embodies a unique system which far outweighs all other systems put together—the political, social and the industrial. It is a very comprehensive system with numerous functions in which a great harmony exists between thought and effort. The subtle body sends out vibrations which in themselves constitute a complete system. No vibration, no movement, is without utility. Each leaves its mark. All those marks are carefully preserved within. Inside, there is an enormous computer which registers each vibration, big or small, and also gives out in course of time the consequences thereof.

Within the subtle body, the *Karma sharir*, there exists a complete discipline of fear, strongly incrusted with atoms of ignorance. These atoms become activated in accordance with the stimuli received, but even if no stimulus is available, these atoms, on attaining maturity, become activated of themselves. For their activity they are not dependent on any stimuli; they operate on their own.

The order of *Karma* is highly responsible. It is so deeply alive to its responsibility that it does not wait for any stimulus to start working. As soon as conditions are ripe, it starts functioning. Fear becomes manifest. Sometimes a man feels he is calm enough, but a strange melancholy afflicts him. Or for no apparent reason, a man is filled with joy, vibrations of bliss irradiating his whole being. Similarly, without any bad news, a man is sometimes filled with sorrow. Why does one suddenly flare up? What is behind a sudden upsurge of fear? Everyone has experienced such a turmoil at one time or the other and one wonders why it happens.

It happens because of the activation of the atoms of fear in the inner atmosphere. This indeed is the greatest source of fear, the basic source, the mother of all sources.

There are latent within us the atoms of unawareness, which is like a fountainhead with many streams. The fountainhead is one, but the streams are many, spread all around. Fear is one of the streams. The originating causes of fear lie within us. But we know very little about these inner goings-on. We view everything in the context of external circumstances. We have become fatalists of circumstance. We seem to believe that man's nature is determined by his circumstances. There is of course some truth in it, but it is not the whole truth. Nevertheless, this partial truth has so dominated the human mind that each man thinks, speaks and acts in terms of it. "What am I to do?", he seems to say, "I have to adjust myself to circumstances!" It is very difficult to get rid of this preconception, which embodies only a partial truth, not the whole truth. The whole truth embodies two things: (i) that man is conditioned by his circumstances, and (ii) that man's action determines his circumstances. Only a synthesis of these two facts can give us an inkling of the truth. In fact, a third fact has to be added to it — that is, maturity. Circumstances, man's action and fruition in time make up the complete triangle of truth. In these three dimensions is truth manifested.

The soul is fashioned by past deeds and it is also influenced by circumstances. And yet it is an entity, complete in itself, with an independent existence. If it were wholly influenced by action and circumstances, it would no longer be a soul, indeed it would become non-soul, with no entity of its own. But that which has come into being even for a second, can never totally disappear. Being is stable and permanent. The existence of the soul is based upon self-consummation. Self-consummation is of two kinds—natural consummation and artificial consummation wrought by skill. The former is concurrent with one's inner being, the latter modified by outer factors. The natural consummation of the soul is constanly in operation and maintains its entity. With the termination of this consummation, the very existence of the soul is ended. This natural fruition is operative all the time, constantly evolving so as to perserve the entity of the soul.

Even when it gets dark, light does not cease to exist. At midday, there may form thick clouds in the sky — very dense and black. There may be total darkness and yet the 'day' is very much there — its existence cannot be denied. There is a difference between the gathering of dark dense clouds in the sky during the day, and the night. Even in the midst of deep darkness caused by dense clouds, one is very much aware of the existence of the day. Just because of total darkness, one never says it is night. What constitutes the dividing line between night and day is the consummation of our being. "I am endowed with consciousness", "I'm a conscious being", "I'm not an unconscious entity" — this awareness lasts for ever. This mature consciousness is accompanied by the consummation of past deeds and an awareness of the prevailing circumstances. The fruition of the three together constitutes our individuality.

Internal causes constitute the fourth big source of fear.

SOURCES OF FEAR

From the four mainsprings of fear result fatalism of circumstance, belief in the doctrine of *Karma* and that of fruition in time.

Most of the time a man is obliged to adjust himself according to his circumstances, reacting to different stimuli. A man is compelled by circumstances to move in a particular direction, with little interference by his awakened intelligence. Mature intelligence starts functioning only when one's very existence is threatened. In that case, it becomes very active; otherwise it goes on at a medium pace.

Most fears are the creation of circumstances. A particular situation arises. A disease spreads and the mind is afflicted with the fear of that disease. The visualisation of old age fills the mind with the fear of old age. We see something and the fear of that is stamped upon the mind.

Lao Tse, the great preceptor of Tao religion came across a horseman during his travels. Lao Tse asked him, "Who are you, brother?"

The horseman said, "I'm the Plague."

"Where are you going?"

"I'm going to Shanghai."

"What will you do there?"

"I'm going to kill ten thousand people."

Lao Tse went ahead. The horseman also moved on. Some days elapsed.

On his return journey, Lao Tse came across the same horseman.

Lao Tse said, "So, you are back?"

"Oh yes, my task is over."

"Why did you tell me a lie? You said you were going to kill ten thousand people?"

"Yes, I did. I never told a lie."

"But you did, for fifty thousand people fell victim to the plague in Shanghai."

"Of course what you say is true. Fifty thousand did die in Shanghai. But, Sir, I was responsible for the death of only ten thousand. The remaining 40 thousand died of fear! What could I do? I never told you a lie."

It is true that certain situations infect a man with fear. Something happens at one place — it might be an explosion — and the man in a remote place on hearing of it suffers a heart-failure. An incident takes place. An eyewitness is not much disturbed, but a distant hearer dies of shock. This is living on the periphery.

We need not discuss fear too much because those who constantly indulge in such discussions are infected by fear. We are aiming at complete freedom from fear.

We have been talking about how fear comes into being. We might now concentrate upon ways of getting rid of fear. What are the methods, factors and sources which help a man attain freedom from fear? Is it possible for a man never to entertain fear, not to be disturbed or to become anxious even when placed in a fearsome situation; to remain firm and steady even when the whole environment is charged with fear; not to be upset or vexed in the face of disaster?

It is certainly possible. *Preksha* furnishes one way of getting rid of fear. *Kayotsarg* embodies a means of becoming fearless. Those who practise *preksha meditation* are actually seeking a means of freeing themselves from their ills. A discussion of the disease implies in itself a search for the cure thereof. The calamity and the way of meeting it are intimately connected. One cannot find a cure without knowing the disease, and one cannot get rid of the disease without finding a cure for it. If we are seeking to conquer a disease, we must know the means of curing it. We shall also have to know everything about the disease before we can cure it. If we want to get rid of evil, we must intimately know how that evil functions, how it comes into being. Evil can be known; it is not something unknowable. How can we end something of which we know nothing? Insofar as knowing is concerned, the good and the evil are on the same level. If it is a question of what is harmful and what is beneficial, we say the evil is harmful and the good is beneficial. But we must know both. Only then shall it be possible for us to give up evil and to accept the good.

It has been concluded on the basis of psychological experiments that attention wavers, that the mind cannot concentrate on one object for more than four seconds. But there is a theory of meditation which does not accept this. According to some believers in that theory, a man can concentrate on one subject for five to ten hours, even more. However, the mind of a person who has never practised meditation cannot be steady; it continually changes from one object to another. In view of this, we are willing to accept the psychological theory of attention not going steady for more than a few seconds. The mind of a person who does not practise meditation cannot concentrate on one spot for more than four to five seconds. Most probably it changes every second; it may even change in a fraction of a second. The mind moves very fast. Within a second, it wanders all over the world. Such a conclusion about the mind's rapidity of movement is perfectly valid, and yet there is no finality about it. If we look upon it as the ultimate conclusion, we might easily go wrong. The moment we accept a conclusion as final, our exploration comes to an end. The process of awareness is then abruptly concluded; the continuity of meditation stands discounted. Then everything is limited and known; there is nothing limitless and unknown. While practising *preksha meditation*, we enter into a state of mind in which we are capable of concentrating on an object without any interruption, in which constant attention is possible. This cannot be a subject of psychological experimentation, nor of reason. Until the doctrine of *Leshya* (perception of psychic colours) is clearly understood, no thorough understanding of the theory of constantly wavering attention is possible. Feelings change and every change of feeling is accompanied by a change in thinking. It might be possible to mark one's thought, but the feeling behind it goes unobserved. Thought has no independent entity of its own. All thoughts derive from feeling, and dissolve with a change in feeling.

There are three orders — the order of thought (the conscious mind), the order of attitude (the subconscious) and the order of instinct (the unconscious mind), The three are intimately connected. Instinct gives rise to attitude, and attitude gives rise to thought. If we make an effort to steady our attitudes, *tejoleshya, padamleshya and shuklaleshya* become stabilised and as a consequence, thought becomes steady. Rather we should say that thought comes to an end. For thought by its nature is fickle, it can never be steady. Thought moves rapidly. Where there is constant movement, there can be no steadfastness. So constantly moving thought can never be steady. Steady thought is a contradiction in terms — steadiness and thought do not go together. Thought is ever restless, the mind is never tranquil. It is the function of the mind to wander, to be in constant movement. Such is the nature of thought. We, therefore, cannot make it steady; thought can never be stable. But it can come to an end. There are two distinct states: either there is thought or there is no thought. When there is right perception, there is no thought; thought comes to an end. This state, when thought is totally absent, comes into being when there is right perception. In this state, all fear naturally ends.

There is only one way of getting rid of fear — the purification of attitude; the cleansing of the heart of all impurities. When the passions are sublimated, the heart becomes innocent and pure and fear then dissolves.

XXII. THE FEAR COMPLEX

Happiness is the greatest achievement of life. Each man passes through joy and sorrow. Joy is no great thing because behind every joy lurks some sorrow. Sometimes there is joy, and at other times man is drowned in sorrow. Sorrow, likewise, is not wholly bad since it is invariably followed by joy.

Happiness lies beyond joy and sorrow. Virtually it signifies the purity of the mind. A mind that is pure is not ruffled by joy or sorrow. In a pure sky, there are no clouds, no rain, no hurricane — there is absolutely nothing. The sky is perfectly clear. All is clarity, brightness; all is light. Happiness is a condition of the mind that is quite unsullied. There are, however, many hurdles and dangers. Even a major accomplishment, if attained without effort, loses something of its stature, and is consequently ranked as minor. How many valleys crossed? How many ups and downs? are the questions posed while assessing a great achievement. The destination arrived at when the feet are tired by walking to the breaking point is all the more significant and memorable.

Happiness is a tremendous achievement. Complete absence of fear and happiness go together. They are inseparably linked with each other. Where there is total absence of fear, happiness is bound to be, and where there is happiness, fearlessness is its inevitable accompaniment. The moment fear appears, happiness dissolves.

Man's life is tied to the wheel of circumstance. It is an interminable series without any break. There are seven circumstances which destroy happiness and create fear. It is essential to know these:

> Fear of this world;
> fear of the other world;
> fear of like and dislike;
> sudden fear;
> fear of suffering;
> fear of death; and
> fear of disgrace.

The first state of fear pertains to the world we live in—the world of human beings. Man fears man. One man creates fear for another. Actually there is no cause for such fear, for basically any one man is like another; both possess a soul, both belong to the same species, both have consciousness, both are endowed with intelligence. So, one man need not fear another. And yet each individual in this world finds himself menaced by others. Man is possessed of greed, and greed gives rise to fear. If a man were not avaricious, he would not be afraid of anything. The root cause of fear is greed. There are great passions and impulses and there are passions and impulses subordinate to these. Greed is the primary impulse, and fear is secondary to it. Where there is greed, there is fear; without avarice fear cannot exist. A greedy man is solely interested in grinding his own axe, and where self-interest dominates, it creates fear all around. Fear is the inevitable accompaniment of preoccupation with self-fulfilment. Why after all, one may ask, is our society afflicted with aggression? What sustains the imperialistic mentality? Thefts, robberies, plunder, betrayals and frauds — all improper conduct flows directly from avarice. These are the breakers from the ocean of greed that rise high up the sky. As long as greed lasts, selfishness endures and one man becomes a danger to another. All talk of going beyond danger becomes unreal in such a context. No trust subsists between man and man. That is why there is such lack of trust in our world. One cannot trust even one's close relatives — father, son or wife. Fear pervades all relationship. Nobody has faith in another; everyone has reservations, secrets, covert schemes, rituals and ways of conduct which are ultimately unshareable. Even a teacher does not part with the ultimate secret; he wants to keep it to himself. That is why many ancient techniques in India have been irrecoverably lost. The master would not share the secret even with his most promising pupil, and the skill was inevitably lost after the master's death. Nobody trusts another. How to create an atmosphere of trust is the compelling challenge faced by man today.

A master-tantrik once saw a rat writhing in fear. Moved by pity, he turned it into a lion. A small rat transformed into a powerful lion! A rat that lived in constant fear of the cat suddenly changed into the king of the jungle, feared by all other animals! Now, as soon as the rat found itself transformed into a big lion, its hunger for food also grew and its first thought was how to appease that growing hunger. The great tantrik, its benefactor, still stood before it. "Here is my food," the rat-turned-into-lion thought, and it leapt towards the man. "What an ungrateful wretch!", said the master of spells, "I changed this fearful rat into a powerful lion, and it is now out to destroy me!" Immediately he cast a counter-spell and the lion once again turned into a rat.

Such is the state of the world we live in! Whom to trust? Even the benefactor who turns a rat into a lion cannot trust his beneficiary.

Life is like that. The world being full of greed and selfishness, how can one man trust another? Faith is just not possible in such a world. That is why our most intimate relationships are characterised by inner reservation, secrecy and fear. Two persons live together—they may be man and wife, parent and child—but between the two there exists a wall of mistrust. Even though near, they are far from each other, never really together.

Man fears man and it is because man is full of greed, selfishness and ungratefulness—the three traits go together.

The second state of fear pertains to the other world which includes the animal world. Man is afraid of other species. In the darkness of night he goes abroad with a stick in his hand because he is afraid of meeting a dog or a cow or another beast that might harm him. Some people are afraid of the cat and the rats. Almost all fear the serpent and the scorpion.

Fear of the other world includes the fear of goblins and sprites. It is really very strange. We all have heard marvellous stories relating to ghosts. In this context we may distinguish between two kinds of fear — imaginary and real. Once I met a man whose nervous system was so weak that he was afraid of every person he encountered; he was afraid that the other person would kill him or give him a severe beating. And he would begin to scream. This kind of fear is purely imaginary. It grows in direct proportion to the feebleness of the nervous system. The state of the nervous system and imaginary fear are closely related. Those having a weak nervous system are for ever afraid of the known as well as the unknown all day and night — it is because of the weakness of the nervous system and the improper functioning of the brain cells.

Sometimes, however, fear is actual, real. A particular situation excites fear. The fear of goblins and sprites is often imaginary, but it can be real too. The mind has formed a concept that ghosts abide in the dark. As soon as darkness sets in, one sees ghosts dancing everywhere. Only that man who is afraid of the dark can tell what darkness and loneliness do to a man. It seems to him that nothing exists in the world except goblins and sprites. He sees a ghost standing upright on the stair; he gazes at a wall, only to find it inhabited by demons. Both fore and aft, right and left, he sees spirits ascending and descending. It is a most singular state of mind. One's whole imagination is pervaded by ghostly beings.

The old Nuns' Hostel at Ladnun is housed in a building which is said to be the abode of Pirji (the spirit of a muslim holy man). It is said that Pirji visits this house every now and then. Once the nuns were shifted to another hostel and the building was occupied for the night by some monks. At midnight one of the monks came out of his room. He saw a man clad in white sitting outside. The monk wondered as to who the man could be. Might it not be the shade of Pirji? The monk was frightened a little but he resolved to explore the strange presence. As he neared the spot, he found that there was no Pirji—only a stool covered with a white cloth. From far it looked like a human being, but actually nobody was there. The imaginary shade vanished in no time.

Such imaginary shades, innumerable images, float before us day and night. The picture of imagination assumes a definite shape and it seems somebody is there. The sight thereof is frightening.

Sometimes one hears a sound and is filled with fear. A torch sighted in the cremation ground at night affords concreteness to the imaginative form of a ghost. The sight of a burning pyre makes one uneasy. If we can put an end to our imaginative apprehensions, we should be free from fear almost 90 per cent. Only 10 per cent of fear then remains. I don't discard all stories of ghosts and sprites as being figments of imagination—these too may partake of some reality, but this is rare. But even factual fear can serve to confound and weaken us. If a man's morale is high, a spectre can do him no harm. As a matter of fact, it is not the spectre or the ghost that excites fear; fear pre-exists in a man's being. If this inherent fear were not there, nothing in the world could do any harm to him. Lord Mahavir said, "Only a fearful man is afflicted by a ghost; the fearless man is not disturbed by any phantom." The goblins and sprites have their spheres of action. They have their limitations and cannot harrass all and sundry. They can only permeate a body that would accept them; a reluctant body they cannot penetrate. A fearful person is the most apt vessel to receive them. It is a noticeable fact that more women are haunted by ghosts than men. It is because they are less courageous than men; they get frightened very soon, and are therefore more apt to receive them. It is a very significant fact that only a fearful person is permeated by a ghost; the fearless is beyond its reach.

The third state of fear pertains to like and dislike, which means the fear of being united or of being separated, of getting things or meeting situations one dislikes. It is such a big fear as to exert its pressure at all times. What is acquired must not be lost, and what is undesirable must never afflict us—such is the eternal tension thereof. When someone dear to us goes on a journey, we are naturally concerned that no mishap should occur to him. And the cycle of union and separation goes on. Nodoby wants to be separated from the pleasant; nobody hankers after the unpleasant. Wherever a man goes, he carries with him his burden of fears. Those who attend *shivirs* (meditation camps) are no exception; they bring their fears along with them. After a few days they are heard to remark, "All fear has vanished!" Those who are full of fear cannot quite appreciate this state of complete freedom from fear.

Masters of *ayurved* say it is not proper to inhibit the senses too much; nor should these be pampered. The children of parents who scold too much are apt to become perverse. But even parents who pamper their children, only serve to spoil their wards. The senses are like children; these need to be handled with care. When treated right, they function perfectly. However, too much concern with the body, with one's looks, constant thought thereof, can create a dangerous situation, both physically and psychologically. It has been observed that those who shirk hard labour and seek too much comfort often attract diabetes. In *ayurved* this malady is significantly called "*Sukhasak*", i.e., "Comfort seeker". Heart trouble, too, is common among those who do not labour, who lie idle all the time. Their arteries get thicker, so the circulation of blood is adversely affected. Physicians of old advised rest to heart patients, but modern doctors counsel otherwise. They say, "Have a stroll. Do some light exercise so that the blood circulation is normalized." The modern physician does not encourage lethargy and may thus be said to be approaching, willy-nilly, a spiritual attitude.

Too much solicitude about any person or thing is also productive of fear. It is necessary to take care that one's clothes are clean and in good taste. But to be preoccupied with clothes to the exclusion of everything else is not at all desirable, for it only serves to create a climate of fear. One becomes more and more obsessed and is consequently steeped in fear. Any kind of preoccupation is bound to create more fear. Search for greater comfort, greater adornment of one's person, too much preoccupation with dress are all ways of nourishing fear. Fear is thus firmly entrenched in our lives.

Sudden fear—unimaginable and unexpected—is the fourth kind of fear human beings are liable to. Such sudden fear may be quite imaginary or it may have a basis in reality. Something happens and leaves an imprint of fear on the mind. There is nobody who has never had a mishap. All of a sudden, like a bolt from the blue, something fearful happens. A man in perfect condition rises to go. Suddenly he stumbles against something and staggers, and fear siezes him. Another man goes for a bath. He misses a step and slips down into the stream, and is about to be drowned. Sudden fear takes hold of him in that moment. Some untoward event occurs and a man is struck with terror and he flees in fear. All these escapist tendencies arise because of sudden fear. Accidents occur in the sky, on earth and in water; these involve pedestrians as well as men travelling by air or sea. All men are liable to these.

The fifth state of fear is that of suffering, of pain. Disease, old age, etc. constitute the root of pain. There is hardly a man who has not suffered from some disease at one time or the other. Nowadays, even a child emerging from the womb is discovered to be diseased. From the moment of embryo formation, it nurtures disease. Thanks to its mother, the child is born a patient. Not to speak of confronting the disease, the very mention of it fills a man with fear. To contract a disease is one thing, to be afraid of it quite another. We must be able to distinguish clearly between fear and the situation of fear. They are two different states, though intimately connected. Yet they remain distinct, never merging into one. Like parallel lines, they run together but never meet. We regard them as one because of our own mistaken view-point; we are unable to trace the fine line of distinction between them.

Disease, old age and death—are the three sources of suffering. But even so there is no cause for fear.

Every man faces disease at one time or other, but the man who recognizes the reality of disease, knows it to be productive of pain and yet is not afraid of it, never feels irrecoverable. Only that patient is beyond recovery who fears the disease. Fear of illness only serves to increase it a thousand-fold, and the malady of a man who is not afraid of it, is considerably diminished. In some cases it disappears altogether.

Many systems of medicine have been invented to remove suffering and disease, so that man is freed from pain. There are different kinds of medicine, witchcraft, chemicals and minerals used for the purpose. But it has also come to pass that without any medical treatment, without any witchcraft or the use of medicines, mere perception of the disease, i.e., to come to know it fully, to bear it without fear, has resulted in an individual keeping perfectly fit, even in the very continuance of the disease. On the other hand, people who are afraid of the disease and have taken different kinds of drugs, resorting to various systems of medicine, have yet remained disease-ridden even though desiring health.

Sanatkumar ruled over the earth. It so chanced that his graceful body was afflicted with 16 diseases all at once, each more terrible than the other. All his pride in the beauty of his body was destroyed. He relinquished his empire and became a monk. For long was he engaged in spiritual pursuit and led a life of extreme asceticism. In course of time, he came to experience the supra-physical state. His achievements were many and great. His diseases continued but they ceased to torment him. There was absolutely no fear in his heart. The sage Sanatkumar, though afflicted with a great many diseases was totally free from fear. Both health and disease continued in him, without causing any conflict. The monk was invested with a divine indifference—perfect non-attachment. He was absolutely without fear. The absorbability of such a man's body registers a tremendous increase, and his capacity for self-preservation grows to such an extent that the diseases with which he may

THE FEAR COMPLEX

be afflicted, torment him no more. His peace of mind is never disturbed.

One day a physician came to him and said, "Sir Monk! The structure of your body indicates a noble origin. However, the gracelessness of your body shows that you are suffering from many diseases. I have a panacea for all your ills. Will you kindly take the medicine I offer? This will enable you to regain perfect health, and you will then be able to intensify your practice of *dhyana* (meditation.)" However, the monk refused to take any drugs. The physician persisted, "Sir, I just want to do you some service. The taking of these drugs will cause you no discomfort On the contrary, these costly and infallible drugs will cure all your maladies, and you will soon enjoy perfect health." The physician persevered in his endeavour to bring the monk round to his point of view. At last the monk, while rejecting his offer, said, "You want to treat me, Sir. You want to cure me of my ills! You want me to enjoy perfect health! But how are you going to accomplish your purpose? Have you got the medicines I possess myself?" And saying this, the monk put a finger into his mouth, brought it out and applied a thin layer of his saliva on his leprous skin. In great consternation, the physician saw the white spots disappear, the monk's whole body assuming a healthful golden hue. The physician's astonishment knew no bounds. He kept looking at the beauty of the monk's body and stood still.

The monk went on, "How did you intend to cure me? Wherefrom will you get the specifics which are found in my body? Through the practice of meditation and asceticism, I have acquired certain powers by means of various secretions of the body.

"Such inner powers are awakened by *dhyana* (meditation) as to render external medicines redundant. A touch of mucus turns the body all golden. The touch of air bearing an enlightened person's sweat, restores complete health to a patient; his malady disappears. So what kind of treatment do you propose to give me? You've only intruded upon my peace. Rapt in meditation, I knew no disease. But you come here with your infallible remedies and are full of arrogance. What are you going to do now?"

The poor physician stood speechless. After what he had seen, he had no words to utter. He prostrated himself before the monk and said. "Sir, I've done a great wrong. Kindly forgive me!"

The sixth fear on our list is the fear of death. Man dies, not of disease, but of fear. Someone is told by a doctor that he has cancer, and the man starts dying from the moment he hears it; he feels extinguished. If he keeps up his spirits, the cancer would not affect him so much. Another person is told that he is suffering from heart disease and from that very moment he goes under and starts withering away. Death kills none; a man is killed by his own fear.

A man had artificial teeth. On retiring at night he put his denture in a bowl full of water. A child happened to come to his room and taking the denture to be a kind of toy, escaped with it. On rising in the morning, the man looked for his denture but it was nowhere to be found. He thought hard and it occurred to him that most probably he had forgotten to take his denture out as usual, and had instead swallowed it in sleep. Immediately he felt an unbearable pain in his stomach. He was beside himself with pain. A doctor was called in. On hearing the story, the doctor said the man will have to be operated upon to extract the denture out of his stomach. The situation became very critical. The extreme pain he experienced was very real but its basis was purely imaginary. Just at that moment, the child appeared with the denture in his hand. The moment the man saw his denture, his pain disappeared. He grew perfectly normal.

Such occurrences in our life show that man is not killed by disease, but by fear.

The seventh state of fear is that of disgrace. What would Mrs. Grundy say? Man is afraid of infamy. He wants a stainless reputation, his prestige high, his name untarnished. To keep up his prestige, he would even take recourse to false principles, and willingly suffer all kinds of inconveniences. Behind all this lies the fear of disgrace. To maintain his reputation, a man would go to any lengths, even to the extent of committing a grievous wrong.

Sadhaks (meditators) practising *preksha* must be able to distinguish between fear and the situation of fear; these are not one but two different things. That is the crux of this discourse.

XXIII. REACTIONS OF FEAR

Preksha meditation is an endeavour for enlightenment. Enlightenment and complete freedom from fear go together, just as darkness and fear are inseparably united. They are synonymous terms — darkness and fear. Fear is darkness and darkness fear. The fear that permeates our life leads us to darkness, to illusion. It may be natural darkness or the darkness of our mind, the illusory nature of our approach. Or it may be the gloom and sorrow of life. Whatever its quality, darkness remains what it is. But someone may say, what is wrong with darkness? What is wrong with fear?

It is a very natural question. The answer would depend upon our approach. It would be wrong to conclude on the basis of a particular point-of-view that fear is definitely bad. For in certain circumstances fear can be good. It all depends on the function it performs. Fear is of two kinds: creative and constructive, and negative and destructive. Likewise, fearlessness, much often constructive, can also be at times destructive. Every fact or thing must be looked at from a holistic, many-sided point-of-view.

Today's discussion on fear will be based upon the reactions it provokes. Reactionary fear—fear that provokes reactions, like disease, old age, death, forgetfulness, and madness—is taboo; it does no good. There are five reactions of fear mentioned above.

The first reaction of fear is disease. It is an indisputable fact that we ourselves invite diseases. How else can so many diseases enter our body uninvited? There may be one or two gatecrashers, but will fifty people come to your house unsolicited? Diseases inhabit our body because we invite them. We tend them so tenderly, so religiously that they do not want to leave us. All disease is a reaction of fear. Man is afraid and because of it he harbours diseases. You witness another man suffering from a disease and you are instantly filled with fear that you might also contract it. This very reaction constitutes an invitation. Most people react like that in the face of disease and become highly perturbed.

The disease in itself is not so productive of pain as disease mixed with fear. Of course any disease causes some pain, but when fear is combined with the disease, the resultant anguish is terrible and it becomes a torture. One disease gives rise to another and all man's power is laid waste.

The second reaction of fear is old age. One grows old fast because of fear. He who is free from fear, never grows old. His hair may turn grey, but his heart remains young. He may enter his 70th year, yet he cannot be said to be old. The body of course grows old. That is but natural. As the years pass, one's hair turns grey. But that does not mean one has become old.

As a matter of fact, becoming old implies the decline of one's powers. It is we ourselves who invite senility, for we never need become old. Willy-nilly we dissipate our energies and grow feeble.

Ignatia, a well-known physician-saint of Greece, was asked: "How is it possible for one to remain young and healthy throughout one's life?" He said, "Mend your mistakes, come out of your illusions, and you will remain young and healthy for ever." Indeed, it is our errors and illusions which invite old age. A man who is careful about his food and conduct never grows old too soon. Carelessness in eating and behaviour is the main cause of early decay. In the vigour of youth, one is liable to give oneself completely to the pleasures of the palate, but complete and blind surrender to gluttonous impulses constitutes the first invitation to old age.

After all the capacity of the digestive system is limited. The liver functions as far as it can. The pancreas too works within limits. So indeed do all the organs of the digestive system. Somebody says, "Here is one litre of orange juice; quaff it off! It's all liquid, like water, would do you no harm." Neither the drinker nor his host knows whether his digestive system can withstand such an onslaught. The capacity of the system is essentially limited. The intestines and the stomach are capable of digesting a certain amount of proteins, carbohydrates, alkalies, salts, and vitamins; it is all settled. Nothing is indefinite. The brain may or may not be so aware, but the digestive system is fully conscious of the amount of secretions required to disgest different kinds of food. It is all an ordered process.

A proper and balanced diet keeps old age at bay for a long time. In the absence of such a diet, old age sets in early.

The physician-saint did suggest an effective resolution of the problem: To be caught in errors and illusions is to invite old age. He who comes out of them, keeps young and healthy for ever. And he keeps so even at one hundred.

The third reaction of fear is death. The fearful man does not die a natural death; he commits so to speak suicide. Natural death comes in its own time; it cannot be forced. One man may live longer than another, but death comes to both in a natural way. However, the fearful person would never die a natural death; he virtually kills himself. Ninety-five per cent of the people die an unnatural death. They fear death and in the process draw it nearer; they die before their time. What they seek to evade comes upon them early. It is as simple as that, and exact like arithmetic. This fact must not be lost sight of.

An employer posed a question: How much two and two make? One of the candidates answered, "Four." Another said, "Twenty-two." Still another said, "Sometimes four and sometimes twenty-two." The third man was selected for the post. It was a simple question which elicited three different answers. Two of the answers were absolute, arising from an inflexible, monistic point of view, while the third signified a pluralistic, many-sided approach. The latter answer was practical, complete, not partial.

The arithmetic of life is in fact very simple, but it has been complicated beyond measure. Here is a verse from one of my poems:

> The book of life is simple and easy to read;
> The translation thereof is ever complicated.

So complicated indeed as to become unintelligible. Many a time it so happens that the original book is very lucid, but the person who translates it into another language, makes it so complicated as to render it difficult to understand. The very purpose of translating a book is to make it accessible to more people, but if the translation is intricate, that purpose is defeated. One needs still another exposition to make the second one intelligible, *ad infinitum*.

Take, for instance, the word "Indra". One translator rendered it as "Shataritu" which is a synonym of Indra. Had he used the original word, all, whether learned or not, would have understood it without any difficulty. But only the learned could make out "Shataritu" — a bookish word not accessible to all. This complication of an originally lucid text is a great fault in translation.

Man's life, too, is very simple. So are his necessities. But the analysis thereof is often so complex as to render it quite unintelligible. A man stands stalled at every step; he can make neither head nor tail of it. For example, take the maxim, "Don't be afraid!", or "Never fear anything!" Complete absence of fear mitigates disease, keeps old age and death at bay. It is a very simple proposition. But man cannot understand it. He fears disease, old age and death. The more he is afraid, the sooner do they assail him. How does it come about? Poor man is not to be blamed! It is beyond him—something hidden in the depths of his being manifests itself.

The internal secretions and the fluids released by the *Karma sharir* greatly influence a man's attitude, thoughts and actions. His basic temperament and emotions are controlled thereby. A man so affected is not capable of understanding the truth, the simple arithmetic of life. No one who is influenced by another can perceive reality as it is. Total freedom from all kinds of conditioning is an essential pre-requisite for the discovery of truth. A man, acting from direct perception of reality, encounters few difficulties, but even God cannot rescue a conditioned entity. When a man hankers after a thing or a person, he stands imprisoned. Until he acquires the thing he longs for, he cannot be at rest. He dreams of it night and day, he would not even shirk from stealing it to satisfy his longing. Likewise he becomes a blind follower of the person he is fascinated by. Or a particular idea might absorb him quite, to the exclusion of everything else.

One of the aims in the practice of *dhyana* (meditation) is to directly experience the unconditioned state — never to be influenced by any person or thing, but maintain one's independence, not to become a victim of circumstance. *Preksha* (perception) can take us there. He who practises *preksha* reaches out to the core of the matter, and his mind is cleansed of all impressions. On the other hand, to be caught in superficies is to be swept by the flow of circumstance. And a man often goes by appearance. He does not probe any deeper than the surface. And this often results in his committing a grievous wrong.

A man told the villagers, "I saw some Jain *munis* drinking water in the canal." The villagers were shocked. A Jain *muni* drinking unrefined water of the canal! It was against the Jain traditions. On reaching the village, the *munis* found no welcome: instead strange looks met them. Nobody came near them. The *munis* wondered as to what had happened. There stood the devotees, but no one bade them welcome, nobody greeted them. The villagers were behaving as if they no longer recognised the *munis* as their preceptors. Nobody came to the place where the Jain *munis* stayed, to hear the discourses. On being questioned, an old devotee explained, "Sirs, you have been guilty of gross misconduct! The village was not far. And yet you could not contain your thirst even for a little while and instead drank the impure water from the canal. Now in the face of such intemperate conduct, do you really expect people to flock to you?" The monks said, "We never took water from the canal!" Further enquiry revealed that the man who had spread the rumour about the Jain *munis* drinking water from the canal, had heard about it from someone else and that someone else had heard of it from still another person, and so on and so forth. Ultimately they reached the man who had originally witnessed the fact. On being confronted, he said, "With my own eyes I saw the Jain monks sitting in the canal and drinking water." A senior monk immediately got to the root of the matter and said, "O devotees, you ought to have enquired out as to whether there was any water in the canal or not. The canal was absolutely dry. We had a supply of drinking water with us. We only sat on the canal bed and drank water there. There is a world of difference between drinking water in the canal and drinking water from the canal."

Generally a man hears something and is overwhelmed by it. He makes no attempt to find out the truth of the matter. In order to know the truth one has to probe deeper. A superficial observer will never know the truth. Those who have found the truth have always delved deep.

Preksha dhyana is a method of going deep into oneself. You begin with the skin, with the surface. What is going on there? Let no one disdain this kind of observation, for a deeper analysis of the physical organism would reveal a veritable treasure-house of energies inside the skin. Deep inside the skin are to be found the ten essences—the five senses with their vital powers, and the power of the mind, the power of speech, the power of the body, the power of respiration and the life-force. One must directly experience these ten powers and the vibrations thereof.

The throbbings of life are not easily apprehensible. We cannot perceive them until our sensibilities are refined. Only a very sensitive mind can do so. There are different kinds of vibrations. All is movement, fluidity. There is nothing that is solid, that is not pulsating. With all this goes the vital breath of life. There is inhalation and exhalation. Not only do we perceive the respiration, but also the power behind it; we perceive the essence of breath itself. This requires a very subtle mind. The breath is something gross, hence easily perceptible. You place your finger on the nostrils. You feel the air going in or rushing out. This is breath, pure and simple. But what is the activating force behind it? What draws breath in and what pushes it out? From the physiological point of view it is the respiratory system which controls the breath. All inbreathing and outbreathing is through the respiratory duct. But that is only a physiological explanation. According to spiritual science, all movement is caused by the life force. If this force is extinguished, there would be no respiration whatsoever, despite the physical organism with its respiratory system.

We speak. Language comes out of us. But language in itself is mute. Whatever is being uttered constitutes language, but what makes the utterance possible is the life force behind it. Without this vital power, language stands blunted, extinguished.

All movements of the body are actuated by the life force. The entire physical organism is permeated with its vibrations. Through *preksha dhyana*, we perceive those subtle throbbings of life.

In the body there are to be found the flesh, the marrow, the fats and semen. There are seven constituent elements of the body, and beyond those elements lies virility. We must intimately know the activities of all the elements; we must perceive through *preksha* the vibrations thereof.

There are many diseases latent in the body. Some are already active, others are in the process of being activated, and still some others are in the realm of potentiality. Do we come to know about a disease the day it is born? Not at all. It takes many days, months or years before we recognize it. But it has been there all the time. Only at maturity does it manifest itself. Through *preksha* it is possible to perceive the secret goings-on in the physical organism.

Acupuncture is the Chinese method of treatment. Its study involves a minute and detailed analysis of sensory centres. A man suffers from pain in the knee. The concordant centre of the knee is situated in the sole of the foot. If you experience pain while pressing the sensory centre in the sole, you will also experience pain in the knee — the two go together. To remedy the pain in the knee, one has only to apply pressure on the corresponding sensory centre in the sole. The concordant centres of all the organs of the body are located in the hands and the feet.

There are many facts relating to the body which reveal themselves only when one delves deep under the skin. *Preksha* furnishes the means for an in-depth study of the physical organism. Sensations and vibrations become the medium through which you perceive the true condition of the body.

When we look at the body in the gross, we are not able to gather much knowledge about its functioning, but if we go deep inside, we find there are hundreds of ducts and passages in the body, specific systems and outlets.

Arteries and veins are nothing but roads and paths, the highways and the tracks. There are more passages to be found in the body than in a big city. Traffic along these paths is conducted in a most orderly fashion. Whatever happens is faithfully reflected through the five senses. The whole of man's conduct can be analysed on the basis of reflexology.

The way to enter these depths lies through *preksha*. It is natural to ask why body perception or perception of the centres of consciousness be continually repeated. And how many times? One should understand that the world we live in is full of innumerable subtleties. With the completion of each cycle we have a glimpse of a few aspects, but the aspects are legion, each phenomenon of life bearing a million aspects, a billion possibilities—there is no end to it all. To know the whole, one life, nay, many lives may not suffice.

We have discussed *preksha* at some length. The reader might think that such a long discussion is irrelevant. But our intention is to make it clear that a thorough understanding of *preksha* would set a man free both from logic and from all obstacles which impede enlightenment and consequently give rise to diseases, hasten the approach of old age and are responsible for premature death. What

REACTIONS OF FEAR

is required is total freedom from the psychology of fear. If one can be free of fear, one can face anything — disease, old age or death with equanimity. Neither death, nor disease, nor old age would then become a problem. Disease and old age would be rare, and even when they come, they would not last for long, their intensity would be greatly diminished. In order to be free from the corollaries of fear, *preksha* constitutes a very important means.

The fourth reaction of fear is forgetfulness. Man fears and because of it his memory gets weakened. Not only the old guard, but even growing children today complain of feeble memory. It sounds so strange. An old man of 80 complaining of weak memory is understandable, but when a child of 12 complains of it, one does not know what to make of it. The main cause of course is fear which so comprehensively pervades every sphere of life. When the sugar gets dissolved in milk, its entity is no longer distinct, but the sweetness in every drop of milk is sufficient proof thereof. Likewise, fear is so inextricably mixed with everyday living that it is difficult to perceive it distinctly. However, rampant forgetfulness or enfeeblement of memory is a definite indication that some deep fear pervades our life. The very fibres of the brain get shrunk and memory is adversely affected.

The fifth reaction of fear is madness. Man feels utterly disintegrated and goes insane. There could be many reasons for it. But the greatest cause is fear which provides madness an easy access into the human organism. A sudden shock benumbs a man so that he begins to rave. The shock of fear is very deep and drives a man out of his senses.

These are the five reactions of fear. There can be many more, but all those could be classified under one of the main five categories.

We have discussed hitherto the sources of fear, the states of fear and the reactions of fear. We have analysed them at some length. Now the question arises as to how does one get rid of fear altogether. Lord Mahavir said: "Have no fear!" That is also the teaching of the Upanishads. Every seeker on the spiritual path has uttered the same warning. Nevertheless, to say "Fear not!" is easy, but as long as there exist the sources of fear and the reactions of fear, the maxim, "Have no fear!" cuts no ice. As long as the causes of fear are present, there can be no deliverance from fear. By merely repeating the maxim "Fear not!" one does not become free from fear. We have to discover a way out. We must find a technique. Only through the practice of the proper technique is freedom from fear possible. To this important task we shall now address ourselves.

XXIV. CREATIVE FEAR

Day and night, night and day — with the twilight dividing these! There is the day and there is the night and in between is the evening. Likewise there is an intervening stage between fear and total freedom from fear. It is neither fear nor fearlessness. It cannot be called fear because of the absence of any perversions caused by fear in the nervous system; nor can it be called pure fearlessness because fearlessness is the ultimate, transcendent state. Between fear and total absence of fear stands a transitional state called 'creative fear'. Fear is of two kinds—destructive and constructive. Likewise fearlessness is also of two kinds destructive and constructive. These are the four alternatives.

The thief was fearless, reckless, unheeding. Every time he committed a theft, he was caught and punished, but on his release from jail he would start again. He had no fear. Once the judge remarked, "How utterly shameless you are! You experience no shame in being brought to my court time and again?"

The thief said, "Sir, judge! Every time I come, I find you here. If you come here everyday, why should I feel ashamed to come here occasionally?"

Abashment, discipline and qualms of conscience are forms of constructive fear—we may call these modesty, self-control or scrupulousness. Because of mental hesitation, a man avoids evil. Discipline can exist even when self-discipline has not yet evolved. The elderly people forbid something; so a man does not do it. This is also constructive fear. Another person has scruples about doing something, saying to himself, "If someone sees me doing it, it would bring me disgrace." So he forgoes it. He abstains from the act out of fear. Such a man might possess no pure vision, no spiritual insight which would make him avoid evil irrespective of whether someone sees him or not.

Where there is spiritual insight, the question of someone seeing or not seeing does not arise. He who is blessed with spiritual vision would never commit an evil act.

The worldly-wise are very sensitive to what Mrs. Grundy would say. But there are reprobates who give no thought to what others may think of them. They care a fig for other people and their opinions. Here fearlessness itself becomes a curse. The big bandits, thieves and murderers show no fear. They would commit all kinds of evil without any hesitation whatsoever. But their fearlessness is destructive; it could not be equated with true fearlessness.

From the very beginning, from childhood, certain beliefs take root in our life — the feeling for discipline and mental qualms save us from committing many evils.

The revered Kaluganiji once told a moving tale about a youth preparing to go to foreign ports for the purpose of acquiring wealth. He said to his young wife, "I'm going abroad to earn money. Family honour lies in your custody now. Please keep chaste! Let not the family name be besmirched. Do take care. Still, the mind is very fickle, and if you can no longer endure celibacy and may want to indulge in sex, search out for your partner the man who goes to the most remote part of the forest for his morning ablutions." For a long time after the departure of her husband, the modest wife observed great restraint and remained chaste. None could find fault with her conduct. But when years passed away without any news of her husband, her endurance broke down and she felt in her stirrings of desire. The human mind functions in a queer way. Even great hermits and ascetics are sometimes assailed by temptation. It is unimaginable how their consciousness lapses, the virtue of a lifetime spent in meditation stands vitiated in a minute. On the other hand, we hear of great reprobates achieving salvation almost on their death bed. Insensitive wretches suddenly regain sensitivity and become enlightened, and people say of such a person, "He pursued all vices throughout, but lived the last ten days of his life in the manner of the greatest ascetics." Such sudden transformations are not unknown. One who is awake may fall asleep; another in oblivion may wake up suddenly at any time.

So the wife who was no ascetic but an ordinary woman found herself assailed by lust. Yet she remembered her husband's counsel. She asked her servant to fetch her the man who went farthest into the forest for his morning ablutions.

In due course, the man appeared before her. The wife asked the stranger why he went so far into the forest. He demurred, "I don't know! I feel so abashed!" On being pressed further, he confessed that he could not endure anyone seeing him naked. "I don't want anybody — not even a bird — to have a glimpse of my private parts," he said. "I feel so shy. Even the earthen pot of water I carry for washing, I keep in a covert place — I won't let even a lifeless object be a witness to my ablutions!"

Thereupon, the young wife said at once, "Sir, I feel very grateful to you for enlightenment. It was kind of you to come here. You may go, now."

She had suddenly grasped the meaning of her husband's parting adjuration! The sense of shame is a tremendous thing; there is great safety in it.

CREATIVE FEAR

The sense of shame and qualms of conscience are forms of constructive fear. Man fears disease and death, and it is a very old mentality. We are not afraid of indulging our own inclinations to the full; but we fear the consequences. It is absurd to be so afraid. What is to be feared and avoided is the mental inclination, not its result. For aeons it has been man's enduring weakness to spurn the consequences and not his mental inclination, to fear the effect and not the cause! But without cause there can be no effect. So one must beware of the cause.

We fear the disease, but not the causes which bring it. If we could fear the causes, that fear would be constructive. One aspect of fear is creative. Excessive eating, for example, brings forth disease. So I shall be afraid of eating too much. Bad, unwholesome food brings disease, so I shall always avoid unwholesome food. Strong emotions cause disturbance and bring disease; if I indulge in anger, I would be inviting heart-trouble; my blood-pressure is bound to go up. The whole system is poisoned. Therefore, I shall be afraid of giving way to anger. If we fear the causes which bring disease, that fear is constructive. But when we fall a victim to disease and fear the disease and moan, "What will happen to me now? O God! Why should I be so afflicted?", such fear is not constructive; it only serves to aggravate the disease, brings more trouble. So let our fear be creative and constructive. We fear death but not the causes which bring death. The prospect of death fills us with dismay. But do we realise that indulgence in like and dislike is the chief cause of early, inopportune death? He who is caught in approbation and condemnation, in love and hate, dies early. Overeating, immoderate sleep, extreme laziness, yielding to strong passions, pride, anger, envy, hatred are all productive of premature death. These we ignore, these we do not fear, but we fear death. Fear becomes constructive when we are apprehensive of all tendencies which bring untimely death. If we keep alert and are fully alive to their danger, then alone has fear a constructive role to play.

Man fears disgrace. He is very jealous of his reputation, of what people think of him. But he does not fear the causes which bring him into disrepute. This is most strange. Our conduct and behaviour is such that it invites infamy. But we only fear dishonour; dishonourable conduct we condone. We say, "Do what we will, we must not be humiliated under any circumstances!" Such fear is futile. If we avoid the causes which bring disgrace, our fear is creative.

In order to make our fear creative and constructive, we must be able to draw a fine distinction between the fear of fear (i.e., our anxiety to get rid of fear) and the fear of the causes which produce fear. These two fears are quite distinct; to be afraid, and to be alert and careful so that fear does not come into being, are two different things. If we assume that fear is always bad, all talk of social security is rendered meaningless. Then the security of the individual, the security of the family, of society and the nation, are all submerged in a vast confusion. The concern for a secure, abiding order is ever constructive; it cannot be destructive. The chief thing to understand is that the maintenance of order is for stability, and not for any destructive purpose.

Imagine a fire burning. No man would put his foot into the fire. We may say that man is afraid of burning his foot but such fear cannot be said to be destructive; on the contrary it is constructive since it ensures safety.

The owner of an ice factory was asked, "What do you do in winter? In the summer season, you make ice, and there is great demand for it. But how do you spend the winter season?"

He said, "I make ice during summer and in winter I eat it."

Quite right! The factory does not run during the winter months. Income from the sale of ice during summer, enables the factory owner to maintain himself. "I make ice during summer and in winter I eat it." The ice supports him, provides him security. Likewise each individual seeks security. He avoids fear and the things that cause fear. No sensible person would deliberately put his foot on the serpent's head; no man would knowingly drink poison. Concern for security cannot be classed under destructive fear. Fear for safety becomes constructive; it is the intermediary stage between fear and total freedom from fear.

Here is a leaf out of my own book of life. I was 13 years old. The revered Kaluganiji was staying at Manasar. I and my classmate Muni Budhamalji were in attendance. The reverend Kalugniji taught us the following verse:

> The fear of God, the fear of the guru, and the fear of
> what the villagers might say, are all constructive.
> He who fears is saved, thus spake Tulsi.

Expounding the above verse, Kaluganiji said, fear is not always futile. There is great wisdom in fear. One who does not fear when he ought to is in for trouble.

That verse, we thought, had great significance for us. We studied under Muni Tulsi and feared him. Now revered Kaluganij had also delivered a warning: "He who fears Tulsi is saved, and the heedless is in for trouble". We did not know at that time that Sant Tulsi Das was the author of the couplet and the word "Tulsi" in the verse referred to the poet himself. We thought then and for a long time were under the impression that the word referred to our *guru* and the verse itself was a salutary warning to his pupils. If we feared our *guru* we would be saved, if we continued inadvertent, we would fall. That couplet, I might say, had tremendous impact on both myself and my classmate, Budhamalji; it moulded our lives.

I feel that constructive fear is creative and gives a direction to our life. When I say, be brave, never fear anything, be totally free from fear, I only wish to underline the necessity of avoiding destructive fear. We are going to talk about pure fearlessness too. Ultimately we must achieve total freedom from fear, so as to awaken pure consciousness in which all fears are dissolved, when all our efforts and our inner impulses are suffused with spirituality without any outside conditioning, when all stimulations, all causes and effects cease, when spiritual consciousness actuates our thought and action from moment to moment. That is the destination we aim at, the ultimate goal. But we cannot afford to be impractical. There are stages in life, childhood, youth and mature old age. Right now we are living in the first stage, when any talk of spiritual inspiration would not be intelligible, would not, therefore, be relevant. What is relevant here is that in the initial stage, creative fear has a role to play. In the second stage, when *meditation* has matured a little, one begins to transcend constructive fear and move in the direction of total freedom from fear, the attainment of which signifies the peak of all spiritual effort and the awakening of a spiritual consciousness in which all apprehensions stand resolved for ever, and where there is complete absence of fear, a state of utter fearlessness, an atmosphere of non-fear, where runs the great stream of fearlessness without any obstruction, where all is courage and self-confidence. Fear surrounds the negligent on all sides, but for one who is awake, fear comes to an end.

All men wish to awaken in themselves the consciousness of non-fear. But how is it to be accomplished?

Two most important systems functioning in our body are the nervous system and the endocrine system. They regulate the working of the entire organism. The external situation and the inner chemistry of the body determine our response. It is a common belief that circumstances make a man. There is some truth in it. But it is not the whole truth. The whole truth is that both circumstances and biochemical reactions within determine a man's nature. We often try to alter the circumstances to suit our convenience, but as often we fail in that endeavour. However, it is the biochemical reactions that influence us most; internal secretions from various glands determine our conduct. With a change in the inner chemistry of the body, it becomes possible to go beyond the circumstances, to transcend them altogether. On the contrary, unregulated biochemical reactions render us a slave to circumstances; we become their victim. Those who practise *preksha* meditation must realise this truth and they should embark upon the process of changing their biochemical reactions, if they would master their circumstances. In today's scientific age, the practice of meditation should not be merely a leap in the dark. Science has developed to an extent that it is not possible nor desirable to ignore the new developments altogether and keep treading the beaten path. The other day we were talking with Professor Sharma, Head, Department of Educational Psychology in the N.C.E.R.T. Dr. T. Bhatia was also present. It was said that the most notable observations made about the practice of meditation related to physiological effects, for example, the lowering of body temperature, relief from blood-pressure, the increase or decrease in weight. I said we do not look upon meditation as a means of treating physical ailments. Nor is the *shivir* (meditation camp) a hospital, though it is an admitted fact that physical diseases have been cured in *shivirs*. But for us that is a secondary issue. Our main purpose is to bring about a transformation of being. The consummation of meditation lies in accomplishing a complete change of heart. Our emotions undergo a mutation. Feelings of violence, of insolence and indiscipline, feelings of cruelty must dissolve altogether. If there is no change of feeling, meditation cannot be said to have reached perfection. There are techniques available to bring about this mutation of feeling. If you concentrate on *Jyoti Kendra* (the Centre of Enlightenment), the emotion of anger is quite transformed; concentration on *Darshan Kendra* (the Centre of Intuition) does away with illusion and awakens inner vision. Our frontal lobe is very powerful; it controls all our feelings. The hypothalamus governs everything. It controls the pineal and the pituitary glands. The pituitary, in its turn, controls all other glands. For a complete transformation of feelings, we must concentrate our attention on the forehead and the front part of the head; without it there could be no change of feeling. When we concentrate our attention on the navel, the centre of bio-electricity, we experience a sudden upsurge of power and high stimulation. There is an unprecedented increase in vitality but at the same time it contributes towards the growth of high passions. All the strong emotions arise from the adrenal.

It is however, possible to control all these. The three psychic centres—(*Shanti Kendra*, the Centre of Tranquillity; *Jyoti Kendra*, the Centre of Enlightenment; and *Darshan Kendra*, the Centre of Intuition, all situated on the frontal lobe above the eye-brow, are responsible for the transformation of feeling. Both desirable and undesirable emotions issue therefrom. We believe that ugly, unpleasant and undesirable emotions can be transformed. *Leshya dhyana* (Preception of Psychic Colours) is an important technique in the Jain system of meditation. Concentration of attention on various colours brings about a corresponding change in feeling. Modern colour therapy has shed a great deal of light on the importance of colours. A lot of research is being done on colour therapy and a good deal of literature has been brought forth. Also treatment through perception of colours, and the use of sun rays occupy an important place in nature-therapy. However, there has been of late a tremendous development in the field of perception of psychic colours which is of great significance in the whole system of *preksha meditation*. Of course all the practices of *preksha meditation* are the means of awakening the consciousness of non-fear, a state of total freedom from fear.

XXV. TOTAL FREEDOM FROM FEAR

Things happen outside, as well as inside. Our being is divided into two — the inner and the outer. The outer world of phenomena is clearly visible, not so the inner world. But it can be perceived, felt, expressed. Our vision is turned outward. How one sits, the shape of the hands and the mouth, the structure of the face and its expression, the fingers — all these relate to bodily posture. The facial expression and the inner feeling are intimately connected; inner feeling determines the outward bearing. When anger arises, the face would automatically assume the pose of anger. One knows that a person is angry without being told. His facial expression gives a clear indication of his inner state.

In ancient Indian poetics is to be found an eleborate analysis of emotion. There are three streams of feeling: the enduring, the indicative and the evanescent. What kind of feelings are inspired by a particular posture? How does an individual manifest himself? The erotic sentiment expresses itself in one way, pathos in another, and disgust still in another way. There is one facial expression peculiar to wrath and another peculiar to tranquillity. There are different gestures for every feeling, every sentiment. Thought, feeling and gesture are linked with one another. Our facial gestures are determined by inward feeling. Fear expresses itself in a way peculiar to itself. The face of a man in the grip of fear shrinks. Likewise his body. Both the body and the face shrink and expand. Fear contracts, and joy expands. Irradiated by joy, the face opens up like a flower. On the other hand, the face of a frightened person gets shrunk. It appears to be quite emaciated. Changes wrought by fear in the outer appearance are quite apparent. However, inner parts of the body also manifest these changes. The heart beats faster, the blood-pressure goes high, the throat gets dry, the glands secreting saliva are inactivated, the face becomes lean, the stomach and the intestines contract; there is loss of appetite. A man who constantly lives in a state of fear has little appetite. The conductivity of the skin stands altered; it grows hyper-sensitive.

A man tells a lie. Telling lies is a crime. He is presented before the judge. The man is afraid of being exposed. But how is the judge to establish that the man is a liar? That he is a criminal? Of late certain devices have been evolved, like the galvanometer. The machine is switched on and the criminal made to stand before it. The man is afraid of being caught. Fear gives rise to excitement. His inner being is disturbed. The moving hand of the galvanometer would indicate this disturbance and conclusively establish that the man is not at ease and he is not at ease because he has told a lie. The galvanometer would thus establish his guilt. All this happens through the conductivity of the skin, which is measured by the galvanometer and which gives us the truth. In a fit of anger or fear or of any other strong emotion, both the outward appearance and the inward state undergo a change, and this change reveals the truth. A man assumes a thousand poses during the course of a single day. With the help of a sensitive, high-frequency camera, these varying postures can be photographed, and the difference between one pose and another is clearly visible. The pose of five minutes ago is altogether different from the the pose of five minutes after. As the inward feeling changes, there is a corresponding change in a man's countenance. The science of face-reading is based upon that. On the basis of the shape and structure of the face, a man's proclivities can be foretold and even his future determined.

Fear is a strong emotion. A man's countenance in a state of fear shows distress and is strangely disturbing. Whoever comes into contact with a fear-oppressed man, would soon imbibe his restlessness. How does it come to pass? The visitor would not know why; but he would be unquiet.

When the feeling of non-fear is awakened in a person, it shows itself in his features. The outward stance of non-fear is gaiety. The face blossoms. There is perfect joy. No problem or any kind of tension whatsoever! Deep tranquillity within. When the current of fear flows, our sympathetic nervous system (*pingla*) becomes activated; whereas in the case of non-fear, it is the para-sympathetic nervous system (*ida*) which becomes active. There is no turbulence anywhere. One experiences profound peace and joy. It feels good to be alive.

The question arises as to how we can live for the most part in a state of non-fear. How to make the current of non-fear flow most of the time? How to experience the state of non-fear? All fear is harmful, whereas non-fear is beneficial. We must relinquish the stream of fear and enter the stream of non-fear. For this are necessary the right technique and the right means.

One of the techniques is *anupreksha* (contemplation). Through *anupreksha* it is possible to further develop the flow of non-fear. Within our body lie many systems of vibration. The paths, the tracks, and the highways are all there, by means of which sound vibrations pervade the entire organism and influence our conduct. The ancient doctrine of vibrations is a very comprehensive one. Not since the development of the Quantum Theory but much before that, about three thousand years ago, this doctrine was well-established. According to it, the world is nothing but vibrations, nothing but wave after wave of sensation. A wave of fear arises and immediately vibrations of fear overwhelm the earth and the sky. If at that time we could somehow start a wave of non-fear, if we could produce vibrations of non-fear, the wave of fear stands dissolved. The doctrine of *anupreksha* is a contralateral doctrine which lays down that one wave can transcend another, that a good wave can be started, the bad one rendered ineffective. Similarly, a bad wave, if stronger, would destroy the good one. Our valour, intelligence and vision determine what we shall do at a particular time, and what kind of effort we shall put in. The man who has practised *preksha meditation*, the one who has perceived the truth that the evil wave can be countermanded by a good one, that a negative wave can be supplanted by a positive wave, becomes very alert so that as soon as an evil thought arises in his mind, he sets about releasing a counter-wave of goodness that would repeal the former.

Three different states arise in life—the state of untruth, the state of truth, and the third state which transcends both good and evil. The state of untruth is an evil one, with a negative role. The second state is that of truth, which is positive and constructive. The third state transcends the other two; it is beyond right and wrong, beyond all options, beyond thought. This is the ideal state, quite remote for us for the time being. Generally, our life is spent between the counter-streams of good and evil. Sometimes the wave of goodness triumphs; at other times, the wave of evil sweeps away everything before it. The stronger our will-power and our resolve to live in the present, the more alert and earnest we are in the practice of *preksha*, and the more constant and regular our practice, the more alive do we become to the danger of evil and wicked thoughts arising in the brain. We are then able to release immediately a wave of goodness and purity. We start practising *anupreksha* and the evil wave subsides.

Anupreksha constitutes an important means of avoiding untruth. The whole of *Japa* (repetition of a deity's name) is based upon that. You are asked to remember the deity, repeat the *mantra*, because if pure feelings and thoughts inhabit your mind, there would be no room left for impure thoughts and feelings to enter there. That is why one takes recourse to *mantra*, the incantation. Some people are reluctant to recognise the utility of the *mantra* in the field of spiritual development. But we feel that the *mantra* has an undeniable virtue which must be recognised. Because all of us cannot directly enter the state of *nirvana* (release from bondages). The phenomenon of a direct leap into *nirvana* occurs rarely. It is possible that an individual here and there makes such a leap. There may be one in a million who can jump down straight from the roof. But if everyone were able to do so, there would be no need for a staircase. As it is, if all start leaping directly from the roof, hospitals would soon become filled to capacity; it would cause an upheaval. The phenomenon of the leap is not universal. It is not valid for all. It could only be an exception to the rule. To reach the ground of *Veetaragta* straight, to enter *nirvana* directly without any intermediary stage, is to make a leap which an individual does rarely on his own. Others must employ whatever support they can; to go to the roof they must use the stairs. One staircase serves to take one up as well as down. It is not that there is one staircase for going up, and another for going down. The same staircase serves both purposes. Likewise, there is only one current of feeling. One can use that current of feeling to rise high or to go down. When the current is attuned to truth, we rise high; when it is allied with untruth, we go down. The development of *japa* or the *mantra* was based upon the feeling that there should be something which calls for exclusive attention so that noxious feelings have the least opportunity to enter the mind.

Another means of attaining the state of non-fear is *preksha*. With the gradual development of the power of seeing, our perception becomes truth-oriented. Whatever fear there is, it is because of untruth. False belief, false doctrine, false conception, false determination — whatever be the aspect of untruth, it only creates fear. As our vision develops, we perceive the truth more clearly. We bid goodbye to fictions. We grow stronger, and fear decreases of itself. There is no fear in facing the fact, but fear is inherent in illusion, in a state of unconsciousness, and in untruth. *Preksha* becomes the means of breaking the cycle of ignorance, and when this cycle breaks, fear dissolves of itself.

Preksha, anupreksha, the repetition of a *mantra*—these techniques were developed primarily for the evolution of non-fear. In every tradition — Jain, Vedic or Buddhist — there exist *mantras* for the prevention of fear. Some people get frightened in sleep; they have terrifying dreams at night. Others take fright for no cause. In order to elude such predicaments, hundreds of *mantras* have been evolved and these have been used to good effect. They help divert attention from fear. The very condition of the mind stands altered. Also a great many remedies have been evolved. There are many medicines, roots and herbs, which if placed beside the pillow, stop fear altogether. All dreams cease. The roots and herbs and the *mantras* have been useful, and research in this direction has yielded good results.

There is another path leading to non-fear. This relates to our character and conduct. Fear springs from violence, from untruth, and from acquisitiveness. These are the three great causes intimately connected with our character. Every man knows what fear acquisitiveness creates. A man leaves for the bazar, but midway to it he remembers that he had forgotten to lock his room. Immediately he turns back in fear lest some thief should get in. Why this fear? Because he is so attached to things which he has accumulated that he cannot look upon with equanimity the prospect of being deprived of these. There are many people who do not even make use of their accumulation. At the time of making yearly accounts on the occasion of Diwali, or Ramnaumi, they calculate what profits they have and how much their wealth has increased, and the very thought of it gives them such deep satisfaction as nothing else in the world can. The mere realisation that "I have so much!" is highly gratifying. Apart from that, their vast accumulation has no meaning whatsoever; it has no utility; it is never consumed. But the very fact of possession makes them so happy that it becomes for them the *summum bonum* of life. And yet this very realisation that "I have so much" can create such fear that the man knows no rest all day and night. He is afraid of being cheated by his manager, his partner, his servant, his workers, his brother and his father. He is for ever tormented by fear. A man finds great psychological satisfaction in possession, but this is for ever accompanied by fear that he may in some way be cheated of his possessions. Gratification is momentary, but fear is constant. Accumulation is the greatest cause of fear.

Untruth, too, is a great cause of fear. Thoughtlessly one tells a lie but afterwards one is constantly possessed by fear of being exposed.

Violence too is born of fear. As long as a man is possessed by violence, untruth and acquisitiveness, non-fear cannot come to him. Destructive desperation, yes, but no constructive non-fear. A man may grow so reckless, that he is not afraid of anything, and in such a state he is liable to commit great atrocities. Such a man will never experience true non-fear which is always constructive.

I happened to talk to Baba Nagpal. I found that the dominant note in his worship of divine power is that of character development. The Baba says, " I have no charm or amulet to give; I don't believe in conjuring. I only say to the people, 'Look to your character; pure food and pure conduct; without these there can be no salvation'." It is a great utterance.

Anandghanji, the celebrated Jain master from Gujarat, was a great *yogi*. He had acquired a great many *siddhis* (supernatural powers). Wherever he went, people flocked to him in great numbers — the rulers and the ruled, the high and the low. It was said that the saint could fulfil every kind of wish. So there was always a crowd beside him. He could not have a moment to himself. It became a great nuisance and the saint sought the seclusion of the forest. The multitude followed him there too. Someone would say, "I've no issue," others sought wealth, still others came to him with different kinds of problems. The saint did not know what to do with them. In order to get rid of them at the earliest possible, he would write something on a piece of paper, make it into a pellet, and give it to the devotee, saying, "Keep it with you but take care not to open it even accidentally. And you must do what I tell you. Will you?" When the man promised to do what he was told, the saint said, "Look, if you want that your desire be fulfilled, for six months or one year, you must not tell a lie, also during this period, you must observe complete abstinence from sex; you must not steal, nor kill, nor indulge in hoarding things. Any lapse on your part would result in the failure of your mission. But if you remain steadfast, you are bound to succeed. Come to me then." After six or 12 months, the devotee's desire is fulfilled. He comes to pay his respects and says, "Sir, due to your grace my work was done." The saint would then laugh and say, "Do you know what brought you success? If you open the pellet I gave you, you will find written there, 'You're the master of your own fate; I've nothing to do with it.' If you've succeeded, it is because of your own character. You lived a pure life, took pure food and conducted yourself nobly. So you are the creator of your own success."

What really works is the strength of one's own character. And as a man's character develops, the state of non-fear, of total freedom from fear gradually comes into being. The strength inherent in non-fear does wonders. Whatever a man does then is right. The greatest obstacle that a man faces in the fulfilment of his tasks is fear, mistrust, suspicion. When a man embarks upon a new venture, he is immediately assailed by doubts. "Will I succeed or not?" he says to himself, "If I fail, what will people say?" How can a man afflicted with fear and mistrust really succeed?

The great secret of success is the development of character. The three great pillars of character development are, non-violence, truth, and non-acquisitiveness.

If we want to enter the state of non-fear, we must develop in ourselves the spirit of non-violence, for non-violence is one aspect of non-fear. We must also pursue truth, for truth is another aspect of non-fear, and we must also cultivate non-acquisitiveness, for non-greed is still another aspect of non-fear. The man in whose heart these feelings abide is bound to enter the state of non-fear. Which does not mean that you must have no possessions whatsoever — no household can run without these. But we must clearly distinguish between the possession of articles and attachment to these articles. They are two different things. Similarly, some kind of violence is inevitable in the nature of things, but to be possessed by violence is quite another matter. There may be occasions when one cannot speak the truth, but to be wedded to untruth and to believe that one cannot survive in the modern world without telling lies is most questionable. What creates problems is our deep attachment to things and persons. There is a subtle dividing line between necessity and desire. Material things are necessary, one cannot do without them. Even a monk has a few possessions. He must have a piece of cloth to cover his body, he carries a bowl, and he has books. He also has pupils. Things and persons are inevitable there in any course of life; one cannot isolate oneself completely from these; indeed one must live with them. But if a man does not attach himself to things or persons, he remains calm under all circumstances and the desire for accumulation has no ground to strike root. On the other hand, any kind of attachment results in acquisitiveness and accumulation. Even a piece of cloth, a book, if one is attached to it, becomes a source of corruption. *Preksha* helps to make it clear how far our infatuations for objects has relented, how far our attachments are weakened. *Preksha* is the means of weakening one's attachments, it is the means of awakening latent energies, of awakening bliss. Not mere power, but power that is roused with full consciousness and bliss. Awareness and bliss are the two banks between which the stream of energy flows. Such power is universally beneficial. But divorced from joy and consciousness, mere power for its own sake is very dangerous. Electricity is very useful, but at the same time dangerous. If one is careless and touches a naked wire carrying an electric current, it would be suicidal. So let there be an awakening of consciousness, let there be full awareness, let the mind be purified, let the heart become entirely innocent. When consciousness is pure, the state of non-fear will arise of itself. The very experiencing of the movement of consciousness constitutes in itself total freedom from fear.

A monk was meditating in the forest. He stood still in meditation. A serpent came and bit him and slipped away. A man happened to be passing there and he saw the serpent bite the monk. So he approached the monk and said, "Sir monk, a black serpent has bitten you. Are you aware of it?" The monk said, "I don't know." The man said, "But are you not afraid?" The monk said, "No, I know no fear." The man said, "How is it you show no fear? Are you not afraid of death?" The monk said, "I'm perfectly at home. There is no serpent here. It is possible the serpent was elsewhere, and has bitten some other person. I am quite all right."

In a state of full consciousness, even a snake-bite does a man no harm. It is only in a particular state of mind that the poison affects a man. It is common knowledge that after a snake has bitten, the bitten man's family take special care not to let him go to sleep; the patient must keep wholly awake, not a wink is permissible. In a state of full consciousness, the poison has no effect; on the other hand if the man goes to sleep, he is not likely to rise again. That is why he is not allowed to sleep. He must keep perfectly awake, for total wakefulness is a powerful antidote to poison. The snake-bite has no effect upon a person wide awake. Wherever there is full awareness, we have a taste of non-fear. Enlightenment is a state of total freedom from fear.

We are surprised when told that Lord Mahavir was bitten by a furious snake named Chandkaushik, and yet remained unmoved. There is, however, nothing uncommon in the occurrence. If the snake had bitten any Tom, Dick or Harry and the man had kept unperturbed, it would certainly be surprising. But for a man like Mahavir, who was constantly and fully aware of himself, the poison of a snake, or a scorpion, was quite immaterial. The man who has reached the highest ground of spirituality is not disturbed by a snake, nor does any poison, whatsoever, have any adverse effect upon him.

The experiencing of full consciousness is the experiencing of the state of non-fear. Likewise, the experiencing of bliss. We are not talking of pleasure or of joy, but of real happiness. There is always fear inherent in pleasure. Joy and sorrow are linked together. Every joy is followed by sorrow, as every sorrow is followed by joy; they make an inseparable pair.

There may be a brief interval between the two; but sooner or later one is bound to be followed by the other. But bliss is beyond pleasure and pain, beyond joy and sorrow. *Preksha* gives rise to waves of bliss—that bliss which is allied with equanimity. In equanimity there is bliss beyond joy and sorrow. In that state there is total freedom from fear.

There are two ways of entering the state of non-fear—the experiencing of consciousness and the experiencing of bliss. *Preksha* develops both. *Preksha* means inner perception. When a man looks outward, he experiences fear. The reason is quite apparent. All our values, standards, and codes of conduct are based upon comparison with another. If I look to another, there can be only two responses. When I compare myself with those who occupy an inferior position, I am filled with pride; whereas in the presence of my superiors, I suffer from an inferiority complex. Both superiority and inferiority complexes are the product of extraversion. All the social values and standards of conduct are the creation of concern with another. "What a magnificent marriage our neighbour organised!", we say, "Well, we cannot afford to be less magnificent! Our prestige is involved." Another's action becomes the standard for us! So we are always at the mercy of another. Dependence upon another always creates fear. In order to get rid of this fear, we must practise introspection. For the man who has started looking within, instead of outside, all values and standards based upon comparison with another become redundant. There is then no fear of what another would say. The development of an inner vision, transcending outside values and standards, in effect, means the evolution of non-fear—that is a state of total freedom from fear.

GLOSSARY OF SOME HINDI WORDS USED IN MODERN JAIN LITERATURE

acharya	Founder or leader (of a school of thought), teacher, preceptor.
anupreksha	Concentration of thought; contemplation; cf. preksha which means concentration of observation.
anuvrat	A small vow; anuvrat is also the name of the moral movement started by Acharya Sri Tulsi in 1949, inspiring people to take vows not to indulge in particular evils. The person who joins the movement and takes such a vow is called an anuvrati.
asana	Yogic posture.
ayurved	An Indian system of medicine.
chitta	Consciousness; conscious mind; psyche.
dhyana	Concentration, meditation.
dharmya dhyana	Concentration on the nature of reality.
japa	Iteration of a mantra or a deity's name.
leshya	Psychic colour; passions.
leshya dhyana	Perception of psychic colours.
karma	Action: according to the doctrine of karma, a man reaps what he sows, i.e., a person's fate is determined by his past actions.
kayotsarg	Rising above the kaya (body); self-awareness by relaxation.
kundalini	Awakening of vital or bioelectrical energy through concentration on different parts of the body, one by one and all at once; tejolabdhi, tejoleshya.
mantra	Spell-word.
muni	Monk, sadhu.
pranayam	System of controlling breath.
preksha	Seeing, perception; concentration of observation.
preksha dhyana	Preksha meditation.
sadhak	Spiritual practitioner.

sadhana	Spiritual practice, constant endeavour to reach perfection in any field.
sadhu	Muni, monk.
sadhvi	Nun.
samans and samanis	A new category of sadhvis and sadhus who are granted certain exemptions in respect of food and travel. Unlike sadhus and sadhvis, they may use a vehicle and are free to accept food specially prepared for them.
shivir	Camp.
shivrarthi	A person attending a shivir.
shrawak	A member of the laity, in contrast with monks and nuns.
shukla dhyana	Pure concentration.
tapasya	Penance, austerities.
tirthankar	Founder of religious doctrine.
tejas	Lustre, light, brilliance, splendour.
tejas-shakti	Luminous power.
tejolabdhi, tejoleshya	See 'kundalini.
veetarag	One who has transcended passions.
veetaragta	State of freedom from passions and affections.